**HAYLEY KATZEN** migrated from South Africa to Australia in 1989. In Sydney, she graduated with an LLB and worked in public law and law reform before making a sea change to the North Coast of NSW to work as a law lecturer and researcher. In 2005, Hayley moved to her girlfriend's cattle farm in the Australian bush and it was here she learned the crafts of short story and essay writing and completed an MFA (Creative Writing). Her writing has won competitions, been read on ABC radio and Queerstories and been published in Australian, American and Asian journals and anthologies including *Australian Book Review*, *Griffith Review*, *Southerly*, *Fourth Genre* and *Kenyon Review*. *Untethered* is her debut memoir.

# UNTETHERED

This book is published by Ventura Press
PO Box 780, Edgecliff NSW 2027 Australia
www.venturapress.com.au

ISBN: 978-1-920727-44-4 (paperback)
ISBN: 978-1-920727-45-1 (ebook)

 A catalogue record for this
book is available from the
National Library of Australia

Cover and internal design by Deborah Parry Graphics
Printed and bound in Australia by Griffin Press of Ovato Book Printing

 The paper this book is printed on is certified against the
Forest Stewardship Council® Standards. Griffin Press holds
FSC® chain of custody certification SGS-COC-005088. FSC®
promotes environmentally responsible, socially beneficial
and economically viable management of the world's forests

# UNTETHERED

## HAYLEY KATZEN

For Jen


and for my mother

*We are entirely made up of bits and pieces, woven together so diversely and so shapelessly that each one of them pulls its own way at every moment. And there is as much difference between us and ourselves as there is between us and other people.*
– **Michel de Montaigne, 'On the Inconstancy of Our Actions'**

# CONTENTS

# PART ONE:
# ROMANCE

*For without hearts there is no home.*
— 'Don Juan', Lord Byron

# 1.

# TYWYAH

'WHERE THE HELL ARE WE?' I said to my game-for-anything buddy. I'd counted four pubs and three butchers as we drove along the main street of the small country town.

'Casino,' she said. 'The beef capital.'

'Where even the radio station's named for cattle?' I said as I read out a billboard: COW FM.

I flicked through the CDs in the console. I couldn't remember any more songs from *Grease*, *The Sound of Music* or *Jesus Christ Superstar*. My friend launched into 'Don't Cry for Me Argentina'.

I joined in for the chorus, replacing Argentina with South Africa. Six and a half years earlier in January 1989, as an impatient and determinedly independent 22-year-old, I'd migrated to Australia. My stepfather, whose oldest sons had already migrated, had facilitated the golden opportunity: a permanent residency visa. My father's sudden death had catapulted my decision to emigrate immediately, ahead of my mother and stepfather: I needed a safe home. I was no Eva Peron but leaving South Africa, mired then in a draconian state of emergency, had felt like a betrayal of the national democratic struggle and of the courageous and moral self I aspired to be. At the same time, I was deeply grateful for migration's privileges: to study and live in a safe and peaceful country, free of the fears and insecurities, the alienation and guilt that came with being white and Jewish in apartheid South Africa.

Lismore, where I taught law at the university, was thirty kilometres behind us. Byron Bay, with its ropey fig trees and camphor laurels, sugarcane and white beaches, an hour and a half behind us. A year ago, hoping to find somewhere I might belong, I'd taken sick leave from my paid and unpaid legal jobs in Sydney, loaded my white hatchback and, together with my housemate, headed north.

As my friend belted out another verse, I examined the mud map on the back of the invitation to Jen's fortieth birthday party. We still had another ninety kilometres to go before we got to Tywyah – and this had all been my idea.

I'd met Jen two days earlier, watched as she'd roped a load of mattresses and bags of horse feed to her blue truck. I was intrigued. I'd never met a woman who talked of 'loads' and 'truckies' knots'.

But on that spring evening, I was more interested in a woman with deep brown eyes and a shaved head. We'd circled each other a fortnight before at a Tropical Fruits dance, and I'd finally found an excuse to drop by the converted stables where she lived. I tried not to look at the bed I longed to lie on. I rolled and smoked cigarette after cigarette. My blood, my breath, my heart all moved too fast. My words tumbled and tripped. I wanted to be there, and I wanted to run away. The arrival of the woman's friends, Jen and her carpenter girlfriend, was a salve. The invitation to Jen's birthday party on her farm was gold: a chance to see my crush again, and a chance to get to know more women in this new community.

'Why would you want to live out here?' I wondered aloud as we drove on, past endless barbed-wire fences, past skinny cows and horses floating in paddocks bleached of colour, and then up and over a mountain range for more barbed wire and lonely houses. As the sun was setting, we clattered over a wooden bridge signposted Hamilton's Crossing and pulled up at the mud map's X: a red mailbox with the sign *Tywyah*.

'Weird name. How do you even say it? Tiwieh?'

'Maybe tie-why-ah,' my friend said.

I got out to open the gate. 'Gross. Can you smell that?'

What a tough, hot, dry, ugly place. I climbed back into the car and notched up the volume on Jane Siberry's 'Calling All Angels'.

We followed the arrows across a mustard-brown paddock; past a cow's body, her ribs a scaffolding without the skin; through a dry gully and up a rocky and rutted driveway. Just when the car demanded another gear, an oasis appeared amid the spotty gum trees: a crowd of women, some standing around a bonfire, some lounging on sofas beneath a passionfruit vine on the wide verandah of a mudbrick house.

I fluffed my short hair in the side mirror, for a fraction of a second not recognising myself. A couple of years earlier I'd cut my wild mane short in the hope I'd look more 'dykey' and find my place in Sydney's lesbian community.

As we hesitantly walked through the open gate, Jen welcomed us.

'Thanks for the invitation,' I said. 'We've been trying to work out how to say the name of this place. Is it Ti ... Tiwi ... ah?'

She laughed. 'Tie-wire. As in tying the wire. You know that wire used in bush building?'

'No,' I said, looking completely blank.

'Everything here was built with poles and wire. So that's what we called the place. We were taking the piss out of everyone buying bush blocks or hobby farms and calling them exotic names like Bella Vista.'

We joined the gathering and, not long after, a friend from town, dressed in red leather chaps, said, 'Hey, you girls, we need some performances. Can you whip something up?'

Someone suggested a song, someone had a guitar, and before I knew it I was led over to the stables into what was called a 'tack room'. There were saddles and helmets, reins and bridles, whips and chains. Why the hell not? I thought, as I stripped down to black bra and denim shorts.

An hour later, in front of a crowd of women, most of whom I didn't know, I mock-kissed a bare-breasted woman in a harness and helmet. I wore elasticised workboots and sported a whip. Bridles, reins and chains trellised my pale freckled nakedness. We were the dancers, the girls behind us the guitarists and singers for a spontaneous performance of 'Wild Thing'.

After our performance, while the leather girls with handcuffs dangling from studded belts gave me approving looks, I searched out the safety of my game-for-anything buddy. Instead I found the woman I had a crush on and, still skating on this bold me, I said, 'How about a night of uncomplicated sex?'

I can't believe I actually came out with that line. Something tipped my usual seesaw from anxiety to adventurous. Maybe it was the costume, the performance amid the safety of a women-only event, maybe it was the unknown crowd and far-away farm, maybe it was another case of fake it till you make it, something I'd become more proficient at since migration. That night I found a bold self – the bravado of the outsider who so wants to belong.

Like many a romantic comedy, Jen and I collided after that weekend. My lover – the first night at Tywyah had led to a second and then a third – had invited me to dinner. Jen was a guest too, and I parked behind her blue truck. The night ended with a bang – between Jen's blue truck and my little white hatchback.

My lover and I discovered the collision as we were leaving. In the moonlight I stared at the damage while she went inside to tell the others. How was I to handle this? It wasn't the dented white duco that worried me. It was the politics of economic inequality – of difference.

On Jen's farm I'd seen the sagging mismatched couches, and heard how she and her girlfriends had built every structure on the block. I assumed that Jen, like some of my other friends, might be on the dole and have no access to extra cash or credit – 'skint', as the girls used to say. What if Jen wasn't insured? What if she couldn't afford the repairs?

If economic privilege is relative, in the class-conscious lesbian feminist community of the nineties, to have a well-paying job, own a home or have savings meant you were labelled as 'rich', and your ethics around money were up for discussion – particularly if you'd inherited money, as I'd done when my father had died, suddenly, tragically, when I was twenty-one, six months before I'd emigrated.

Where my South African political education had focused on Steve Biko and Franz Fanon's writings about black consciousness, in smoky Sydney pubs, around kitchen tables and from Audre Lorde's *Sister Outsider* I'd discovered feminism and 'the personal is political'. I learned about the complexities of power and choice and the words that described experiences I'd known of but had no language for, like incest and domestic violence. I learned too that feminists had overlooked the blacks and gays, the elderly, the poor and the dis-abled – what is these days known as intersectionality. And I'd learned about hierarchies of otherness: to be black or poor was 'worthy'. I, on the other hand, was suspect: middle class, Jewish, heterosexual until recently – all privileges some associate with power. Worse still, I was a white South African who'd benefited from the privilege of whiteness.

So staring at Jen's truck up against my dented duco, I wondered whether I should just say, 'I'm happy to pay.' Or would that offend Jen? And if I didn't offer, would the privilege police accuse me of being a typical ungenerous rich white Jewish South African?

When everyone came out to look at the smash, there was laughter and disbelief.

Jen looked at the two vehicles, opened the passenger door of her blue truck and said, 'The handbrake must've slipped; the truck's rolled back. I'll call the insurance people on Monday.'

My shoulders dropped. This wasn't ethically complicated. Jen saw this as her responsibility. I wasn't expected to pay simply because I could afford it. Perhaps, despite differences, I could still fit in here, still make this place home.

'The pool's completely private,' the elderly woman told my house-mate and me as we stood outside the blond-brick house on the hill. I nodded and smiled. What a view. To the west were rolling paddocks, south and north were ocean glimpses, and the house was only ten minutes from the quaint village of Bangalow, where you couldn't do the grocery shopping but you could post a letter and buy Persian carpets. It was also only a half-hour drive to the university where I worked.

'We're active in Rotary and the Country Women's Association so we built the house for entertaining,' the woman said as she gestured through the glass screen doors to the large paved area.

I pictured ladies in linen lunching at white-clothed tables and men in open-necked shirts leaning over the built-in-bar.

'Do you entertain much?' the woman asked.

My housemate and I avoided each other's eyes.

'A little,' I said, as I imagined the parties I might host. I pictured groups of lesbians lazing naked beside the private pool, smoking, drinking, dancing, perhaps even performing – surely that raised din-ing room with the wooden bannister could become a stage.

I wanted to do cartwheels across the acre of lush green lawn. I saw security, and a happier, more balanced life. How fortunate I was. If a migrant, rather than an expat, is defined by some 'need', my need for physical safety had surely been met. I sang a few lines from *The Jungle Book's* 'The Bare Necessities' out loud.

Ten years earlier, as a university student in Cape Town, I'd stood amid the wreckage of homes that had been bulldozed by the South African government, handing formula and nappies to women who had nothing to feed their babies and nowhere to shelter them. Later, as we'd driven home to hot showers and warm beds, someone had started singing 'The Bare Necessities'. I'd joined in, but as we sang I'd looked back at the hundreds of homeless people camped in Red Cross tents.

How very grateful I was then – and now. Unlike the residents of that township of Crossroads, unlike so many South Africans and Australians, I had the necessities in peaceful, safe Australia. Here, I'd be able to send down roots. Under the tutelage of my gardener–writer housemate and her girlfriend, I'd take up gardening, which they said would help me manage the stress of my academic job, perhaps teach me what I needed to learn: patience, and the natural order and cycle of life. What really mattered. This would be a place to belong.

'Can you convert this into two offices?' I asked Jen's girlfriend the carpenter as we stood beside the carport's brick pillars. Apart from the countless sliding glass doors, which made me wonder if I'd ever feel safe on my own, the house had one major drawback: there were only two bedrooms, both too small to accommodate a bed and desk, and I now needed to work harder than ever. An inheritance might've helped buy the place but I'd pay the mortgage and maintenance from my university salary. I had to show everyone I worked for it all – how else would I gain my community's approval? Buying the place had felt like another coming out: I could afford a place that my closest friend described as 'over the top' – again, a relative term. Only a handful of the women I knew owned houses.

The carpenter walked around, measuring, tapping, suggesting, jotting down figures with the pencil she pulled from behind her ear. Each office would have doors to the outside and she could cut through the brick wall to create an entry from the house via my wardrobe. Like the magical portal of C.S Lewis's *Narnia*, I imagined sliding the mirrored wardrobe door, pushing aside my buttoned shirts and waistcoats and stepping into the world of my legal work.

Afternoons I came home from my job at the university to find the carpenter, cap on backwards, listing what she needed for the next day while Jen, her girlfriend and assistant, wound cords, put away tools and swept up wood shavings. In her builder's apron and cut-off denim shorts, Jen was friendly, tidy, reliable, personable. With her slim hips, muscled shoulders and arms and playful brown eyes, she was spunky too, but as someone else's girlfriend, she was beyond my mental bounds. Sure, I was always happy to see her, but with lectures to deliver and the legal publisher breathing down my neck for the administrative law textbook I'd been contracted to write, I wished they'd hurry up and finish.

After the job was finished, I arranged to buy wood and hay from Jen. She'd deliver eggs with sunshine yolks, firewood she'd chopped and hay she'd baled. As I handed over payment, she'd say, 'Thanks, that'll pay for my trip to town.'

One day, as we drank tea in the shade of the pool's pergola, Jen explained that the farm was too far from town for a regular job and local farmers wouldn't hire a woman for cattle work, even though they'd all seen her ride and work cattle at the area's campdraft events. Making a living from the land wasn't really possible either: her two hundred acres could only run thirty head of cattle, and distance combined with poor soil meant it wasn't viable to sell vegetables. She'd tried, once growing seven hundred lineal metres of snow peas.

'So,' Jen said, 'I'm a self-made peasant.'

'Would you ever leave the farm?' I asked.

'And do what? Go back to teaching home science?'

I laughed. Jen was nothing like my home-economics teacher, Mrs Maggs, with the high bouffant and large bust, who'd patiently tried to teach teenagers who'd grown up with domestic workers how to separate eggs and bake scones.

'I'd have preferred to become a mechanic but that wasn't an option for girls in the seventies,' Jen explained. She told me how, growing up in the country, she'd liked taking things apart and putting them together. She'd spent only five years living in the city – she'd had fun at the lesbian bars but not teaching home science – and then she and her girlfriend Ash, who also wanted to 'live simply and simply live', had left Sydney and taken a motorbike trip north.

'Tywyah is rocky, tough country,' she said. 'But it was what we could afford.' First they lived in a large tent, cooked on an open fire and bathed in the creek. They ate dried beans and tinned food because they had no refrigeration, and once a fortnight drove to town for a steak at the pub. By the time Ash's children, a ten- and eight-year-old, had joined them, they'd laid poly pipe to pump water from the creek, built a shack from bush poles and scantling, bought a milking cow and chickens and started breeding horses.

They seemed the epitome of hands-on feminism and pioneering self-reliance. 'I'm amazed you can do all this stuff,' I said. 'All I can do is convert a power plug and hammer in a picture hook. Who taught you?'

'Not our fathers. I had country common-sense but apart from horseriding, girls weren't taught traditional boys' jobs,' Jen said. 'Luckily Ash and I were both pretty practical so at Tywyah we learned on the job and from some neighbours.'

Unlike Jen, I'd not lived in one place longer than a year since I'd left my childhood home. I'd never been financially insecure and my longest relationship had lasted about two years. I knew of lesbian communities like Amazon Acres where women lived cooperatively and without the crutches of worldliness, but I was not such a woman. I knew myself to be hopelessly urban and middle class. The closest I'd come to pioneering life was admiring Laura, the compassionate and feisty hero of *Little House on the Prairie*, the television series I'd watched as a child.

But as Jen talked, I nodded. Ostensibly, the words she used were familiar: home, poor country, drought, the price of cattle, the financial complexities of relationship endings, even the form required for the fortnightly dole. After all, my businessman father had gone from insurance broking to chicken farming, my mother's family had farmed sheep in South Africa's Little Karoo and I'd worked in social security law and researched the legal recognition of lesbian and gay relationships. Naively, I thought I understood what Jen's words meant.

I prodded her with questions. After five years another girlfriend had followed Ash and she too had matched Jen physically. Together they'd built a bigger house – mudbrick and recycled timber with sand, cement and sawdust walls. But since that relationship had ended, Jen's girlfriends had all been women who'd lived in town.

'Not sure what sort of woman would stick with life out on the farm,' Jen said.

# 2.

# COME MAKE HAY

'A WOMAN WHO CAN put petrol in her car to drive to the farm, who has a job with a regular wage, is a non-smoker – and has a swimming pool.'

That was Jen's list of what she wanted in a girlfriend, or so she told me as we lay naked in her white sheets the morning after we became lovers.

When her relationship with the carpenter ended, Jen had taken to dropping in for a swim – just for a visit, no business transactions.

One December day, the swimming pool water cool against my skin as I watched Jen tumble turn for another length underwater, I was surprised by a race of desire. The newly single Jen, a woman with whom I'd enjoyed an easy friendship for some two years, suddenly seemed sexually attractive, urgently so. Was it her open face, her perfect lips or her lightness and laughter? Or her body – those muscled arms and back, her horserider's thighs, the slender hips with the tattoo on the hipbone? But I'd seen all that before; everyone swam naked in our very private swimming pool. Perhaps desire is often about timing. It was two years and two months since I'd last had sex. In that time I'd not been attracted to anyone and now Jen, with that playful glint in her hazel eyes, was clearly available.

With our elbows on the pool edge, we chatted about love and, as lesbians do, we told each other our coming-out stories. She'd fallen in love at teachers' college in Newcastle.

'Did you know you were a lesbian before that?' I asked.

She hadn't, although no one believed her. 'And you?' she asked.

'No idea.' I laughed. 'When I first emigrated I went out on all these dates with nice Jewish boys. But then law school started and I met this woman, and her friends. Lesbians. I'd never been attracted to a woman before but suddenly I just couldn't stop thinking about her. She had a fetish for Italian leather shoes, wore white shirts with the collars raised and oh my god, the way her fingers would nimbly roll cigarettes – greyhounds she called them.'

'Who made the first move?' Jen asked.

I grinned. 'Me. I'd sent a shipping container of stuff from South Africa and when it arrived, I asked her to help me convert the electric plugs. But as she was levering the back off the first plug, I took the screwdriver from her. She said, "You didn't ask me here to help you change the plugs, did you?" So I kissed her, and then ... mmm ... I couldn't believe it. It was so right, like this was true desire. I'd had consensual sex, good sex, with a boyfriend at uni in South Africa, but oh my god, this was a whole new eroticism and intimacy. It turned everything I'd always expected completely upside down. I realised I had choices.'

'And when that ended? Did you go back to boys?'

'No. I tested out sex with a guy – he was my accountant, but we'd become friends. It was clear to both of us I just wasn't really into it.' I lay back in the cool pool water. 'For me, lesbianism's felt like way more than sex and love. It's about politics too, and I completely love being part of this community.'

'I know what you mean,' Jen said, smiling. 'And what about your family? Are they all back in South Africa?'

'Oh no. Only my stepmother and aunts and cousins are there. My folks split when I was six and my dad died six months before I emigrated. My mom's side are all in Sydney, bar one stepbrother. Two married stepbrothers emigrated first, then I came, then my sister and her family and then my mom and stepdad.' I paused. 'Now they're all in Sydney and I'm here. You know, families. Now tell me about your first girlfriend at college.'

I urged Jen on with questions about her relationships, about the women's community in Sydney in the late seventies, about her links to the lesbian community after she moved to the farm in 1981. Eleven years older than me, she'd come out into a more discriminatory world and a more separatist lesbian community.

'It was so different,' she said. 'I wasn't at the 1978 protest – the first Mardi Gras – but my ex, Rob, was.'

'Another ex?' I teased.

Jen smiled bashfully. 'Rob was dragged away by the cops and when her picture was flashed across the papers she almost lost her job at a private girls' school.'

I shook my head. 'And look at us now, rehearsing our Byron Bay Surf-broads routine for the Mardi Gras without a concern for our safety.'

I wanted our conversation to last, not evaporate like the squiggles she drew with water on the hot pavers. Again I wished I'd spent more time studying the art of seduction than the options for legal recognition of lesbian and gay relationships.

When Jen dropped in early one morning a few weeks later, after I'd fried eggs and made toast, she asked, 'Is there something we need to talk about or should we just leave things the way they are?'

'Well,' I said, resorting to the only type of seduction I knew, 'what I'd really like to do is race you off to bed right now.'

She laughed and said, 'Well, that's not going to happen. I've got to get back to the farm and it's not long since my breakup. Anyway, neither of us is after a one-night stand.'

She was right. As much as I longed to be the kind of girl who'd had more lovers than notches on my belt, my heart was sensitive and I wanted more than sex.

'How about dinner?' I asked.

'It's too far to town from the farm,' she said, laughing. 'I'll call you.'

When I leaned forward to kiss her, she presented a cheek, hopped into her truck and said, 'Good things come to those who wait.'

I groaned, and not just because I hate clichés.

We courted by letter and phone. The publisher's deadline for the law textbook was drawing near but the case law on the right to a fair hearing no longer seemed compelling. I pruned every hibiscus and bougainvillea in the garden, oblivious to the scratches the thorns left behind. I thought only of Jen – well, of sex with Jen.

Eventually the invitation came a fortnight later during a phone call. I was on my bed, fantasising about Jen beside me, when she said, 'Do you want to come make hay?'

'Sure,' I said, interpreting the invitation metaphorically.

'I'm serious,' she said, her tone teasing. 'I'm baling the Mill paddock.'


On that first hot summer night, as cicadas sirened in the gum trees, as I sat at a table covered by a patchwork cloth made by her mum, Jen announced – to my awe and amazement – that everything on the plate was homegrown: the new potatoes, the lettuce, cucumber and cherry tomatoes confettied with herbs, and the rump steak.

All I wanted was to gaze at her slim hips in the faded hipster Levi's, listen to her soft laughter, touch the shaved chestnut hair at the nape of her neck, smell the remnants of the day she'd spent hay baling and taste her, not the pepper sauce that burned my mouth. All I could think was: who's going to make the first move?

Instead I said, 'So, did this cow have a name?'

'Easter,' she said smiling, her eyes glowing in the candlelight. 'Or Christmas, or Dinner.'

Later, as I leaned my elbows on the wide windowsill of her bedroom and looked up into the velvety sky, Boxer and Topdeck snorted and sneezed down at the stables. In the dark I could just make out Jen's shadowy figure walking towards the barn to let them out. My blood shook and spun up and down my veins. I really liked this woman and her blend of softness and toughness, and I feared the strangeness of her world.

I took a deep breath, inhaling the sandalwood oil at my wrists and, over the top of it, pungent mosquito coil, manure and lawn clippings. Intoxicating blends everywhere. What was I getting myself into? This place in the Australian bush where she farmed chickens and cattle and rode horses seemed so much more than a workplace or even a home. It was certainly how others knew her. It was perhaps even who she was.

And it was a two-hour drive along winding country roads from where I lived. Culturally the distance was possibly even greater. Jen and I came not just from different countries but from backgrounds poles apart in almost every way. My parents were middle-class Jewish professionals and intellectuals who'd never done a day's manual labour. During our poolside conversations Jen had told me her father, who'd survived the Thai–Burma railway as a prisoner of war of the Japanese, had been employed as a station's stockman; and her mother, before she became a barmaid, was a full-time homemaker who cleaned the employer's house and sewed wheat bags during the harvest for sixpence each. That was how their family could afford a fridge and an annual holiday to the coast.

As I tried to rein in my mind, Jen appeared, scooped Puss off the bed and put her outside, closed the French doors, and kissed me on the back of my neck.

Over the days as we discovered each other, we found too that our skin told our stories. I, who'd grown up wrapped in cottonwool under the watchful gaze of my nanny Ellen and my mother's 'be careful, don't hurt yourself', was pale and freckled and scarless apart from the recent bougainvillea cuts. Jen's broad and calloused hands were marked by abrasions from fencing, digging, gardening, building and cattle work. There was a scar to mark her fall from the roof when she was building the mudbrick house, scars from welding, and a long scar above her bellybutton that involved a steel post and a broken wire from when, as a twelve-year-old, she'd gone out to get a rabbit for dinner at her mother's request. She was a good shot and some nights they'd go spotlighting – a pair of rabbits brought forty cents. She'd begun riding horses when she was two and hunting wild pigs on foot with a single-shot .22 when she was nine.

If my house with the swimming pool and a full tank of petrol were part of what drew Jen to me, I was drawn to her abundance of things money couldn't buy. Over the months to come, we wooed each other with kindness, affection and attention – and our different resources. Our kisses and bodies were breathless and bold.

I arrived for weekends on the farm with smoked salmon and mangoes, and whisked Jen off to luxurious rainforest retreats and city weekends. I was the adventurer, the city slicker, wresting Jen away from her country comfort. Jen's response to these trips was, 'What I love about going away with you is coming home.'

Jen treated me to bonfires and billy tea, nights in the swag under the stars, horse rides and naked swims in the cool waters of a creek visited only by wildlife.

In the evenings, as we sat on a log in front of the bonfire watching the moon rise gold through the gum trees, I pinched myself. This woman. This space. This freedom. I remembered Marlowe's line: 'Come live with me and be my love.'

'The rural idyll,' I said, leaning into Jen. This was the antithesis of my busy work life. The antithesis of my Johannesburg childhood of bars on every window, high fences and security gates that were locked at night.

Jen laughed. 'Don't romanticise it too much. I'll get you out working soon.'

One weekend Jen led me away from the white sheets and mosquito net down to the stables where she was building a fence. I'd only ever hammered picture hooks into plaster. She showed me how to place the two-inch nail against the wooden paling and tap its head. The first nail catapulted into the dirt. As did the second, third, fourth and fifth. Even when I managed to get the nail to bite the wood, and swung hard as instructed, the nail barely moved. When it did, it was bent. I bit my lip, confused, surprised. How come I could whack tennis balls with ease and grace but not a nail?

'Don't worry, it's very hard wood,' Jen said.

I relinquished the hammer and, with a roll of my eyes and a mock shimmy of my hips, said, 'Does that mean my only role is beautiful assistant?'

As I traced the initials – Jen's and her previous girlfriend's – carved into the cement of the feed shed, I marvelled she knew how, and physically managed, to do such heavy work. But my awe was creased with concern: were we just too different?

On another weekend visit, at dawn I went outside to the shower before I left to drive back to town to teach an early class. Most nights we showered together under the stars, to my delight and relief: who knew what creatures lurked in the open air and dark of the night? The truth was, where raw country coursed through Jen's cells, I was no Emerson, no 'lover of uncontained and immortal beauty'. Like many urban South Africans, I'd been to the game reserve as a child. From the safety of the car I'd jaw-dropped at lions and elephants and giraffes, but otherwise, in my heady Jewish family, 'nature' was mostly described generically, as in 'tree' and 'bird', and only ever scientifically differentiated as 'big' or 'little'. I'd never been camping and the spectre of untamed nature had always seemed more dangerous than city laneways and the bricked paths of botanical gardens.

Now, as hot water washed over me, I looked out to the sunlit spotty gum trees, filling myself with fresh air, marvelling at the extraordinary freedom and privacy of this life. Suddenly, something rat-like raced across the edge of the cement where I stood. I hopped from foot to foot, screamed and ran stark-naked along the timber walkway to the back door.

'What's wrong?' Jen said, meeting me at the door.

'There's a rat. It came right near me,' I said, my face crinkled with horror. I didn't want to be the woman in the cartoon who leapt onto a chair as I'd once seen my mother do, but rats and mice freaked me out more than spiders and snakes. 'Nearly across my feet!'

Jen laughed. 'Ah, that's Martha. She's an echidna. She won't hurt you.'

I shuddered. Martha. She even had a name.

'What's an echidna?'

'Like a porcupine. They're good eating. I had some Koori mates who used to take me hunting. Quite rich. Did you turn the water off?'

'No, sorry,' I said, blushing. This was hardly the way to impress this woman.


As Jen and I gradually opened our hearts and souls to each other, my limitations and fears didn't seem to matter – to either of us. I was a visitor from another world. So, when the pink twine cut into my palms as we swung rectangular hay bales onto the truck's tray, Jen kissed my soft office hands. When I couldn't fathom how to open the strange lever of wire and wood Jen called a 'cockie's gate', she climbed down from the truck and we flirted as she unhooked and levered wood from wire. When I pulled out the whole silverbeet plant instead of picking the leaves, when I didn't think to light the woodstove three hours before I wanted to bake a banana cake, we laughed. When I leaned over the fence, watching as she broke in her mare Topdeck, we joked that she was breaking in two of us at once. When I asked why there were filing cabinets in the paddock, Jen said, 'You mean those bee boxes?' and we laughed. It was easy to shrug off my ignorance and incompetence – after all, we shared values and pleasures and we were newly in love.

We decided we were each other's favourite waste of time. We couldn't get enough of each other's bodies or hearts or minds, and there was no risk we would: we lived two hours apart and both had busy work lives. We inhabited separate spheres and saw each other for a three-day weekend every fortnight. The rest of the time my life carried on as before. I worked long days finalising the textbook and teaching at the university. Home was the sanctuary I'd created with my housemate and our community of friends in a landscape so beautiful that I pinched myself whenever I drove up the driveway and looked out to the hills.

Neither Jen nor I had any intention of changing where and how we lived. Separateness and differences seemed intrinsic to our relationship. Perhaps even its aphrodisiac.

# 3.

# THE REALITY OF JEN'S WORLD

ON ONE WEEKEND VISIT, during the early months of our romance, after Jen had ushered me in through the iron gate, after we'd kissed, uncorked the wine, set out the smoked salmon and cream cheese, Jen said, 'Jack and I've got some work in the yards tomorrow. You up for coming along?'

I agreed, imagining I'd watch Jen and Jack. I'd met him briefly, a sixty-something white-haired man with a big smile. Early the next morning, still humming from our night together, I perched on the top wooden rail of Fletchers' yards wearing my belted Levi's and elasticised boots, a stiff cotton shirt with the collar turned up and my balloon of curly hair tied up in a ponytail. I was safely above the huge black and red cows milling and mooing, peeing and pooing. Not even a slightly squeamish distaste at those bodily fluids dulled my delight – the fresh air, the blue sky, the magpies yodelling, the wind in the dusty eucalypt trees. Magnificent wide-open space. Even if Jen had a 'no affection in front of Jack' rule, I was the star of a rural love story, miles from my legal job – oh, if my mother and friends could see me now.

I'd expected to watch sexy cowgirl Jen in her cream moleskins, blue buttoned-up shirt and akubra hat – until she tossed me a piece of black poly pipe.

'Take this cow basher,' she said. 'We could do with an extra body. Stand over there and just wave it around if any of them charge you.'

With my fingers gripping the black poly pipe, I stood amid the rising dust and bellowing cows, their necks and heads thrust up in the air. When I wasn't making sure I was safe or wondering if the word 'bellows' came from the way their bellies expanded and con-tracted with each vocalisation, I looked over to the other yard. There, with arms outstretched, Jen and Jack were making *sh-sh* sounds and saying 'come on, little fellas' to the calves they were directing towards an open gate. As Jen walked up the side of the race she called me over. My back to the post-and-rail fence, eye to eye with those great big cows, I inched cautiously towards her.

'You can be secretary,' she said, positioning me next to the head bails beside a rusty forty-four-gallon drum that served as a table. She explained that Jack would push the calves up the race, and then she turned and tugged a lever that opened the two steel posts of the head bails. 'When they poke their heads through, I'll catch their necks like this and then we'll put a tag in their ear and cut the boys.' She pulled down on the lever and the steel clanged shut.

I shuddered: this was the clang of the prison door.

'But doesn't it hurt?' I asked.

'Not if they don't wriggle. It just contains them. Like when a limb's immobilised by a splint or something.'

I wasn't convinced. From her top pocket she took a little book with a red plastic cover and 'Elders Stock Agents' printed in white script. She flicked through the pages, each one headed with a date and then 'Bush Paddock' or 'Creek Paddock' and then some numbers.

'We need a tally of how many heifers and how many steers.'

I gratefully took the little book and stub of pencil. At last, a realm

I was proficient in. A job that would keep me safe from the cattle but close enough to Jen, who was lithely climbing over the rails.

She caught me looking and winked. 'You watching?' she asked, gesturing to the race where Jack, with his bowlegs and long black gumboots, was saying, 'Come on, little fella, up you go,' as he walked behind a red calf. And then, as the calf stepped forwards, Jen caught his neck between the steel rods. I flinched for the calf and marvelled at Jen's quick reflexes.

'If you lose one it's more work 'cos it'll go back in with the cows,' Jen said, 'and then you've got to go through that whole process again of separating the calves from the cows and getting the calf back into the forcing pen.'

I nodded, wordless.

'We're gonna cut now. You okay with blood?' she asked.

'Fine, thanks,' I said, not knowing if I was, or what they were about to do.

She spat on a long sharpening stone, pulled a pocketknife from the pouch on her belt, ran it up and down the stone, then against the leather of her boot, and then against the fine fair hairs on her arms. 'Knife's got to be really sharp,' she said.

Trying to be cool, I said, 'Hey, I'm a Jew. We do it when boys are eight days old.'

'That's foreskin,' she said. 'This is the testicles so they can't reproduce.'

I blushed. I knew that. But still, it was all in the same sensitive region. Not that this was what I expected when I came to visit my lesbian lover.

I was relieved when Jen handed the knife to Jack, but then she said, 'Sometimes I do the cutting but today I'll hold.' She grabbed the calf's tail, twisted and pulled it up. 'Some farmers say holding like this numbs them at the back,' she said over her shoulder. 'I'm not sure it's scientifically proven. Main thing is to keep them still and do it quickly.'

Bent over behind the calf, Jack slit the testicle, then set the knife down on the wooden race, pulled on something cord-like, cut again and then tossed a pink sac of tissue and flesh outside the race to the waiting kelpie. She leapt, caught it and gobbled it in one mouthful. Jack repeated the process. It was quick. The calf hadn't moved or cried out, but blobs of bright red blood spattered the dirt beneath him.

It might be different from circumcision but as I stared at that little calf, I remembered my godson's *bris* in Johannesburg a decade before. How before the ceremony, after I'd handed my godson to his godfather, my cousin had grabbed my hand and we'd hurried down the passage to the bathroom. When my godson's cry seeped under the door, we winced with him. Now I was wincing with a little calf. Sure, I couldn't know what he, or his mother, felt, but didn't that cut hurt the calf? Didn't that separation upset the cow? Yes, I might be anthropomorphising, but why not?

Then Jen climbed back over the rails, pulled the lever on the head bails and the calf leapt forwards and trotted into the yard where the cows waited. After a little mewl and a responding bellow from his mother, he found her. She sniffed him and soon he was bashing her bag of milk and sucking a calming glug.

When I turned back to the race, another calf's neck was caught in the bails, Jen was holding his tail and Jack was feeling around for the nuts. It was all so fast. I marked down another stroke. I counted up the little lines and then looked to where the calves were reunited with their mothers. I didn't want to watch the next operation.

'You okay?' Jen asked when Jack was out in the forcing pen getting a calf.

I grabbed a breath that seemed the first in ages. 'Yes,' I said. 'It's just a bit brutal. Those poor little calves.'

'Now you know why all the boys in the area cross their legs when they see me coming,' she said, laughing as she jumped into action and caught another calf.

Over at the dam there was a splash, a flock of wood ducks skimming along the water as one of the dogs swam along the edges. Some of the calves had followed their mothers to stand in the shade of the trees, some had stayed in the yard sucking, and others were lying down. Despite Jen's assurances that the calves would be fine, my heart sank. Would they? How could she be so matter-of-fact about inflicting pain on a defenceless animal? And then, with a mind that tends to mountains not molehills, I wondered about this affair. If weekends on the farm weren't simply about lust and love, if they sent me seesawing between disgust and desire, did I really want to be lovers with Jen?

Job done, Jack washed his hands in the bloodied water in the bucket and Jen packed the applicator and eartags into a fishing tackle box. For them it was simply all in a day's work.

I handed Jen the little red book. 'Thirteen boys and fifteen girls.'

She frowned as she looked at the page. 'Don't you know how to do a tally?'

'Draw a mark for each one and then add them up,' I said defensively.

'That's not how you do a tally. You do four marks and then for the fifth you draw a line through the four. That way you easily see how many you've got.'

There was obvious sense to her method. For the first time in my pen-pushing life I felt stupid and useless.

Then Jack chirped, 'C'mon, Fwankie's makin' ro' ca'es for mornin' tea.'

At the Fletchers', where Jack lived with his three brothers, all bachelors, I followed Jen up onto the verandah. Norman, the only one who could read, was peering at the local paper, his puffy ankles pooling over the top of his slippers.

In the kitchen I was introduced to Frank, who was standing at a burn- and blade-marked formica kitchen table with a jam tin of lard and a tub of vegetable scraps. The second youngest of the four brothers, his red face peaked in a Tintin tuft of rice-white hair and wiry whiskers sprouted from his blotchy skin.

In the bathroom I washed my hands with a nub of soap that teetered on a ledge of decayed wood. The lino beside the shower was blue floral with a smudge worn to white where the brothers had balanced their bodies to scrub a raised foot.

When the clock on the walnut sideboard ding-donged half past nine, everyone took a seat at the round dining table. Its plastic cloth was patterned with purple pansies, and at its centre was an aluminium teapot and a tray of tomato and barbeque sauce, salt and pepper, Vegemite, golden syrup and toothpicks.

There was a dusty curtain of cobwebs over the windows and the framed photographs on the wall beside them drew my gaze. Jen had told me what she'd heard of the brothers' story. How they grew up during the war, in Green Pigeon, way out in the bush. How they chopped wood, carried water, dug lantana and milked cows. They didn't go to school or learn to read and write. Instead, they learned which seeds were poisonous, that pigeons not crows are good to eat, and how to wring a chicken's neck. Twelve children, until the three girls went to live with the nuns.

'Here,' Jack said, pulling out a padded chair beside him. 'Ha' Bwucey's. He a' work.' Bruce, the fourth bachelor brother, worked on a nearby farm and owned the wooden lion on the sideboard, a gesture of thanks from the Lions Club for the many sausages he'd barbequed.

The Fletcher brothers talked in stop-start phrases, their voices hee-hawing and stuttering over each other. It was English they spoke, but to me the conversation was indecipherable. From their teasing tone I assumed they were bullying or blaming. Jen winked at me: she'd warned the brothers were even harder to understand when they were together, and that locals referred to their language as 'Fletcherese'.

She'd known these men for sixteen years and still, sometimes, only context clued her to meaning.

I listened intently to their conversation, bringing the same concentration my rusty Afrikaans demanded when I visited South Africa. Still, I understood little and occasionally nudged Jen for translations. *Lash* was latch, *Tussex* was Sussex, *showed* was closed, *booze* was bruised, *awigh* was alright, *icey* was pricey. I noted words in search of a pattern. But just when I decided Rs and Ls were spoken as Ws, I heard them articulate the R in 'rats' correctly. It wasn't that they had strong accents but rather that they spoke so quickly that some words were skipped altogether, others elided or left hanging, only half said, like *shudow*, which meant shut down. As I sat at that table I wondered what my speech therapist friends would say about their language, if it was simply relative isolation that had nurtured their family code. I was fascinated. They seemed like characters from a novel.

When one of the brothers addressed me directly, I played for time. I had no idea what he'd asked and blushed. If only my alien status wouldn't flash in lurid neon. These men may never have learned to read and write, never have heard of South Africa, but, to my surprise, around them I felt ignorant.

And then Jen said, 'Hayley wants to know if nutting hurts the calves.'

I swallowed. I didn't expect to have a conversation about castration at a table of men I barely understood.

Frank jumped in with a comment and they all laughed.

Jen translated: 'No one eats bull meat cos it's tough and tastes bad and you can't leave them like that or they'll end up like Maclean's.'

'Which means?'

'Inbred. Maclean's our neighbour. His cattle were on the road yesterday; they've got a particular look – skinny, block-headed and sickly. He overstocks so they're always hungry, he never sells and doesn't castrate his calves. It's shameful.'

Norman said, 'Siwy bugger,' and I smiled – I'd understood something.

'They ge' mad if you don't cut 'em. Always fightin',' Jack said, leaning back in his chair. And then he told a story, with Jen translating in asides, about someone who'd lost some bulls – 'gone off into the hills' – and by the time they were found they were crazy: 'Had to shoot 'em.'

Jen chimed in then. 'They grow better if they've been cut but the main reason we cut is so the restockers will buy our weaners and then fatten them up on good country. Restockers only buy steers and heifers. If the bulls aren't cut, you limit your market – they can only go straight to the butchers.'

'So it's a business decision?'

'Kind of. Cost and management,' she said. 'This way, apart from drenching and inoculating, we leave them out in the paddocks until we're ready to sell when they're seven to eight months old.'

When Frank set down a plate of hot 'rock cakes' – date scones – the brothers dived in, slathering them with margarine. They chewed tremulously and went back for a second or third. I stopped at one: rock cake was an apt name.

Frank, I discovered, cooked all the meals: breakfast was cereal and toast; lunch was cold rissoles with onion, tomato and white bread; and 'tea' was three types of meat and boiled veg. In summer he preserved apples that he bought cheap by the box. In winter he pickled chokos from his own vine. He told me – Jen translated – that as a little boy on a wooden stool at his mother's side, he learned to bake and stew and roast. Unlike his brothers, he didn't learn to use a gun or a chainsaw. Then he went working – cooking – for harvesting contractors and weed sprayers.

When I asked for black tea, Jack smiled approvingly and, as he did for himself and his brothers, put cold water in the base of my cup before pouring from the aluminium pot. As I sipped the best cup of tea I'd ever tasted, I was grateful for this tiny twinge of compatibility.

I was grateful too that if this was Jen's life, I had my own – a home, work and friends who spoke my language.

On another weekend we went along to 'hall night', the fortnightly bar and barbeque at the local community hall. I ordered a glass of red – cask wine – from a big-bearded man behind the bar, and steak and fresh salads for five dollars from a bright-eyed, chirpy woman in the kitchen, and then followed Jen out to the barbeque where Frank was cooking steak and onions. With Jack we sat down to eat at a trestle table inside under the fluoro light. As I looked around at the high ceiling, the mudbricks, the regulars' board and low wooden stage, Jen explained that until about a year earlier there'd been no hall: the community had met at the fire shed. Over the last ten or so years the community had fundraised, then the Fletchers had donated a piece of their land, the government had given a grant and members of the community, Jen included, had been employed under a work-for-the-dole scheme to build the hall. In the early days when the community was even smaller, there'd been no fences and gates and people had visited each other's homes, but now the hall was the social hub – playgroup, music jam sessions, an annual fun day and New Year's Eve parties.

'How big's the population?' I asked.

'What do you reckon, Jack?' Jen asked, and property by property, up dirt road after dirt road, they named people and when they'd come to the area, identifying fencing contractors, a top diesel mechanic and a carpenter. Ridge Road they called 'Von Ridge Road' because of the German and Bavarian families.

'About eighty permanents, including children,' Jen finally said.

'And then there's the fishermen,' Jack said. The weekenders who used the fishermen's cottages on the Clarence River, or camped on their bush blocks.

'I can't believe you know everyone in the community,' I said, wondering if such familiarity would be comforting or boring.

As I looked around at the men and women leaning over the bar or sitting up on stools at the high metal table outside with the jam tin of cigarette butts, I imagined my mother describing this as a community of 'dropouts'. This, I knew from countless fiery conversations, was what my mother had feared when I'd left my city job to live in an area where the local paper's news pages were dwarfed by a classified section bulging with yoga and spiritual healing, ballroom dance and mudbrick making, astrology reading and drama workshops. Known as the 'rainbow region', the north coast celebrated difference: sea changers, alternative communities, traditional farmers – and the largest lesbian and gay community outside a metropolitan area.

I thought of the other labels I'd heard applied to communities like this, both in Australia and South Africa: pioneers, ferals, non-conformists, dreamers, idealists, alternates. Some pejorative, some positive, all with a core meaning referring to people who'd opted out of conventional urban life. What, I wondered aloud, had drawn these people here? It seemed most of the residents had moved to the area from somewhere else. Had they walked away from families and convention for good reason? Were they environmentalists following a belief in sustainable living, or visionaries creating new ways of living? Were some hermits or people who preferred solitude to society?

'Anarchists,' Jen said. 'Most people out here want to do their own thing, be their own boss, free of authority.'

# 4.

# ARE WE TOO DIFFERENT?

I'D ONCE ASSUMED my life partner would be someone consistent with where I came from, what I was passionate about and who I thought I was – that imagined and assumed 'people like us'. Literature provides few lesbian couples as role models but like those heterosexual stories of Romeo and Juliet, Tony and Maria, Elizabeth Bennet and Fitzwilliam Darcy, I'd begun to suspect that differences were not obstacles but rather the drug of desire. Or perhaps all relationships, but particularly same-sex relationships, thrive on a tension between the familiar and the mysterious.

On the farm and in private, love and desire ruled. Jen's differences – including her use of a dictionary to write me love letters – were completely intoxicating. But on my turf, even though I welcomed Jen with kisses, I was tense and awkward when she first walked through the glass sliding door, and at some point she'd frown and ask, 'Do I need an icepick to relax you?'

We had many friends in common. Amid the safety of a lesbian and gay party we glided around the dance floor, glued to each other, oblivious of others. Off the dance floor Jen often gravitated to the crowd at the bar, I to the smokers at the bonfire.

One night, at a Byron Bay restaurant, Jen joined me for a friend's birthday dinner. The other guests were middle-class professionals who'd not met Jen before.

'So if they're not dairy cattle, what do you have to do?' one asked.

Jen's answers were soaked in blood and tissue and manure. She illustrated with an outstretched arm how she'd once shoved in a cow's prolapsed uterus.

Another woman grimaced. 'Do we have to talk about this while we're eating?'

'But it's interesting,' someone else said. 'I want to hear more.'

I sat silently, watching faces blanch, wishing we could talk about books or films or people – anything other than farming. When someone asked a follow-up question, I interpreted the interest as middle-class politeness. Jen didn't: she embroidered her story with more gory details and gestures. I glanced around the table, trying to read if my friends thought her cruel and barbaric, if they questioned why we were together.

An internal voice warned: *You're too different. This can't last.*

Just as I was familiar with the heady blend of attraction and fear, so too had I heard that warning before – countless times. Again, I tried to discount it as my mother's voice, as a voice from a place where I no longer wanted to belong. My mother, along with the South African Jewish culture we came from, had taught me to admire intellectual work – lawyers, doctors, teachers, businesspeople, writers and artists. Not manual workers.

When I'd bolted nine hundred kilometres north of Sydney, I'd hoped, tried, to put my oil-and-water family behind me. It might have been a family created by circumstance, a home riddled with the uncertainties and frictions endemic to blended families, but my mother and stepfather's marriage had held together since I, the youngest, was seven years old. Even if my father, a charismatic and kind man, had continued to represent safety, this blended family was the unit in which I, a thin-skinned child with porous and penetrable borders, had been raised. Here I'd learned about 'us' and 'them', and when as an eight-year-old my only blood sibling – a sister seven years older – had graduated from a closed bedroom door to moving to live with our father, I'd looked to my stepfamily and peer group for friendship – love.

Approval and cooperation, I discovered, were the path to inclusion. Work hard, get top marks, play sport, don't cry so easily and never ever behave like or become a kugel, the South African version of a Jewish-American princess. Adaptable and hungry for approval from everyone, as a child at primary school I allowed searching square-edged fingers. I never enjoyed the status of 'boyfriend and girlfriend' but still I did as told with hands and mouth to make that sticky, creamy body fluid appear. I obeyed instructions prefaced by 'I'm going to teach you about sex'. Later, as a 22-year-old alone in a foreign country, I attempted to weasel away from other unwanted approaches without making a fuss.

Within two years of migrating to Sydney – a place I'd expected to be my raft of safety – my relationships with my family, both blood and step, had unravelled. Some family members had rejected me, others I'd refused. After what feminism had taught me about power, I could no longer maintain the pretence of 'family'. For me, family was not a site of safety and support, of belonging. There was no one I could completely trust. The path to freedom lay in speaking out, but I feared the consequences. Fear and confusion multiplied inside me and I felt really, really stupid. I hadn't protected myself; I hadn't spoken out. Not as a child, not as a young adult. Shame dug its crippling claws deeper into me. Silence seemed the only available tool. Exile the safest and most sensitive path.

I deleted phone messages and scrunched up invitations to Shabbat dinners and Passover Seders. I told myself I didn't need this family; I would be the brave and singular heroine who created her own happy chosen family.

Like so many stories, that was a hopeful oversimplification:

family, whatever our experience of it, is our first home. In every phone conversation with my mother, the others – and the wounds that had led to my exile – were there. Beneath our once profoundly companionable conversations writhed a pit of family conflicts and compromises. When I visited my mother in her Sydney lounge room, as her pink lips moved I saw not love but her continued relationships with people who caused me pain. Pain she now knew about. She'd come to embody the unspoken and unresolved. As I sipped South African Five Roses tea, I held myself tight. How was I to handle all the silences and charades? On guard with my mother, I was graceless and quick to anger, poised for escape should any of the family turn up.

On one visit, I noticed my childhood matryoshka doll, which I called a babushka, on the ledge of a cabinet, the painted wood chipped, its yellows and reds faded.

'I haven't seen that for years,' I said as I twisted the doll at the waist to reveal the next doll and then the next and the next, down to the eighth doll, just a little larger than my thumbnail.

'The boys love it,' my mother said.

The boys. Nephews I didn't know. I set the babushka down. Despite my resolve, despite my rich adult life and 'chosen family' of friends, still I ached for that other family.

Relentlessly, my mother pursued me by phone and letter. I fired volley after accusing volley: You ask too much of me. You don't stand up for me. Where's your loyalty to me? Your ongoing relationships with them are a betrayal. My mother raised her shield: I love you. Distressed, bewildered, angry, frustrated, I prickled back: You're all words, never action. Your grand declarations of love mean nothing. I can't trust you. She repeated her catchcries: Let the dead past bury its dead. And: When you're happy, I'm happy.

When I eventually told her about Jen, she said she wanted to meet her. My mother had come a long way.

I came out to my mother at the end of my first year in Sydney, during the university break. She'd not yet migrated. We were seated on opposite couches in her Johannesburg lounge room, the Persian carpet visible beneath the glass table, the antique carousel packed with well-thumbed biographies and barely touched international recipe books.

There was a brief, tense silence after my announcement. My mother's folded arms seemed to tighten and her head bowed even lower. Then she – always the high-school English teacher – shot back with a quote: 'Glory be to God for dappled things.'

'What's that supposed to mean?' I asked.

'Don't you remember, Hayley? "Pied Beauty" by Gerard Manley Hopkins?'

I shook my head, masking an intellectual inadequacy I often felt in my mother's company. 'What's that got to do with my being a lesbian?'

'It's proof of the beauty and importance of difference,' she said. 'One has wonderful, deep friendships with women. You know how important my friends are to me, but that's what they are: friendships. One marries men.'

'But why limit yourself?' I said. 'I don't hate men, Ma. I've just discovered I like women more – in every way.'

'But, darling, I don't want you to be lonely.'

If, to my mother, lesbianism was synonymous with loneliness, I couldn't tell her that in Sydney some weekends my only companions were the plaintiffs and defendants of the case law I was studying. I'd leave my desk to wander through the fig trees of Centennial Park just to see other people, to maybe exchange a few words with a stranger. I couldn't tell her why I'd distanced myself from 'the family', about my fear of becoming one of those people whose dead bodies are found only when their piled-up mail becomes a public health hazard. The lonely death. We'd always shared confidences but now I couldn't admit that my affair with my classmate was brief, that my new friends were busy with their weekend jobs and families and friends, that I didn't feel that the family we had in Sydney could provide any safety. I couldn't tell her that I didn't know if I was straight or gay, who I wanted, or who would want me.

Instead I said, 'It's not like that, Ma. You're stuck in what you've learned from books, and that's an outdated literature. I read Radclyffe Hall's *The Well of Loneliness*, but really, it's not like that.'

My mother was pensive. 'I've always thought someone like you would marry an erudite man, someone who could match you intellectually.'

'What, a nice Jewish doctor?' I laughed. 'Seriously? You know I've never really fitted in those worlds. I tried, but it wasn't right. At uni in Cape Town as soon as I split up with Paul, I migrated from the Leslie Canteen with the Jewish kids to the Students' Union where the lefties hung out.'

'I wouldn't care if your husband wasn't Jewish or even if he were black. But Hayls, lesbianism will mean you won't have children.'

'I still can, if I decide I want to,' I said. 'You know work has always been more my thing than kids.'

My mother shook her bowed head sharply as if to dismiss this news. 'Darling,' she said, 'I just so want you to be happy. When you're happy, I'm happy.'

I sighed. It was a line I'd heard all my life, a sentiment I interpreted as pressure rather than love.


My mother and stepfather came to live in Australia earlier than planned, seven months after my coming-out visit back to South Africa. One Saturday afternoon we chatted in my mother's Sydney lounge room, seated on those same couches, surrounded by those Persian carpets and paintings and a carousel of books: the trappings of home transplanted to another country.

'What are you doing tonight?' she asked, one of her perennial questions.

'Nothing,' I said.

'Oh, darling,' she said, her voice dripping pity. 'You could stay for dinner ...'

'No, thanks, it's fine,' I said, painfully aware she thought I was fulfilling her 'lonely lesbian' prophecy. Painfully aware too that if I'd been able to cooperate with the pretence of family, I'd not be so alone.

I picked up a video and bottle of gin and went home to my cold, silent flat, a floor below street level. As I sat in the armchair I'd brought from South Africa, staring at my books and paintings, the air smelling of subterranean damp, my independent life seemed to have lost its lustrous possibility. Under my mother's watchful and disapproving scrutiny, my Sydney life seemed a vacant dead end. Maybe I had to stick with the structures I'd been raised for. Maybe my mother *did* know best: I'd be a lonely lesbian. But I wanted to be with women, not men. It suited me – emotionally, politically and definitely sexually.

Voices floated in from the street outside. What to do. I was reeling from an accusation and ensuing fight that I, the youngest and the favourite, was 'killing' my mother with my lesbianism. Certainly my mother didn't approve, and love, in my experience, was conditional and synonymous with approval. I was used to my mother saying with pride, 'You're so like me.' To flaunt her approval was to risk losing her love – the only love I'd trusted since my father's death. And it was potentially foolhardy: if I was so like her, should I heed her experience? Did she know best? I'd tried to strike off on my own but I was teetering on thin ice: not yet connected to secure friendships and still bound to a family rife with decades-old compromises.

I contemplated what seemed like a Hobson's choice. As the sky lightened, I swallowed a whole box of heavy-duty prescription painkillers with yet another stiff gin. I hoped I'd never wake.

Through a fuzzy haze I heard hammering on my front door and my mother's voice. 'Open the door, Hayls. Please, open the door.'

As always, I cooperated: opened the door, walked as commanded, threw up pills and gin and bile, and then went to see the therapist my mother had arranged. The therapist insisted my mother come too.

When I narrated my experience of the family, some of which my mother hadn't been aware of, she buried her head in her hands, and, as she'd always done, asked, 'What do you want me to do?'

I answered as I'd always done. 'You've been asking me that question since I was little. Why must I take the responsibility and tell you what to do? You're the mother.'

She said she'd failed me. She declared her love. She quoted poetry, 'let the dead past bury its dead'. She did nothing.

The therapist encouraged us to appreciate how neither could legislate the other's choices or behaviour, the lifelong challenge of any enmeshed mother–daughter relationship.

I planned the meeting between my mother and Jen carefully – timing, food and company. My mother would fly up for the local writers' festival, and Jen would drive to town to meet her. My writer-housemate and her Cambridge-educated artist-writer girlfriend would be the reinforcements.

As soon as Jen's truck lights flickered against the wall I raced outside.

'Do I pass?' Jen asked, gesturing to her black jeans and white shirt.

'Absolutely,' I said. 'Don't worry. That's not my mother's focus.'

My mother and Jen greeted each other warmly, probably even kissed. Then, even before dinner, perched on the sofa, legs tightly crossed, my mother shot Jen a volley of questions including, 'What are you reading?'

'Oh, I don't have time to read,' Jen said. 'Too buggered by night-time.'

I laughed nervously and stole a look at my mother.

My mother's eyes widened; she parted her bright pink lips, held them open, wordless, and then clamped them shut. Jen's response was bound to fuel her disapproval and concern.

'Dinner's ready,' I said, cutting the silence.

Dinner was a roast, red wine and a bookish conversation. A passion for reading fiction had become the only combat-free territory for my mother and me. I shot my well-read housemate and her girl-friend grateful looks and relaxed a little.

After dinner, as Jen lay on her side in front of the fire, she asked, 'Do you lot ever talk about anything other than books?'

We all laughed, my mother included. I studiously avoided her gaze.

# 5.

# CUT LOOSE

TOWARDS THE END OF our first year together, in 1998, Jen proposed in an old church. Although it was now a home, the house retained its cathedral ceiling, high windows and a few pews. The scents that night were coriander and basil rather than frankincense and myrrh, but the collection plate hovered in the candlelight: the night was a fundraiser for the people of a remote Indian village. After dinner, there were raffles with prizes of paintings, pottery, massages and a ceremony donated by a marriage and funeral celebrant.

The gathering of lesbians wore leathers or flowing silks, long hair or short hair; we were artists and welfare workers, professionals and party girls. We identified as feminists who saw ourselves as independent, autonomous women and most of us, even those in monogamous relationships, were averse to the patriarchal and heteronormative institution of marriage and even chose not to live with our lovers.

After dinner of rice and dahl, a glass was clinked for attention and the raffle was drawn. Jen won the celebrant's ceremony.

She stood to the applause, the single sleeper in her ear and the buckle on her belt glinting in the candlelight. From across the crowded church hall, I watched her, pinching myself that this extraordinary woman was my lover.

Suddenly, she placed her hand on her heart and called out, 'Hayley, will you marry me?'

I stopped breathing. If sex marks the beginning of a relationship in stories of an unlikely couple that overcomes obstacles to be together, marriage is traditionally the event that marks the couple as 'hitched'. But what if the law doesn't allow you to marry? What if same-sex marriage hasn't yet become the mantra of equality rights, and floats in the Gay and Lesbian Mardi Gras aren't yet featuring brides in white tulle or tails? What if independence had always been your goal and marriage never on your wish list, not as a young heterosexual woman, not as a lesbian? What if you'd spent three years in Sydney as a member of the Lesbian and Gay Legal Rights Service researching and writing a community discussion paper called *The Bride Wore Pink* and advocating publicly for the legal system to recognise relationships in new ways rather than impose the dependence straitjacket of hetero-normative marriage on a community where relationships take multiple forms? What if you saw marriage as an anachronism – an institution that had once defined women as property, denying freedoms including the ability to say no to sex? What if it was currently used by governments to limit people's independent rights to benefits such as state support?

What if you'd already assimilated as a migrant and saw no reason for lesbians to assimilate into the mainstream? In fact, you were proud to be part of an outsider subculture interested in alternative ways of living. It had seemed a place to belong.

Sitting in that converted church hall with sixty eyes turned on me, I wanted to slip under the table and cloak myself in the fringed tablecloth.

Now I wished I'd not been so earnest, so attached to revolutionary, intellectual arguments and my identity of 'law reformer'. After all, I knew Jen wasn't serious – she'd told me that she too had no interest in marriage. A 'yes' would've been the gracious and playful response.

But back then, caught in the glare of all those eyes, I couldn't see

Jen's invitation simply as a playful celebration of our love. Saying yes would have run counter to everything I believed, everything I'd written in law reform submissions, everything I'd said from podiums in Parliament House and at legal conferences.

I shifted on the church pew, pushing curly hair off my face. With a playful smile I looked at Jen and said, 'I love you but I won't marry you.'

A chorus of 'Why not?' and 'Ah, Hayley' rose from the crowd.

I opened my mouth but nothing came out. This wasn't a conference where my audience had no idea what it was like to live as a lesbian in a world of compulsory heterosexuality. Should I say I didn't want to be a 'wife'? That it wasn't 'fair' because the gold standard of marriage invalidates all sorts of other significant relationships? Should I say I didn't believe in staying in relationships that were damaging, and I'd seen too much of that in life and in case law? That it seemed heterosexual couples often got married around the time a lesbian couple might split? Should I say marriage wasn't the kind of glue I wanted to sustain my relationship?

The hall was pin-drop quiet. Everyone was looking at me, waiting.

My response erupted: 'It just adds pressure.'

There were friendly boos.

I blushed, and to those close by I said, 'Didn't those girls who had a commitment ceremony split up just months later?'

And then Jen came over and, circling me in her arms, she whispered, her breath hot against my ear, 'You know I was only joking.'

'You bugger,' I said. 'Talk about pushing me to my limits – again.'


Two years later I sat in front of the dean of the law school's rosewood desk. I took a deep breath and said, 'I'd like to give notice and leave at the end of semester.'

Three months earlier in a bland room at a health centre, the women I'd interviewed about their experiences with police had flicked through the thick spiral-bound report entitled *How Do I Prove I Saw His Shadow? Police Reponses to Breaches of Apprehended Violence Orders*. Hands gripped behind my back, I scratched at the skin around my thumb. I was terrified. Might the police come after me when they saw the report? Might these women change their minds when they saw their stories in print?

Some of the women laughed at the details I'd altered to hide their identities, some nodded knowingly at others' quotes or stories. Most said they were proud to have participated. One woman left without saying a word. I watched her through the window, lighting a cigarette, taking a slow drag. I wondered if she felt too exposed. Maybe she was back with her ex-partner now; maybe she, like my mother, wanted to 'bury the past'.

After the last woman had left, after I'd binned leftover sandwiches, I'd sat in my car rolling and smoking cigarette after cigarette. I imagined these women and their children's futures and wondered if their generous sharing of their stories would lead to any change for them or other women, personally and legally. And then it struck me: these women looked to me for help, and yet they'd done what I'd never been able to do – they'd shed shame and fear. They'd stood up to bullies and perpetrators and then told their stories publicly. The 'I' pronoun was completely absent from this 300-page academic work, even from the acknowledgments section. Yet always beside me, despite the self I projected professionally, were my own fears, my own experiences of abuses of power and sex, and the ongoing torment of silence and lack of resolution. Feelings which this professional work had uncorked all over again.

Once the report had been published I'd gone back to teaching my usual classes, but when I'd stood under the fluoro lights my voice was dull, my energy lukewarm. The stories of violence and abuse, of isolation and lack of community support that I'd heard from the women I'd interviewed now cycled through me along with my own. More than ever I doubted the ability and commitment of the law to keep women and children safe. As the weeks of semester had worn on, I'd begun to doubt myself as a teacher too. Without passionate conviction in the law's capacity to protect people, how could I inspire the next generation of lawyers to work for social change? During weekends with Jen on the farm, I cried too much, smoked too much and slept too little. I was afraid – for the participants and for myself. If we teach what we most need to learn, perhaps we write about others what we most need to write about ourselves.

The dean's face drooped with concern. 'How about you take a semester off?' he said. 'Or we could give you a lighter load.'

When the dean got up to take a call, I stared at his framed degrees: LLB, LLM, PhD. This was the future I'd been reared for, but was it the one I wanted? And then I thought back to a series of weekend acting workshops I'd done after a therapist had encouraged me to 'do something creative'. At the first workshop one of the participants had called out, 'Give up your day job.' I'd laughed but later, as I drove home, I'd thought maybe I should – could, would. During the second weekend workshop, I'd learned about 'status' and in improvised scenes competed for the upper hand. On the Sunday evening, as the dusk darkened, I'd sat in my car, feet resting on the running board, smoking and thinking about all the things I depended on for 'status', perhaps for protection: academic job, role on the community legal centre's management committee, big house, friends, parties I threw, girlfriend, and funny and smart housemate. Who, I wondered, would I be without all those 'things' and labels; where would I fit? What would keep me safe? I even wondered whether Jen might be less interested in me – after all, she seemed quite tickled to have a girlfriend who lectured law and had a big house with a pool. What did I – independent of my mother and my friends – truly want to do? What did I value?

'So?' the dean asked when he returned. 'How about half a semester off or a lighter load? A casual could teach welfare law from your distance ed materials.'

'No, thanks,' I said. 'I'm going to retrain as an actor.'

Even if the dean and everyone else thought I was certifiable, this, rather than law reform papers or textbooks, was how I wanted to contribute to the world. Discovering a little of what it was to walk in other people's shoes and presenting those lives on stage.

The dean insisted I take unpaid leave. We'd discuss the resignation in a year. He reminded me how fortunate I was to have a permanent position at the university.

When my housemate declared she and her girlfriend were going to travel around Australia for an unknown period, I put the house on the market. Gracelessly and defensively, I shrugged away concerns and claims, and the significance of a home that had been a sanctuary not only for myself but also for my housemate and close friends. It was time for change. Time to be free of the financial burden of a large property; time to live in a place where I felt safe alone. I accepted the only halfway decent offer and, four months later, I slid shut the glass front door.

In the apricot sunset, I stood on the cement water tank looking west to the mountains, conscious of how attachments – or the meanings we give them – shapeshift. What an abecedarium of changes I'd made by the age of thirty-four: country, family, community, sexuality, cities, jobs, friends, housemates, lovers and preoccupations, never mind the more superficial changes like cutting long hair short and putting on and taking off weight.

Each change, despite others' warnings, despite intense fear that I was further deconstructing my rickety safety raft, had seemed clear. Each change, I knew, had been facilitated by my advantages, economic and educational. Out loud I said, '*Siyabonga*,' the Zulu word for 'we thank you' and the name we'd given to the house. Thank you for this era.

Twelve years ago, I'd decided to emigrate the day I'd heard my father had died. Now, on the brink of the new millennium, I'd abruptly rid myself – and my housemate – of home. I had a storage shed jammed with books and teaching materials, the remnants of the furniture I'd brought from South Africa and what I'd accumulated over the last eleven years. In the boot of my car was a suitcase, my favourite mug and a box of books. Untethered from a home and a job and a precious big sister–like housemate, again my education and the money in my bank account felt like my only security.

But as I drove towards Jen and Tywyah, I was comforted by the thought that in a fortnight I'd be on a plane to South Africa. I was going home for the third time since I'd migrated. But this time Jen would be coming with me.

At the end of our first year together I'd 'gone home' with Jen to the flat country and wide-open skies of her youth: Tycannah, a large sheep station in outback New South Wales. In nearby Moree she'd ushered me into the country outfitters, a long narrow shop with akubra hat high-rises. While she'd assessed the hats' brims and bowls, I'd read out names like Cattleman and Campdraft, all so magnificently, quintessentially Australian.

The salesman had come over, surveyed my jumble of thick hair and asked my size. I blushed and apologised. I didn't even know hats came in sizes – caps on a tennis court were all I knew of hats.

'Try the Colly,' he'd said.

As we drove out of Moree, I examined my new hat: its broad brim, crocodile-leather band, high crown with the runway crease and the three holes punched in a triangle. The colour was a little ordinary – plain old fawn – but its body was at once firm and smooth and soft. How many rabbits, I wondered, had died for my hat.

'Collarenebri,' I read out the sign as we drove into the next town.

'Not bree – bry like fry,' Jen had said, chuckling.

'Is this another case of Gwydir?'

She'd laughed. '*Gwy-dah*. You've gotta get the Aussie drawl, mate.' She dropped her voice and accentuated her accent. 'Gwy-dah, like wider.'

'Okay, this one's easier – braai like *braaivleis*, as in a South African barbeque?'

'What are you doing here with me?' Jen had said as she pulled up under a red gum on the banks of the Barwon River.

Now, two years later, I'd show her my landmarks and introduce her to my people: stepmother, aunts and cousins, and my two 'happy families' – families I'd grown up with, the parents my parents' friends, the children my friends. I'd also show Jen my three sanctuaries: my father's and the two happy families' homes, places that had been my refuge from the complexities of my mother's house.

I'd migrated to Australia for the safety of a passport, and for twelve years I'd lived an assimilated life: my accent had softened and developed the Australian end-of-sentence upward lilt. I said mandarin not *naartjie*, passionfruit not granadilla, and caught myself before I uttered South African phrases like 'ag shame' or bastardised Yiddish phrases like 'oy ayoy'. And yet, still I thought and talked of South Africa as 'home', still those three Johannesburg sanctuaries occupied a permanent corner of my consciousness signposted 'safety' and 'belonging'.

# 6

# SANCTUARIES OF OLD

FROM THE AIRPORT the taxi drove us to the home of one of those 'happy families' where we'd be staying. As we turned into the street, I caught my first glimpse of my sanctuary: the tennis court where, as teenagers, we'd battled out tie breaks as Borg and Navratilova. There was the paling fence, the white-walled gateposts free of Johannesburg's ubiquitous wrought-iron gate and intercom. We whizzed up the curved driveway, past cherry blossom trees and rolling lawns, towards the Spanish-style house. There were the high rendered white walls, courtyards and crevices where we'd played hide-and-seek as children. I was back; even if the four sons now lived elsewhere and the parents were away, it was all still there welcoming me.

Jen's jaw dropped. 'And I thought the Galls' house was grand,' she said, referring to the employer's house on Tycannah station where she'd lived as a child. A house she'd only entered for the annual Christmas visit made awkward by the firmly written class lines.

After we unloaded our bags I told Jen how once, playing taxis in my mother's car, I'd released the handbrake and rolled perilously close to the edge of the white rendered wall. 'Follow me,' I said as I squeezed past the cars in the garage and entered through the pine kitchen door, as I'd done for decades.

Now again I found Evie in the kitchen. Evie, who'd ironed our school uniforms and fried fish and chips for dinner, just as she was doing now. She laughed as she held me at arm's length and said, 'Ooh, look at you, a grown-up lady now.'

We passed the room off the kitchen where each of the four boys had carved their names into the round pine table, and I led a wide-eyed Jen up the spiral staircase to the guest suite where, for the first three years of high school, I'd stayed for the month my mother was in London. For those months I was so happy: never shamed, never bullied.

I felt like a character in an out-of-focus movie: there were multiple versions of myself. A bucktoothed seven-year-old leaning over the arm of my mother's chair as she and her friend gossiped and laughed. A teenager in a grey school tunic, playing Scrabble with Daniel, the oldest son. And I was also a 21-year-old, disoriented by my father's death, seeking advice as I sank into the feathery couch.

On day one Jen and I sank into those same feathery couches and dunked in the clear blue swimming pool where I'd once played Marco Polo.

For lunch I raided the fridge, introducing Jen to Provita biscuits and Mrs Ball's Chutney.

'They're not nearly as tasty as Vita-Weats,' Jen said slathering on butter.

'I know. That's what I keep telling my mom when she buys all this stuff from a South African deli in Sydney. I don't get that ghetto mentality,' I said.

On day two the security alarm went off, screeching and insistent. My imagination catapulted. The house had a million entrances and exits. Where was the intruder lurking?

'We probably set it off somehow,' Jen said.

'You can't know that,' I said, astonished by how unruffled she was. Was I unhealthily fearful or was her ignorance a consequence of foreignness?

Flustered, I searched for the security code and stabbed at the keypad until the alarm stopped. The phone rang – the security company would be sending someone round just to check. Within minutes a man in a bulletproof vest appeared at the door.

'I'm so sorry,' I said. 'We don't know if we set it off.'

He said he'd look around anyway and when he returned, I found myself gabbling about how we were visiting from Australia where I didn't even have bars on my windows. I made out that it was safe. It was – to Jen. Nothing was to me.

Jen explained she lived on three hundred acres, that she left the keys in the truck and her house didn't even lock.

He was flabbergasted. 'You can't do that here,' he said. 'Even in the township where I live, the *tsotsis* will come and take your things.'


The next day there was lunch with my stepmother, Genee, in what I still described as my father's house.

'This is how I learned to reverse,' I told Jen as I drove up the long panhandled driveway of 48A Fourth Avenue and looked up at the house's high walls, a blank sandy render but for a few high windows. Jen seemed a little nervous.

'It'll be fine,' I said. 'Genee's lovely.'

I led Jen through the vast open wooden door, chess-boarded with dark mouldings, and into a foyer with a flight of stairs. There were three stairs up in one direction, then a run of fifteen. On my first visit to this house, when I was six, I'd gazed up and seen a woman with a swathe of shiny chestnut hair and revealing cleavage, framed by chocolate-brown walls.

'Bonjour,' Lesley had said, looking down at my father and me.

I'd put my head down and run up to the top, to another world. For years to come – after Lesley went back to Paris, after my father married Genee when I was fifteen – whenever I climbed those stairs I'd laughed and relaxed.

Now again, fair Genee stood on the landing, lit by the skylight's beam. It was twelve years since my father had died. In that time, with no one to share my memories of my dad, my only links to him had been phone calls with Genee. Now here I was, back in his house, smiling up at Genee from the bottom of those stairs, saying, 'This is Jen. Finally, you get to meet her.'

The house at 48A Fourth Avenue was an archaeological dig of my dad, every corner a memory trigger. To Jen I pointed out the walls where one night the naked picture hooks had announced Lesley was gone for good, the studded leather armchairs where I'd sat arguing politics with my conservative dad, the silver cigarette-holder from which Genee's son and I had nicked cerise cocktail cigarettes. Everywhere were physical connections so overwhelming that they seemed to subvert my adult self.

Next stop was a visit to Ellen, my nanny until I was twelve. As a baby, when my mother was out – teaching or playing tennis or bridge or visiting friends – I was with Ellen. As she pegged washing and washed dishes, she carried me on her back, secured by a woollen blanket. Her work done, she'd carry me to her room and lift me onto the thick cotton bedspread of her bed, high up on milk crates to keep away the demonic spirit known as the *tokolosh*. She'd turn on her radio and out of it would stutter a blur of words in Xhosa and then a township jazz of guitar, saxophone and drums. Ellen would hang her apron over the chair and pull the *doek* from her head, revealing her head of tight black twists.

When we heard my mother's anxious call from the back stairs, Ellen would open the door and call, 'I'm here, ma'am, Hayley's with me. Don't worry, ma'am.'

Then she'd again drape herself in doek and apron, strap me to her back and say, 'Let's go back to your mummy, *mbumbu*.'

*Mbumbu*, she told me, meant 'my baby'.

As I child, I went to Ellen not my mother after a dog bite, and spent hours sitting on the kitchen bench quizzing her about her mythical home in that place called the Transkei, a place she went to for four weeks each year. I wanted to know where she had a bath, where she slept and ate, what she did during the day. There were no jobs there, Ellen told me, that's why she had to live with us, leaving her son, Vusi, three years younger than me, to live in the Transkei with his grandmother.

'When can I come see your house, Ee?' I'd ask.

She'd laugh and say, 'You can't come home with me, *mbumbu*.'

'But why, Ee?'

'You must ask your mummy.'

My mother gave no real explanation either but the rule was immutable: I wasn't allowed to go home with Ellen.

Decades later, Ellen still worked in the northern suburbs of Johannesburg for a Jewish family. When she buzzed Jen and me through the security gate, we hugged and hugged and all my longings and fears melted as they'd always done. Even Jen got a hug, although I wondered if Ee realised we were lovers. For all my brazen gay activism and my annoyance that Jen wouldn't show affection at her community hall, I wasn't sure how to break the news of my lesbianism to Ee.

'Sit, sit,' she told us, leading us into the employers' lounge room, laughing when I suggested we go to her room.

I sat close to Ee on the leather lounge as she told me Vusi and his wife had both died from pneumonia, about her two grandsons living with their other grandmother, about her husband, Simon, and about when she might retire and Vusi's sons come to live with her. A story of so many African families in a time when HIV/AIDS seemed to have wiped out a whole generation.

'I can help you buy a house, Ee. I have money here – from Daddy – that stays here,' I said, pierced as always by the inequalities of South Africa and by the unearned advantage of inheritance. 'How much is a house in Soweto?'

Ellen shook her head. 'The government must give me a house in Soweto. Madiba said they would.'

We talked about the reconstruction program, about buying land in the Transkei and the plans to bring running water and electricity to rural areas.

Jen explained that on the farm she didn't have mains power or water. She pumped water from the creek into a tank, had a gas fridge and solar panels which gave her lights.

Ellen put her hands to her mouth in surprise. 'You live like that, *mbumbu?*'

'Not me – Jen.' I laughed.

'It's my choice though,' Jen said. 'Because of where I live, and how I want to live. It's cheap. No bills.'

Ellen explained that she'd put in her application for a house in Soweto, and then she added, 'I like it here with Miss Irene. I have nice rooms and a bathroom, and my friends, and my church. In Soweto there's lots of *tsotsis.*' And then she placed her hand on my arm. 'Now, *mbumbu*, tell me, how's your mummy?'

'Would you like to go out for lunch?' I asked, eager for us to lay down pathways away from the white child–black nanny skeleton, eager to experience this new South Africa where anyone could eat in a restaurant regardless of skin colour.

'No, let me cook some *pap* and *boerewors.*'

And then we laughed together, as Ellen told Jen how I'd liked to sit with her in the sunny backyard, rolling clumps of stodgy *mielie pap* and dipping them in tomato gravy.

'Remember, *mbumbu*, how your mummy would get cross? She'd say, "Ellen, you're making my baby fat."'

After I'd given Ellen the usual envelope thick with notes, we stood outside the high wall where sweet peas scented the air. Falling into her long goodbye hug, it was as though everything was still here for me. Even if the alarm system had reminded me I was only a visitor, even if I felt uncomfortable with the continued inequality and the persistent real or imagined threat, here in South Africa I was safe and loved by people who'd known me forever.

As Ellen stood on the step waving us goodbye, we climbed into the car.

'She's gorgeous,' Jen said. 'But how weird that we sat in her employers' lounge room.'

'Sucks, doesn't it, that she lives in someone else's home?' I said, aware that in contrast to Ellen I'd just voluntarily given up my home, confident I'd be able to rent another place. 'Did you get how buying property works in Soweto?'

'No idea.'

'It sounded like you don't just go buy a house. Maybe there are way too few houses for the number of people. Or maybe Ee doesn't know 'cos she's never had the resources to buy a place.' I drove on, replaying the conversation with Ee. 'And did you hear what she said about feeling safer here than in Soweto?'

'Her friends who live here,' Jen asked, 'would they be domestic workers?'

I nodded. 'I'd bet these houses are mostly still owned by white people,' I said, looking at the high walls, some topped with coils of barbed-wire, others with shards of glass. 'Imagine if I could afford to buy her a house here. Would she even want to live here with her grandsons? How would it be for them?'

'Slag-it?' Jen said, reading out a sign.

I laughed. '*Slag-gat* – pothole. The Gs are all guttural. It's Afrikaans.'

Jen tried again.

'This'll be your version of my Gwydir River,' I said, and we laughed.

I slowed to a stop at a traffic light where a man walked up to my window holding a cardboard sign inked with 'No job no money no home'.

I scrabbled for some coins from the purse we'd stashed in the console and dropped them into his paper cup.

'There's someone at every single traffic light,' Jen said, shaking her head.

'Yup, and if that guy gets nothing here, no department of social security is going to give him the dole.'

I felt that familiar sinking feeling. All this was what South Africa, my homeland, had been when I migrated: bewildering, overwhelming inequalities jostling against a deep sense of belonging. I watched a man in a wheelchair, his cup lodged between his knees, his hands at the ready to roll out his chair when the lights changed to red. Should I be living here and contributing my Australian knowledge of income support and administrative law to this new South Africa? I remembered the conversations I'd had on my last trip to South Africa, how my descriptions of Australia's system were met with comments like, 'This government couldn't afford that.' I didn't know how to translate the Australian experience to South Africa – or if I really wanted to leave peaceful, safe Australia.

'I mean, you do see some people begging in Australia, but nothing like this,' Jen said at the next traffic light as she dug out more coins.

'It's only six years since the 1994 election. Hopefully it'll change. We're still seeing the unwritten apartheid where mostly it's rich white people and poor black people.' I sighed. 'This place does me in. The streets are the same but I'm ignorant about the new South Africa. I don't understand how things work. My memories and fantasies about what a post-apartheid South Africa would be like – everything's out of date. Like an imaginary homeland. Maybe it would've been different if I'd been part of the transition.'

Jen's hand crept across and squeezed my leg and, grabbing hold of that hand, I accelerated away from where home could've been.

# 7.

# TUGGED:
# OLD MEETS NEW

OVER THAT MONTH IN SOUTH AFRICA, I bobbed along on the familiarity and comfort of people and traditions I'd known all my life. Here I was with my cousins and my happy families, warm and kind people. Here too was the security of Jewish family cohesion: seats were occupied by three different generations and conflicts suffused – or held at bay – when everyone turned up for a Shabbat dinner.

Exiled from most of my secular Jewish family in Sydney, I'd had little to do with other Jews in Australia. Solidarity or even contact had felt dangerous: it could lead to encounters with one of my estranged family members, or an awkward moment during a chance game of South African Jewish geography when someone asked, 'So are you related to x and y?' which was usually followed by, 'And how are they?'

In my second year in Sydney I'd pounced on a listing for a Shabbat dinner in a lesbian magazine, hoping that Jewish tradition might provide some belonging, some continuity between the past and my alienated present. When a girlfriend and I had rented a house together, I'd offered its large lounge room for the Passover Seder dinner. Twenty women squeezed into chairs crowded around the white-cloaked tables, some Jewish lesbians, some partners, some mothers, including my own. She was bravely trying to find a way to maintain a relationship with me. A feminist Haggadah, *kneidlach* in chicken soup, sweet nutty *charoset*, matzah, chopped liver, the treacle-sweet aroma of *tsimmas*, voices reciting the prayers, haphazard singing as Jewish women from different places tried to find common tunes. All the elements of a Seder; all the promise of a chosen Jewish family.

With the dishes piled high on the kitchen bench, I'd looked at my mother a few places down. Her head was bowed, her face strained. She and I were both haunted by hurts. She was torn between three points of a family triangle: her husband and his family, my sister's family, and me; I was adrift from everyone but her.

A knot twisted inside me: the Seder felt like an awkward recreation and reminder of the conflicts in my family. This was not the bridge between the world I'd come from and the world I'd chosen to inhabit. What's more, privy to unguarded conversations among my non-Jewish Australian law school classmates and work colleagues, I'd often heard members of Sydney's South African Jewish community dismissed as pushy, arrogant, showy and rich. I'd made stabs at calling out the anti-Semitism but my shame about myself had steadily increased. I was determined not to be lumped in with any 'them', although South African Jews had once, superficially at least, been my people. To stand out, proudly defining myself by my demographics, was not the path to freedom, nor the way to find my place in Australia. For that, I'd decided, I needed to fit in with my Australian friends.

At most South African dinner tables, when someone sought to include Jen, the conversation followed the familiar refrain: 'So, do you have to milk the cows, Jen?'

'No, they're beef cattle, they don't need as much work. I used to have a milker but I gave her to a neighbour so I don't have to milk at five every morning.'

'Thank god,' I'd say.

I'd shift in my seat, uncertain about the meeting of my two worlds – and to which one I truly belonged. I'd been trying to work out how this aunt, this cousin, this old family friend was dealing with my lesbianism. Now I also tried to gauge how they were dealing with my partner being a farmer. I waited for the typical next questions. First, 'How many cattle do you have?' and then, 'And how many staff do you have?'

'None,' Jen said. 'It's just me and my mate Jack.'

The table was silent, then came the disbelieving follow-up question from people who depended on domestic workers: 'You do it all yourself?'

I'd feel proud of Jen – and of the possibilities Australia presented. 'See,' I sometimes said, 'women can do anything, and in Australia they do.'

On one occasion the conversation took a different course. Around the table were the 'children' of my happy families, the men and women with whom I'd had sleepovers and smoked first cigarettes. The good people I'd always considered my people, my flock. There was one stranger: a man from the United Kingdom. Afro jazz was playing on the stereo and the yellowwood table was studded with empty bottles of South African wine. As usual, conversation turned from South African politics and books when someone made an effort to include Jen. I felt a flutter of peevish resentment: I was loving the conversation, I didn't want to talk about farming.

When she mentioned castration, the stranger said, 'That's barbaric. In the UK you have to get a vet to do it.'

Jen's face flushed. She explained that in Australia, distances and large herds affect management issues and vet availability, that it's legal and common practice for farmers to castrate without anaesthesia as long as the animal is less than six months old, that farmers get good at it because they do it more often than vets.

The knots of the riempie chair dug into the underside of my thighs and I crept my hand up to squeeze her leg. I knew she sometimes experienced the awkwardness of the outsider when she came to town after being on the farm; here in South Africa it was amplified. To my relief, someone changed the topic.

After we'd gone to our room, Jen raged about the man's arrogance and accusations. 'He's got no idea how cattle are farmed, or how things are done in Australia,' she said as she paced.

I was surprised how the conversation had affected her. She was usually so easygoing and self-reliant; frequently she'd told me, 'What others think of you is none of your business.'

'Don't worry,' I said. 'He has no idea how amazingly you care for animals.'

She slumped on the bed and said, 'It's not just him. It's your friends. What will they think of me now?'

I certainly wondered what everyone would make of Jen, but her farming practices had never been the reason I'd imagined they might not take to her. 'It's incredible what you do,' I said, 'and everyone here thinks so too – particularly that you do it without "staff".'

She smiled. 'Apart from that idiot, do you think it went okay?'

I said nothing. All night I'd been wondering what my successful and intellectual friends – writers and lawyers and economists and educators – thought of Jen. She was intelligent and common-sense savvy, she was funny and playful, gentle and charming, but her work and passions were manual, and her conversational style – like her whole family's – was not to ask other people questions.

'Well, I thought it went pretty well,' she said.

I harrumphed. I knew it was unfair to want her to be someone other than she was and to measure her against structures and people which, on the surface at least, were separate from our current lives. Still, I homed in on the castration conversation and said, 'Why'd you have to go into such graphic detail about cutting?'

'They asked,' Jen said. Frowning, she added, 'You're ashamed of me, aren't you?'

I denied it. I said I admired and respected her. This was true, but after we turned out the light, I lay awake, blaming her for the now-familiar track of dinner conversations, wondering why love hadn't followed a more convenient and logical course. In fact, it would be many years of similar dinners and sleepless nights before I could recognise that my embarrassment about 'castration conversations' had little to do with how people felt about likeable, easygoing Jen. It had more to do with my own frail desire to be approved of, and my struggle to adjust my own expectations about who I was, who was worthy of respect and where I belonged.

Outside the Johannesburg crickets wailed. I was nuts about this woman. I respected her, I liked her – loved her, really, with a love that seemed to have infiltrated my every cell. Yet here in South Africa, amid my people, I wished she was more 'like us'. How odd. In Australia, where I lived apart from such people, I wanted to differentiate myself from a family that had caused me such pain.

Did Jen also wish I was more 'like us' when I came into her family? I pictured us going to the movies with her mother and sister Kay on the Gold Coast, and the nights I'd begged off watching television to read a book. I thought about the Christmases at her sister Joan's equestrian centre where I'd often wished I was more of a drinker: there was champagne for breakfast; for lunch there were the family's famous drunken grapes and ice cream laced with rum, accompanied by beers and wine; and then late afternoon Kay would produce 'brown drink', a potent mix of whisky, coffee and ice cream. Horses, food or people from their country past were the topics of conversation. In Jen's family, I felt like a fish out of water. And yet, I was welcomed with kisses, my absence met with surprise. Maybe 'fitting' with a partner's family really is hitting the jackpot, or maybe some of us are always uncertain about how 'family' works – how to belong.

As I rolled towards Jen, spooning around her body, I wondered if and when I'd ever situate myself with my partner, not my past. An image of my friend, his hand on his wife's shoulder, popped into my head. He, like so many others, had found belonging with his partner. Despite the many years of exile from South Africa and my family, despite Jen and our three good years together, still I hovered untethered. Was it the separate and independent way we lived, the consequences of our relationship not being recognised by government? Or that we were from such polar opposite worlds?

8.

# GETTING HITCHED

IF THE LAW DOESN'T LET YOU get married or you don't want a part of the institution, historically, the next step for a couple has been to 'shack up'. Almost five years after Jen and I first became lovers, we still hadn't done so.

One hot spring evening in the north coast town where I rented a railway cottage during my break from law, I nestled into Jen. She smelled of sun and dust, and the backs of her hands and forearms were sunburned dark. It was three long, slow weeks since I'd seen her.

I wove my bare legs under her blue jeans and imagined wide red skies as she told me about working for her sister and brother-in-law way out west, filling up water tankers, driving a spray rig they nicknamed 'The Bat', drinking with the blokes at the pub. I listened with an outsider's passing interest in an alien world – the same way I listened to the tales she brought to town from the farm.

When Jen described her brother-in-law as a 'really good bulldozer driver', I was bewildered by the awe in her voice. I submerged that *What are you doing with this woman? You're too different* voice and instead told her about the acting classes I was taking and that I'd been cast as the indomitable Madame de Merteuil in the play *Dangerous Liaisons*.

'Now law seems easy compared to method acting,' I said, laughing.

'I'm meant to think about when I've felt like a manipulative mistress. Any suggestions?'

I wanted to disregard the difference between our interests: the pretence and public face of acting, and the gritty reality of farming. I wanted to believe everything could be shared, any difference bridged or accommodated.

I could rattle off this relationship's assets: desire, ease, friendship, generosity, harmony, independence, kindness, love, passion, respect and support. On the debit side were the limited time we spent together and an eleven-year age gap – Jen was forty-seven, I was thirty-six. I suspected that to balance-sheet a relationship indicated dissatisfaction. The age gap seemed irrelevant. My concern was that because we only saw each other for a long weekend every fortnight, we weren't sharing our lives. Partnerships need time together, like blood needs oxygen.

'Michael from the acting workshop invited me to his birthday party up at Wilsons Creek,' I said.

'Did I get an invitation?' she asked.

'No,' I said and then added quickly, 'he probably assumes you're not around. He knows about you. I'm sure you can come if you're in town.'

She looked at me with guarded eyes but said nothing.

'What?'

'I think you're more interested in Michael than you're letting on.'

She wasn't the jealous type. I was the one who'd wanted to bolt from dances when she'd flirted with other girls.

'No, I'm not,' I said. Admittedly, I enjoyed his company and attention, and he did look at me with sloppy deep eyes, but then everyone at acting class seemed to long-hug and double-cheek kiss. I had no designs on Michael: I was a lesbian, and the lesbian and gay community was my only home. I insisted: 'I'm not interested in him sexually. We just work together.'

'Yes, and they all want to convert you to heterosexuality,' she said, rattling the ice in her scotch glass.

I puffed up defensively. 'No one's converting me. I'll make my own choices.'

Jen said nothing, just watched me.

'God, Jen, our lives are so separate and different – you on the farm, me here,' I said. 'It's like we're living in parallel.'

From my desk I picked up the month-to-a-page calendar with the image of the beach at Byron Bay. At Jen's suggestion – she'd negotiated long-distance relationships before – I'd coloured in the time we spent together: yellow highlighter for time spent at my house in town, green for the time on the farm. The last three months were mainly white space with a rare green mushroom of togetherness.

'But you're always saying distance keeps the passion alive and our relationship fresh,' she said. 'That you like your independent life.'

'True,' I said, 'but we're more like playmates than partners. I want more. I don't want to spend so much time apart; I'm lonely. I want a partnership.'

'So sublet this place. Come spend the summer on the farm. It could be a three-month free home trial.'

I stared hard at her. *Live there.* Images flashed before me. Of the first time I drove to Tywyah for her fortieth birthday party. Of the long, winding two-hour drive. Of the emptiness I'd felt one day alone at the house when Jen had gone out to do a job, the fear of vanishing into thin air out there. I liked visiting – the romance with Jen, the freedom, the quiet, the fresh air, the magnificent spaciousness – all of it fitted my fantasy of the rural idyll. But live at Tywyah permanently? No way: too remote from town, work, friends and entertainment. 'Life', as I'd been raised to define it.

But I'd reached a crossroads: should I go back to law or move to a city where there might be more opportunity to reinvent myself as an actor or find other work? After the dissolution of the home with housemate and after the weeks in South Africa, I yearned for family – for an anchor in Australia. I was unsure whether to buy a place and set down roots, unsure where this relationship was going. Jen, I knew, had no intention of leaving the farm. A three-month free home trial could at least clarify if I wanted to continue this relationship.

'Okay, three months. No more,' I said. 'But can the two-in-the-morning rooster go live next door?'

She laughed. 'You want to get rid of the rooster, you cut off his head.'

On 23 October 2002, two weeks before that free home trial was to begin, a bushfire blasted everything apart. At sunset I drove up the hill to Jen's house. She sat in the passenger seat, shoulders hunched. As I steered, I searched out her hand, brought it to my lips and held it there, wishing I could kiss away the pain of this loss.

Usually, at the particular point on the rutted driveway where the car demands another gear, the oasis appeared amid the spotty gum trees. Usually, my heart lurched at the sight of Jen, sitting on a log beside a bonfire.

This time, as the truck topped that rise, russet leaves crinkled on black trees and twisted tin arched over the ruins of the mudbrick walls. The high-ceilinged barn with the sulky hanging from the roof was gone too. Stables: gone. Outdoor bathroom: gone. Machinery shed: gone. Gone too were the callistemon bushes and palms, the pink bougainvillea and wild rosemary, the crucifix orchids and citrus trees. Only the blue plastic clothes pegs dangled from the wire limbs of the Hills hoist.

Slow the truck and steal a look at Jen. She's staring; she's silent.

Because the post-and-rail front fence has been swallowed into ash, park just outside the yard. Walk hand in hand to what was once Jen's home.

Hear her say, 'There's no sign of the cats.'

Say, 'Maybe they got away.'

Jen's sister Joan and her daughter Janelle drive up in a white ute.

Hear Jen say, 'We have to go look for the horses.'

Together with Janelle, watch them drive off in a fume of exhaust smoke. It's twenty-four hours since the firestorm swept through the farm – five hours since a tearful Jack had rung with the news – but still the air is smoky and pungent with burned eucalyptus, still the pall of grey-white smoke lingers. It's as if there are no other living beings in this annihilated landscape.

The ground is black, talcum-powder fine but a glimmer draws you to a solid weight the size of a fist. Wet your finger with spit and rub at the hard surface. Revealed, the substance is blue-white, almost turquoise, layered like sedimentary rock. It takes a moment to work out that it's glass that has lost its transparency; glass that's nothing like the delicate soap bubble of the glass-blower's studio. The fire had hardened it, made it earth-bound, like the quartz of its constituents.

Look up from where you're squatting amid the ash as your mind manufactures the louvers of the spare room, and beside them the mottled glass of the sliding windows of Jen's bedroom. Warm to those memories of your first night together and then flush, hoping Janelle can't see your thoughts. How bizarre to reminisce about hedonistic romance when all around is savage destruction. Maybe this is the mind's way of denying reality, a coping mechanism for shock: to see memories rather than tangible, harsh reality. Detect bewilderment in your thoughts – disbelief. How can there be nothing left of a place where so much happened for so many people?

Your heart clenches and twists for Jen. For her, this was so much more than a series of romantic hotspots. For twenty-one years this had been her home, her work, her creation: her identity. Her history was etched in this place. Remember the square photograph stuck to the fridge beside the 'Dip me in honey and throw me to the lesbians' sticker: Jen at twenty-eight dressed in the blue overalls of 1970s feminism, leaning against a truck parked beside a Kawasaki motorbike and an army tent. She called it 'moving in day'.

It's much more for Janelle too. Years ago, when she was still at high school, for a few years she'd lived with her mother and two brothers in a little cabin up the back paddock. Uninhabited for years, now it too was burned, leaving nothing but a cement slab.

Walk down to where the barn used to be, calling 'Puss, Puss', 'Bug, Bug', shaping your mouth into sibilant sounds. In the darkening light pass concrete slabs with burned-out posts like primitive totems – all that's left of the feed shed and tack room.

The chicken coop is now nothing but the half tyre into which you'd drizzled grain. There's no sign of the Rhode Island reds or the white Plymouths or even the rooster that tormented you at 2 am. Wonder how feathers smell when they burn, or whether they also vanished into ash. Find no evidence of chickens, dead or alive.

Notice the four outdoor stables are untouched. So too the paling fence that was part of your courtship, and to the east a stand of spotty gums are unburned. The wind must've changed direction. Perhaps the chickens escaped. Head down the hill, away from the burn site, calling out the cats' names and then 'Chook, Chook, Chookie'. Walk and call until you see the chickens huddled in an unburned patch of short stubbly grass – even Chookie, whose leg Jen had amputated after a fox attack. Exhale. Something has survived. When they cower away as you step towards them, leave them for now. Maybe the cats are also alive. Call 'Puss, Puss' and 'Bug, Bug' and walk further into the bush.

When there's no sign of the cats, assure the chickens you'll be back and walk up to the 'house', past bench ends without their wooden seat; the rims of tyres; and a bicycle lying on its side, its front wheel tortured into an oval, handlebars twisted. The tin of a shed has fallen into itself onto the steps of a ladder to create a teepee. A wheelbarrow lies face down, bent and buckled. Only metal and stone have survived.

Trip and stumble. At your feet is a hole a foot deep where a post must have liquefied to ash, and a jumble of pie-shaped blades and metal that's lost its identity.

Walk around the back of the 'house' and look down the hill into the bush where the fire has been fiercest, rampaging through the crowns of the trees. There are swathes of blackened trunks and russet foliage. No blade, no leaf, nothing spared.

Turn away to what has survived: the rock walls of the new outside bathroom are cloaked with a tablecloth of bronzed tin, and the green bath's paintwork is blistered. Step through the side of the bathroom that was always open to the west and look down at more unrecognisable metal and Mediterranean blue tiles set into the cement like paw prints. Remember the many nights Jen had led you by the hand, love songs swooning out the kitchen window as you'd stood together under the plume of hot water.

Over to the west, stomp your boots against the crossword of loose blue tiles. This was once the kitchen floor of the pole-and-scantling shack Jen had built with Ash. How ironic that name seems now.

Walk around the front of the house and join Janelle who sits on a log that, oddly, has burned at only one end.

'You wouldn't know what was here before,' she says.

Nod. What a leveller fire is – a grand home or a tin shack are all reduced to the same jumble of tin and ash and misshapen metal.

From your back pocket pull out your red and gold pouch of Dr Pat tobacco and scatter shreds along a tally-ho paper. Mindlessly roll this cigarette tighter than your usual skinny racehorses. Pass the tobacco to Janelle and say, 'Sorry, no lighter.' You both laugh, dry hollow laughs, and light your cigarettes from a large log speckled with embers still glowing.

Say, 'We could boil a billy on that and have a cuppa ready.'

But you can't. The billy is now burned or buried, and truth is, you've never boiled the billy. That's another of Jen's many seductive skills – swinging the billy and making damper on a fire down at the river.

Stretch your legs out and look up into the blackened bush of tall gum trees with names you never remember. Sometimes you recognise the silver-leaf ironbark, but that's only because of its silvery leaves. Today the crinkled and crisped leaves don't aid identification.

Say to Janelle, 'Guess that colour's burnt orange.'

Then there's nothing more to say. You've read about the murderous roar of a fire but here in the aftermath, the silence is eerie without the usual evening cackle from the kookaburras or high-pitched calf cry. Sit and smoke and listen to the screams of tin twisting away from the flames, to the firing of the mudbricks in the giant open-air kiln, to ghostly voices whispering from the verandah, deep and high laughter, the strumming of a guitar.

Wonder what this loss will mean for Jen. Think how the farm was not insured – something you, the daughter of an insurance broker, never understood. Think how recently Jen had been struggling to find ways to earn money and wondering what else she could do. Wonder what she'll do without this place that's been her life and identity. Wonder if the fire might provoke her to move or do something different.

Think too about your relationship balance sheet. Now you're ashamed you ever resented this place. Just as the fire erased everything, so too your petty dissatisfactions and privileged aspirations seem irrelevant, wasteful deviations from the truth. Now you push aside your mind's attempts to control and compensate and you see it clearly: there is only your fierce love for Jen. A love you could count in seemingly new ways: selfless, willing and committed.

When Jen returns at dark, having found the horses in a burned paddock, we go down to the community hall where rows of red fire trucks and white utilities are parked. A woman from the Salvation Army is pruning the partially burned lime tree. She offers bacon and eggs. I eat; I always do, even in times of stress. Jen doesn't; she drinks. She can't swallow food.

The hall has become the fire communications centre and desks line the wall where blokes usually hold up the bar. Voices drone from two-way radios and the low stage is crowded with tables of men and women in fire-brigade yellows. On the noticeboard is a large map, black arrows showing the direction of the fire as it came out of the forest, crosses marking houses that have been lost. Beside one in capitals is 'Lewis' – Jen's name. At last count, three other houses have been destroyed, four saved. No human fatalities but a group of kids just off the bus came close to being incinerated in the bush. Brigades have arrived from nearby areas and further afield. More trucks are expected later that night; helicopters will water-bomb in the morning.

I unfurl the borrowed swag outside on the hall's verandah and we lie awake under the fluorescent light, listening to the voices inside, alive and disembodied. Jen is cold and wired with shock. Suddenly, she's shrunk; she's smaller and frailer in my arms than ever before. I hold her tight all night.

The next day when two friends arrive with clothes and food, we take them to the house site. Bug, the front verandah cat, appears from the bush. The undersides of her feet are raw fleshy wounds instead of leathery black pads. With damp hessian sacks we douse flames that whirl like dervishes around the neighbour's hayshed.

Back at the community hall, I boil frozen peas, heat pies and steam potatoes to feed firefighters in yellow uniforms streaked with charcoal. I show the two burly paramedics the cat's pads and hold her while they wrap bandages around her little feet. I give her water and stroke her soft white belly. After a few days she goes to live with Joan.

A local woman, barefoot and lean, is so exhausted and drunk she forgets about the next tray of pies in the oven. It was her husband who saw Jen's house go up. 'He got there just as it went,' she says. 'They watched it burn; there was nothing they could do. He's a mess.'

After a couple of days, we move our swag into the small library attached to the hall. Its walls are lined with *Reader's Digest* classics and the complete set of *Carry On* videos. All night we hear fire crews coming in and out, hear the two-way radio, hear about the section where the fire got away, hear about a new fire raging to the west.

When more friends come out from town, they bring clothes from my house, gourmet food, gifts, donations – and a bottle of scotch. Now Jen has jeans and shirts and socks, and a box of linen including fifty-five mismatched pillowcases. I amuse myself by counting them, imagine each donor wanting to help, try to remember who gave what. But there's nowhere to keep anything and Jen says she wants nothing, so she gives things away as fast as she's given them. Even I, who'd always equated possessions with safety, get an inkling that it's all just 'stuff', perhaps not totally replaceable, but still just stuff. Nevertheless, I stow away some towels and work shirts; after all, she has nothing but the purple T-shirt, blue jeans and leather backpack she'd had with her at my place in town when the house burned down. Without everything she owned and built she says she feels lighter than ever before. She laughs as she, never religious, says, 'I feel closer to God.' I wonder if this feeling will last, and how fire seems to trivialise all but life itself.

I spend days helping Jen deliver bales of donated hay to cattle in burned-out paddocks and fill out claim forms for a woman with a nose-ring whose arms are bandaged from burns she sustained while trying to save her husband's home brew, and for a man who has lost his tin-shed home. I realise he's probably on psychiatric medication and wonder when he took his last dose. A woman tells me she hid in the dam with her four-month-old baby and a kangaroo as the fire raged over them and everything went black. As I jiggle a rattle for the blue-eyed baby, I wonder if she'll remember this moment or only the stories the adults tell. Any blue sky is masked by fog-like smoke and at night we can't see the Southern Cross or the Saucepan.

It's hot and dusty and I've never liked the taste of beer but it's the only drink that's cold. So I take the brown bottle coddled by a stubby holder with the words 'Pub with no beer', and this time the beer is deliciously drinkable. Years later I'll look back and wonder if that moment marked the beginning of my life as a country girl.

At night, I talk to people about things – weather and land – not ideas, feelings, literature and social justice. Watch as people glug down beer the way I drink water. Listen to the sobbing bald-headed man who'd watched Jen's house burn. Tears run clear rivulets down his blackened cheeks. He keeps saying sorry, he keeps saying he wished he could've saved her house. He says, 'It went up with a big bang.'

Jen says, 'Must've been the hundred bales of hay in the barn or the gas bottles and oxyacetylene tanks.' Then she drapes her arm round his shoulders and says, 'It's not your fault. There was nothing anyone could do. It was a freak firestorm.'

This is what I will tell her over and over in the coming months when she again questions why she'd left that day to come to town to see the old friends who were driving through. Again and again I will say, 'Thank god you weren't there.'

Daily, the smoke lifts to reveal a little more blue sky. Areas have been 'blacked out' and 'mopped up'. I learn that 'mopped up' has nothing to do with cleaning floors; it means putting out embers and checking that a burned area won't reignite. 'Blacked out' doesn't mean burned by wildfire; it means intentionally burned so new fires can't get away. After another week, the hall empties out, the fire trucks drive off, the helicopters fly away. The emergency is over.

The local councillors come to see the devastation and I guide them through the ruins of Jen's house. They're silent as they step through charcoal and ash in their suits and heels. They act decisively, arranging for council trucks to remove the rubble from the burn sites, and for the excavation of a hole the size of a football field next to the hall for disposal of rubble.

The local firefighters – men with beer bellies and big beards – peel the tin off the mudbrick walls. Finally we can enter the house. In the bedroom I find a shard of paper from the law textbook I wrote, a soporific Jen had kept beside her bed. The passage was from the chapter on procedural fairness, about the right to a fair trial. My favourite ground of review. It's yellowed and burned unevenly round the edges like the pages of a school history project. I laugh at the law's stubborn survival, and the exhausting density of that book. Nearby are mounds of blackened coins: the loose change Jen kept in a glass jar. As advised, she'll try submerging them in Coca-Cola but the coins will never again shine silver and, despite intentions to cash them in, they'll stay in a saucepan for decades.

We find a buckled potato masher, a toasting fork, a porcelain cup with a gold rim round the top, a shard of pottery from a salad bowl, a cast-iron frypan that has blistered. Jen runs her finger over the buckled and contorted slow combustion stove. She shakes her head at the intensity of the heat.

In the concrete laundry tub up at the site of Joan's burned cabin, we notice matted hair and find the lifeless body of the other cat, Puss. I hold Jen as she shudders and cries. Cries like she hasn't yet cried.

# 9

# PICKET-FENCE HOME

I'D SUBLET MY HOUSE in town for the three-month free home trial, so we were both essentially homeless. Jen's absentee neighbours offered their A-frame doll's house with a loft bedroom and we sizzled and sweated through the summer heat.

Back at the farm I found shards of pottery and tiles. 'We could do a mosaic,' I said, imagining the past re-formed into something new.

Jen shrugged and I felt stupid for even suggesting it. Over where the toolshed once stood we picked through the remains. I found a crowbar cowed by heat and then fished out a pair of boltcutters and some chisels.

'What about these?' I asked.

Jen shook her head. 'There's no point,' she said and then gave me a physics lesson on radiant heat and how it affects the strength of steel, the temper. I lost track of the science; I was tickled by the notion that even steel can become vulnerable.

When I pulled out molten shapes with sharp points and flattened globules, Jen weighed them in her hands and explained they were the aluminium from machinery motors. To me they were sailing ships and castles. Even though there really was nothing to salvage of her old life, I kept sifting through the ruins and playing the game of 'what's that?'. I learned about triple grips that hold rafters together.

I learned about house construction from the burned remains.

As I picked through the rubble, I mused on how the fire had both purged and immortalised the past, including the work of Jen's previous partners, friends and family who'd shovelled, carried, lifted, hammered, painted and etched their names into cement slabs. I thought about how both her previous long-term partners had been so invested in this property, how skilled they were and yet neither relationship had lasted more than seven years. How different I, a pretty rough version of a South African Jewish princess, was from all these women. Would I, I wondered, be able to give Jen what she might need and want at this potentially life-changing juncture, and in the future?

Then I went back to sorting through the rubble – wondering how to salvage some of the past – memorialise it, and planning lunch.

One weekend we left the farm and headed to my hometown for a fundraiser arranged by friends who'd started a Tywyah email list and opened a bank account for donations. Everyone knew Jen's home had not been insured. In a quaint country hall with a view of the Byron Bay lighthouse, while friends decorated the hall with palms and gingers, Jen set a table with contorted cutlery and glass louvres that had melted into layered clumps. Friends had formed a band for the event, others a choir. Artist friends auctioned their photographs and brightly coloured ceramics, and the cooks fed Jen's mother and two sisters and the hundreds of guests who'd dressed up in cowgirl hats and boots. The night was a blast: chat and laughter, music and a pumping dance floor. When Jen and I took to the stage, as tears rolled down her cheeks and she squeezed my hand, I read out her speech of thanks. I looked into an audience of shining eyes and smiling faces. For Jen it was a lesson in receiving; for everyone else it was a heartening reminder of the strength of our community.

Two months on from the fire, after fences were repaired, after council had excavated a hole next to the community hall, a posse of girls from town came out to help load rubble onto a borrowed tip truck and twenty-one loads clattered down the truck's tray into the big hole. The phrase 'to clean up after yourself' had developed a whole new meaning. Twenty-one years of work and possessions, if not burned then buried.

'You could come live with me in town,' I said to Jen.

She smiled wryly, sadly, and said, 'You sure you didn't burn the place down?'

'Busted,' I said, clicking my fingers. 'It was so much easier than chopping off that rooster's head.'

Jen didn't know what her next step would be. Even if she came to live with me she needed somewhere to store things on the farm. So, on hot December weekends, two builder friends built a cabin on the slab of the old tack room. What was to be a storeroom soon became a place to stay.

And so it was that my understanding of construction – and my vocabulary – expanded, although not commensurately with my skill. Under instruction, I cut donated corrugated iron with tin snips, drilled roofing screws into the tin, steadied old lining boards as Jen ran them through the thicknesser, pasted cement into holes to ward off rats, and jested and jousted with Jen to keep her spirits up. My office-white hands blistered and cut and cracked. At lunchtime I set up an iron table in a burned paddock, clothed it in white, and poured water into ruby-red goblets.

At the end of a long day's building or fossicking amid the ash, our legs were black to the tops of our workboots, and my face was streaked grey where I'd swiped at my unruly dark hair. At night I fell asleep by eight, barely able to hold a conversation, let alone read. I was in my body, not my head. It was as if the fire had given me a new skin. To my surprise, I was happy. For once, there was no internal questioning.

We took breaks at the beach but no matter how much I duck-dived under the waves, I couldn't get the smell of burn out of my nostrils. Jen was thin now; kilograms had melted off her. She went warehouse shopping for clothes and I mentally catalogued the provenance of her new wardrobe: the red trousers from the surf shop, the black trousers from my closest friend, the belt from Melbourne friends. One afternoon when we were staying with friends in town, she came back from the washing line empty-handed and tearful. 'I didn't know which clothes were mine,' she said.

When a steel recycling company came to collect car bodies, they took the tin boat that had melted to a puddle, an old car body and then lifted up Jen's blue truck on a hook and squashed it. Jen cried as she had when she found Puss.

The council sent B-double trucks and diggers and we watched mudbrick walls tumble and metal claws dig down to unearth the huge footings that had supported the house. Sixteen loads were taken away.

The bulldozer driver said, 'You made sure it wasn't going anywhere.'

Jen nodded. 'Worked, didn't it?'

After the truck drove away I stood beside Jen and Jack, my hands behind my back, surveying the great big empty space where the house used to be, the ruins of the bathroom's rock walls, and the burned-out horse trailer saved as a monument.

I looked from the house site to the bush. It was four months since the fire had struck. Now the blackened trunks were dressed in green leaves.


Then there was nothing more to do. So, just as I'd once dreamed, Jen moved with me to town, into an affordable house I'd bought in the small town of Mullumbimby. It was two and a half hours' drive from the farm.

Every morning Jen walked Yup, Spook and Lucy, her three working dogs, on the beach; the rest of the day she lay on the couch. She didn't know what to do, whether to rebuild or sell up and move to town and do something different to earn an income. Was the fire the end of her twenty-one years of living as a self-made peasant?

'I'm not used to living with a flush toilet,' she said jokingly, 'so don't expect me to remember to flush it or clean it.'

The house had a backyard large enough for one-legged Chookie and three others; the rest of the chickens stayed with Jen's neighbour Jack, who kept an eye on the horses and cattle. Jen planted lettuce and winter vegetables but nothing flourished. She said the large mango tree shaded the garden, the soil was too poor, and she didn't understand coastal conditions. At night when dogs barked up and down the street, she harangued the irresponsible owners as she tossed in bed.

Mostly, she said little of how she felt. Sometimes I eavesdropped on her conversations to find out if there was more going on for her than I knew. When she couldn't make decisions, I made them for her. When she couldn't deal with the government bureaucracy that was distributing money to low-income and uninsured people who'd lost their homes, I went into feisty legal advocate mode: made calls and wrote letters. I could do something concrete and useful, and I relished it. I suggested, arranged, organised and did – for her.

Until months later, she snapped. 'Stop organising me,' she said.

I walked on the beach, the wind and sand smacking at my tears. It was Jen's loss, not mine; she was even living in town with me as I'd once dreamed. Yet nothing felt right. As my feet sank in the sand, I pictured her lying on the couch where I'd left her: aimless and uncertain about the future. Despite my sweet little house, I felt similarly unmoored. Without my university job I didn't know what to do or who I was. But Jen had had this situation thrust on her whereas I'd chosen this strange, unstructured life without a workplace as identity and anchor. Now helping Jen seemed the only thing I wanted to do, the only thing that gave me a true sense of purpose.

I threw myself into a job producing a play – coincidentally about couples who spend their time in crunchy silences – and flitted between marking papers for the law school and reading the job classifieds. Then I started rehearsals for the play I'd been writing about attitudes to asylum seekers and applied for a job setting up a philanthropic organisation. Despite Jen's reservations about the job's inflated expectations, the low pay and how it'd tie me to town, I took the job. I dusted off the black jacket with the velvet lapels from my city law job, got a haircut and bought a skirt and blouse under Jen's mother's guidance. I grew inside: again I had a role in the world where I could use my skills to do something that might help redress inequality. I wrote websites and brochures, researched the complexity of charitable giving and other foundations. Each week I'd meet with potential philanthropists. It was intriguing – amusing even – to step into homes with marble and stainless-steel surfaces and meet people like my parents and their friends, like older versions of who I was meant to be.

But the gritty reality of the farm pulled me: when Jen went to do cattle work, I went too. We called the cabin 'the love shack' and played cards and Scrabble by candlelight. My face reddened and my hands blistered when we dug holes for fencepost strainers; I 'showered' bent under a tap in the stables and carried buckets of water to wash dishes. When Jen connected a pipe to the sink in the cabin, I whooped as the water first gushed out of the tap. I was awed by the simplicity, and the tangibility, of the workings of living.

# 10.

# MAYBE A BABY

REMEMBER THE SCHOOLYARD CHANT? 'Tom and Lisa sitting in a tree, K-I-S-S-I-N-G. First comes love, then comes marriage, then comes the baby in the carriage.' I was never popular enough with the boys to be the target of this chant but it comes to mind now when I think how, a year after the fire, I started questioning what was 'next'. Even if removing 'marriage' messes with the rhyme and substituting two women's names disrupts the hetero-normative progression, I began to question if, subconsciously, I'd cleared the cluttered career decks to make headspace for motherhood. Maybe a baby was next? Maybe a baby would help me create the stability of home?

Jen's disinterest was unyielding. 'Why would I want to do that? I'm nearly fifty,' she said. 'I've never wanted kids.'

I didn't push it. A baby seemed theoretical. I wasn't sure if I really wanted to parent, if I was looking to fill the gap vacated by my career, if Jen would continue to live with me in town, or if I just wanted to fit in: the lesbian baby boom was in full swing.

'There's going to be a consultation in Lismore on lesbian parenting,' I said one Saturday morning. 'The Gay and Lesbian Rights Lobby is doing a follow-up on *The Bride Wore Pink*. They're calling it *And Then … the Brides Changed Nappies*.'

'So?' Jen said, stretching out on the couch with the newspaper. 'We don't have kids. Why would we go?'

'It's still about how our relationships are treated. Even if the state government changed the law to treat us as de facto relationships, they haven't changed the laws around kids. We still can't adopt as a couple and there are heaps of issues for non-biological mothers, like child support and custody and access.'

'You go,' Jen said, 'I've got nothing to offer.' She flattened her newspaper.

As I stood in the doorway staring at her, the thought struck me: did I have anything to offer? Or was I just clinging to an old identity as a law reformer? An old label, an old home. I felt a sudden stab of loss: not because I didn't have kids but because I no longer had a role in the political campaign. Now that I wasn't teaching law, I'd stopped keeping up with the legislative changes, stopped being the person to update the lesbian and gay section of *The Law Handbook*, stopped being invited to speak at conferences. Jenni who was coming from Sydney to run the consultation now did all that.

As nostalgia pinched, I reminded myself I was happier out of the public role. I'd chosen to step back, hadn't I? I was done with law and its injustice, with worrying whether I was the right person to represent community views. There'd been that lesbian parenting conference in Canberra where, although I'd been invited to speak, I'd felt like an outsider in friendly but unfamiliar territory. After I'd listened to a panel of children talk about having two mummies, and to co-parents describe their experiences, I'd felt awkward, as I'd sometimes felt all those years ago in Sydney when I, a white Jewish ex–South African lawyer, had taken the stage to 'represent' a diverse community's views on relationship recognition. Some of the women were mothers and lawyers; they, not I, should've been the 'voice'.

'I'm not sure I have anything to offer either,' I said, joining Jen on the couch. 'But I think I'll still go. This matters and it'd be awful if Jenni came up to consult with regional dykes and no one turned up.

I might ring Marianna and see if she'll go, and see if Jenni wants to have dinner after.'

In a dusty room above Lismore's Winsome Hotel, together with a reluctant Jen, I joined the group of lesbian 'mummies' for the consultation. As everyone squeezed onto the sagging fawn couches, someone said, 'This is the first time in a year we've been out without the kids.'

Another woman nodded. 'I keep checking to see where they are.'

Jen found a seat and I sat on the wooden floor, my back against her legs. Although this time I was participant not facilitator, I was wide awake to every comment and nuance. Perhaps we never really slough off old passions and professions. Old homes are always with us, haunting us.

In our small regional lesbian community we all knew each other, but for Jenni's benefit we went around introducing ourselves. Jen and I, and Jenni and her girlfriend, were the only women without children. One woman had had a child during a previous lesbian relationship; the others had had their children during their relationships. In two of the couples both women had had a child using sperm from the same donor; in one case the donor was the non-biological parent's brother.

When it was Jen's turn, she said, 'No kids but an ex had two.' She paused. 'I'm only here 'cos Hayley made me come – and to go out to dinner.'

There was a titter of laughter; then it was my turn.

'I never thought of having kids. I was so career-driven but …' I looked across at my friends and said, 'Because of Isa and Massi, I've started wondering.'

My friends laughed heartily and nodded. 'Those kids are cute.'

Massimo, with his whimsical smile, was born just before I'd taken leave from the university. For weeks I'd peered at him from a safe distance until one day Marianna had passed me the swaddled bundle and said, 'Hold him, he won't break. He's nice.'

Since then, every week I'd visited, carrying Massi around the garden, giving him sniffs of mint and coriander or setting him down among the nasturtiums. I'd even changed his nappy – under the direction of two-year-old Isabella, his bright, chatty sister. I was besotted with them both.

Someone asked Jen how she felt about me having a child.

She shrugged. 'I won't stand in her way but it won't be my kid. Hayley can change nappies and clean up vomit and get up at night.'

There were shocked gasps and giggles. I watched dust float in a shaft of sunlight, uncertain whether to position myself with the mummies or support Jen.

'There are enough kids in this world,' Jen said. 'I don't need to add more.'

Afterwards, as we sat on high stools in the pub downstairs sipping cold beers, Jen said, 'I felt the wave of judgement when I spoke. Maybe it's generational. In the seventies and eighties, no one was having kids. We were more concerned about losing our jobs if we came out. The only mention of parenting rights was when dykes who'd been married lost their kids in family court.'

It was not the first time our eleven-year age difference was apparent. Whereas she'd come out in the separatist 1970s when many women were closeted at work, I'd come out in 1989 when separatism jostled against coalition politics and anti-discrimination legislation had been passed.

At her local community hall or around the Fletcher brothers, Jen never kissed or touched me. It was as if we were friends rather than partners. I'd even been introduced as such by some members of her family. Even walking down the street in town, if I took her hand she'd usually hold mine awkwardly and drop it soon after.

'I don't get it,' I once said. 'You're an out lesbian.'

'Of course people out here know I'm a lesbian. I just don't show affection in front of them,' Jen replied. 'Especially not Jack. I don't want to embarrass him. But also, there's been a long history out here. When we first came to the area some people saw us as ball-breaking lesbians, and as witches who made sacrifices and danced naked around fires at full moon. There've been "incidents" too. That family fun day down at the hall, just before we got together. Some girls from town came and one of the locals bailed me up: "What the hell do you think you're doing? This is a family day!" I thought he was going to punch me out until his wife dragged him home.'

None of this made sense to my firebrand lesbian self but this rural community was Jen's world. Who was I to buck it?

The decision to have a baby was different. It was my future. I was thirty-six. If I wanted to fall pregnant, I'd have to act soon. Would our relationship survive it?

After dinner, as I drove home through silent villages, I said, 'Sounds like I do have to choose: you or a baby.'

Out of the corner of my eye I saw Jen shake her head.

'That's not what I'm saying,' she said. 'Don't take things to the extreme again. I won't leave. If you really want a baby, go right ahead.' She paused. 'As long as you're clear why you're doing it.'

Silently I fumed: why couldn't she just say, 'Sure, I'll support you'?

But was I clear? My biological urge didn't seem as strong as some of my friends'. Maybe, at this crossroads in my professional life, I was just following a path I thought I should – one of those internalised narratives. Maybe I was just gooey about Massi or wanted a substitute for my job or family of origin.

In the months to come, as I watched friends go through IVF and advertise for donors, I realised I didn't want sperm from an unknown donor. I listed my male friends and got no further than Daniel, the oldest son of one of my 'happy families' in South Africa. He had good genes. He was kind and open-hearted and brilliantly clever. I trusted and respected him – and he'd also turned out gay.

There's a photograph of Daniel in an album my mother gave me before I migrated, as if to remind me of my roots. On a page headed

'These were such happy times' is a photo of my older sister in a red parka, Daniel in a white V-necked jumper and I'm dressed in a pale pink party dress, clutching the corners of my black velvet bolero. If Daniel's five, I'd have been three. He's smiling, engaged with the camera; I'm all smiles and chubby cheeks and buckteeth, distracted by what's happening off scene. My sister stands slightly apart; Daniel and I stand close, our arms touching.

'Will you give me sperm?' I asked Daniel a few months later, before we'd even got through the main course. The Johannesburg restaurant was crowded with loud voices and spicy slow-cooked *potjies*. Although I'd been back 'home' a few times since I'd emigrated, on each visit I'd felt more disoriented. So much had changed in the fourteen years I'd been away: the place and its politics, the people I'd once known, and myself. The impetus for this trip was the news that my beloved aunt had lung cancer.

Daniel's partner, Pravin, stared at me. Jen shook her head and said, 'Oh, Hayley.'

Daniel laughed and his face lit up: he was interested in having kids.

'Imagine our mothers' faces,' I said. We laughed about the ironies of the two gay children having a baby and whether this might satisfy or upset our atypical Jewish mothers.

'But how would it work?' Pravin said. 'You live in Australia.'

'I'll be ovulating while I'm here,' I said, picking up my fork. 'We could just give it a go – with a syringe, of course.'

'We'd have to check for Tay-Sachs,' Daniel said.

Jen and Pravin looked at Daniel and me blankly. We explained that because we were both Ashkenazi Jews we'd have to get tested for this rare genetic disorder.

Daniel said he'd think about it, and then, looking at Pravin, he hastily added, 'And we'll have to talk about it.'

As Jen and I climbed into bed, she said, 'I can't believe you asked so bluntly – and before we'd even eaten.'

'I couldn't wait,' I said, laughing. 'Anyway, we've known each other all our lives. What do you think? Do you reckon he was keen?'

'Maybe,' she said. 'But I don't know about Pravin.'

'At least he didn't say no,' I said, snuggling into her.

'You sure this is what you want?'

'I think so,' I said. 'Anyway, it's up to Daniel now.'


A fortnight later, after an antipasto and crusty bread lunch, Daniel and I adjourned to the upright chairs of his study, leaving Jen and Pravin to nap on the sofas.

'Why do you want to have a baby?' Daniel asked. 'Is it redemptive?'

There was no hiding here. Daniel knew of the familial estrangements, and how fraught the relationship, once so close, with my mother had become. I admitted he could be right: I longed for family. Again, decision-making rather than biology or 'social infertility' was my hurdle. Perhaps it was so for all women who didn't 'fall' pregnant. Motivation was under the microscope.

It's often difficult to tease out the precise origin of decisions. Now as I write, with more than a decade of distance, I'm equally unable to answer Daniel's question. As much as I loved being part of a sub-culture, perhaps at thirty-seven, the part of me bound by social and familial expectations was surfacing. Maybe the hetero-normative progression is as deeply ingrained as ABC, maybe the biological clock is the handmaiden to the powerful cultural imperative: to be a woman is to be a mother. Or maybe I was searching for that illusory guaranteed human relationship, hoping that a child with my blood and genes would assure me some enduring connection. Some belonging. A home.

Daniel didn't only question my motivation. He questioned too why I'd asked him. 'You still seem really attached to my family,' he said, 'but I feel I barely know you. We haven't been part of each other's lives for years.'

I swallowed hard but couldn't dam the tears. His parents had been my kind, wise advisors, he and his brothers my playmates, his family home my sanctuary. If not with my own family, at least with my 'happy family' I'd assumed I would always belong by being, not doing. Daniel had left South Africa to study in America when I was sixteen and by the time he returned I'd emigrated. But hadn't he signed his first book, just seven years earlier, 'to my sister found'?

'I've been wondering if you hope to cement your bond to our family through a baby,' he said.

Without weekday traffic the Sunday afternoon was quiet. I sniffed, then blew my nose. Until that moment I'd assumed – hoped – this old connection was deep and enduring.

When our conversation turned to the present, Daniel was practical. He was concerned about the implications for his relationship: Pravin wasn't interested in parenting.

'Ditto for us,' I said, relieved to be in the present and discussing something we shared as adults. 'But if relationships don't always last, I'm not sure Jen's disinterest is reason not to have a baby.'

'I'd really want to be involved in my child's life,' Daniel said. 'If you lived in London or even the US it'd be easier. But Australia?'

To me, for once, even geography didn't feel like an obstacle. Our child would have the best of many worlds. Details could be ironed out. Our lifelong goodwill would help us negotiate. Ostensibly we left open the idea of having a child together.

Later, as Jen comforted me, she said, 'Maybe it will still happen. You've been thinking about this for months. They might need more time.'

I rang a pathology service to find out about Tay-Sachs tests but my enquiries were half-hearted.

Before we left South Africa I tore off the tape on a pregnancy-testing kit. As I fingered the plastic components, I imagined watching the strip change to positive. For a moment I considered looking for another donor, even an anonymous one. By passing the decision-making baton to Daniel, was I letting go of something I wanted and wimping out of making an irreversible and significant decision, one that would create new life and possibly destroy my relationship with Jen?

I shoved the kit in its box and threw it away, oblivious that in two years' time the still-unresolved decision would be made by my body: my uterus would swell for the one and only time, not with new life but with multiple, potentially malignant melon-sized fibroids.

# 11.

# A WOODEN BABY

AFTER A YEAR IN TOWN, as parrots squabbled in the golden rain tree outside, Jen said, 'I can't think what else to do. I think I'll take the easy way out and rebuild.'

My heart seesawed: sinking for myself, soaring for her. She was so deeply connected to Tywyah, her place in the bush. I still couldn't imagine living out there but I was certain of one thing: I wanted to share a life with Jen. After all my evangelism about the recognition of alternative families, after my share-housing experiences, after living alone, it now seemed that to live with Jen – to live in a settled relationship with a lover – was to turn a house into a home.

One bright sunny morning we sat in a carpenter friend's place, playing with house designs. We came up with a studio-style house with a tiny space for a study, although I still couldn't imagine living full-time on the farm. If the fire got us 'hitched', Jen's decision to 'take the easy way out and rebuild' seemed like our baby.

My new job with the philanthropic foundation fired me up and filled my days. But on weekends I happily swapped silks and linens for jeans and work shirts to head out to the farm with Jen.

As the winter drew closer, I groaned about showering bent under the cold tap in the stables until one weekend, as I drove through the gate, I saw smoke curling up from behind the cabin. Jen had driven out to the farm a day earlier. A blue bath – once a horse trough – now stood beside a forty-four-gallon drum of steaming water that rested on a rock cave where a fire danced. A pipe from the drum carried the hot water into the bath, the garden hose provided cold water and a wooden dais of old bridge timbers would keep feet clean. As I submerged in steaming hot water scented with spruce and looked up at the starry sky, I was tipsy in love with Jen and the rural idyll.

We drove around the property looking for usable timber. Jen tapped red gum and ironbark trees; she hugged them for size and looked up into their crowns. When she'd selected the red gums, she and Jack carved out the scarf. I held the dogs as trees screeched and crashed heavily to the ground.

'It's brutal,' I said as we stood over the felled tree. 'Untimely ripped.'

'Better than buying timber from a yard and transporting it out here.'

'We should've gone for a steel frame.'

'That would've cost more,' Jen said. 'This is a useable, free resource and it's renewable.'

Like the old house, this one would have solar power and a long-drop toilet but, to my relief, it would be more user-friendly: solar hot water and a gas stove meant we wouldn't have to light the woodstove to cook or heat water except when it was cloudy for days.

'And we need rainwater tanks,' I insisted.

'What's wrong with pumping up from the creek?'

'The cattle poo and wee on the banks of the creek. I don't like drinking water with floaties.'

'What's the matter with you?' Jen said playfully. 'I've been drinking that water for decades. Tanks will cost a few grand.'

I shut my mouth. She'd played the money card.

It was ironic – and ethically questionable: in 1999 same-sex relationships that were 'marriage-like' had finally been recognised under New South Wales state de facto law. But at the time of the fire in

2002, although we'd been lovers for five years, we didn't tick most of the law's boxes: we didn't live together, weren't financially interdependent, didn't have property or children together or perform household duties. If we had been living together, my income and assets would've disqualified Jen from receiving a lump sum payment from the government given to her because she'd been on government benefits and uninsured when the area was declared a natural disaster.

The government payment had given Jen much more than money – it had given her autonomy and freedom of choice at a life-changing juncture. Independence. Perhaps it was the differences in our bank balances, perhaps a manifestation of our feminist politics or because we'd both had relationships where endings had been financially uncomfortable, but for us financial separateness was a given. It was one of the manifestations of how we prized our individuality and autonomy.

I, among others, had made a donation to Jen's bank account after the fire. But now when I offered to pay – for house construction, whitegoods or a new stock saddle – Jen refused: she'd build the house to her budget. So, even if we'd designed the house together, even if I wound up covering half the costs, Jen insisted on tallying my contributions. The agreement was clear: Tywyah was Jen's; my assets were mine.

One autumn weekend a giant of a German man arrived at Tywyah with his mobile sawmill to cut up the red gums Jen and Jack had felled. With exacting accuracy, the scaffolding and sharp blades were set up over each log. Everyone – including two neighbours and our carpenter friend – was allocated a job.

'We pay per log,' Jen had explained as we looked at the timber list: four-by-twos, six-by-threes, three-by-twos, joists, beams, batons, rafters, hip rafters, studs, bearers, ridge plates. Another new language.

I did as told, stepping away from the squeals of the machinery until my cue: load timber onto truck, drive up the hill, unload onto gluts. What was once a burn site became a timber yard.

The miller had advised leaving the timber to dry but council had approved the plans and the local builder, Rang (short for Orangutan because of his broad feet), was available. Now closer to fifty than thirty, Jen had decided to get help building this house.

'But I thought you weren't meant to build with green timber?' I asked.

Jen shrugged. 'It won't make that much difference, and anyway, it'll be six months before we use most of it.'

With pink string line, Rang and Jen pegged out the house: eleven by six metres with room for three and a half–metre verandahs on two sides. How incredible, I thought, as I stood in the 'house' defined by the pink string line, to choose to return to the farm – even to build in precisely the same place. Jen might dismiss her choice as taking the easy way out, but to me – who'd not gone 'home' when the new South Africa was declared, who'd long been estranged from family, who'd left my profession – to do it all again seemed resilient and brave. And unfathomable. Was this, I wondered, what it meant to belong somewhere, to know one's true home?

'This would be too small for a study as we planned,' Jen said, as she joined me inside the string-line house and led me to the south-western corner. 'We'll make it a walk-in-wardrobe and instead block in a section of the verandah for your study. Like where the old dining room was.'

'That's the best view in the house,' I said, tickled by her decision. 'But what about the rest of the house? Isn't it a bit small?'

'Just wait,' Jen said. 'It'll change.'

It did. As the stumps and joists were hammered into place the house grew, and then, when the stud walls rose, it again shrank.

Weekends I'd drive out to the farm where Jen was working with Rang and his offsider Hugh, men whose names I'd learned when we'd worked side by side clearing tin from the burned house.

After twenty-one work days, Rang and Hugh packed their tools. The house was at lock-up.

'But it's not finished,' I said. It was no more than an outer shell.

The 'finishing off', I discovered, was the time-consuming job. No way Jen was paying anyone for that – even if I paid. The friends who'd built the cabin would do the deck, and our carpenter friend would help secret-nail the teak floorboards that had lain in someone's paddock for decades – after I'd belt-sanded each one. The rest Jen would do herself, with my help.

So I held the dumb end of the tape; carried timber and gyprock; passed nails and screws, tape and plaster; sanded and oiled timber; wielded a paintbrush, hammer and belt sander; and held timber for the sliding compound mitre saw. Manual work that looked simple but wasn't. Manual work that one had to learn slowly by doing, not from books.

Throughout the day I'd hear 'Put more paint on your brush', 'Go get …', 'Don't do it like that', 'Try this way', 'Can you …'

Again and again I'd say, 'I'm sorry, I'm trying. I thought I was meant to …'

I was afraid I'd mess things up. I counted the minutes to knock-off time.

'You are a real help,' Jen would say. 'I couldn't do it without you.'

I doubted that but I knew she liked having me around – and even if my limitations frustrated me, even if this was a tough lesson in humility, I so wanted to help and so loved being with Jen. I even enjoyed the actual physical 'doing' – when my arm didn't go numb and I wasn't corrected. Sometimes fear flickered: if I ride Jen's bandwagon am I foregoing my own? What now is my life? And then the practical present pushed aside those feelings and thoughts.

On the sixth of January – the anniversary of my emigration – we dragged couches and mattresses into the backyard of my

Mullumbimby house, cloaked trestle tables with my African print cloths and draped a tarp over the Hills hoist. As I'd done for a decade wherever I lived on the north coast, I'd invited everyone I knew to welcome in the new year; some of my friends had taken to calling it the annual general meeting for the diverse lesbian community. So close to Chanukah and Christmas, this was my attempt to counter the invisibilities and absences caused by estrangement from my own family. It was a celebration of community in all its diversity. Everyone was welcome: 'just BYO drinks and a salad or dessert and we'll provide the barbeque.'

By mid-afternoon I stood surveying the gathering of a hundred people: the kids playing in the mango tree; the women in leathers or flowing cottons, punk haircuts and grey bobs; the dancers on the brick pavers; those sitting deep in the couches or lounging on mattresses under the shaded clothesline. I thought of these as my Gatsby moments, the watcher at the party, checking if anyone needed company or introductions, if the watermelon needed covering, if the fly-veil had slipped from the salad table. I breathed in that tribal feeling, like the one I had on the dance floor at Mardi Gras or at a Tropical Fruits party. This was a beautiful belonging.

Lunch was over, and we'd played the adult version of pass the parcel and the potato dance, where a couple must keep an uncooked potato between their foreheads while they dance. Jen's nephew was blowing up balloons and twisting them into poodles and flowers. Behind me someone heckled in a loud voice. I turned to see who it was and that's when I saw it: Jen's mouth over another woman's mouth, in broad view. I turned away quickly.

Around me, everyone was applauding the performance. I clapped too but all I could think was *that's it, relationship over*. I felt sick fury. How little Jen cared for me, how little she respected me. She'd been tossing back beers for the last few hours; there was no point saying anything to her. I eyed out escape routes. Oh god, we'd been together seven years, had so much fun together and been through so much tough stuff. I'd even begun to consider going to live with her on Tywyah. And now, just like that, in front of all our community, it was over.

In the days to come Jen explained, 'I'd said "shush" and "please stop talking" but she just wouldn't shut up. So I said, "If you don't stop talking, I'll kiss you." And it worked. Come on, I was just playing; it had nothing to do with sex or even attraction.'

'You do that again and we're over,' I told her.

'It didn't mean anything,' Jen said. 'Don't make my paddock smaller.'

She repeated what she'd told me on another occasion: 'Flirting's completely different from hunting. I flirt, I don't hunt.'

I couldn't grasp the difference. Kissing is kissing. A leads to B. Chemical reactions create explosions. If intentions and actions aren't transparent and clear, I panic.

I made an appointment for us to see a therapist. We sat on a couch, leaning on opposite armrests but still touching toes during the session.

'I felt completely betrayed and just so embarrassed – so ashamed,' I said. 'Like the fool everyone was laughing at, standing by watching Jen with someone else – someone she'd rather be with than me. Why else would she do that?'

'If Hayley makes my paddock smaller,' Jen said, 'there'll be no room for me to just be myself. I won't know who I am. This would just be the beginning.'

'But we're in a monogamous relationship,' I said. 'That means we don't kiss or carry on with other people.'

We reached an agreement: no kissing other people.


As the time drew nearer for Jen to move back to Tywyah, I took a deep breath and said, 'I'm coming too.'

In years to come the reasons for that decision would seem glaringly obvious, making it inevitable even. How slippery and subconscious motivation is, plain only in retrospect once we've learned what we had no idea we needed to learn.

Back then I answered others' surprised questions with pragmatism. I didn't want to go back to law or keep working for the philanthropic organisation. The north coast offered no other appealing jobs – for that I'd have to move to the city. If I moved to the farm, I'd be free to have a shot at writing a novel. The income from renting out my house combined with the farm's low cost of living would obviate the need for a regular job. It would also allow Jen and me to contribute in our different ways so that we could both live without financial stress.

Of course love, not money, was my real motivation. Walking together through the loss and recovery had deepened our love and knowing of each other. Perhaps it had taken the rebuild to really get us 'hitched', for me to set aside the balance sheet and admit that this was more than a long-distance affair. Without Jen I'd be inconsolable. As different as we were superficially, we fitted on both a deeper and a day-to-day level. In Jen's steadiness and sensuality, in her intelligence and ease, I'd found something more wondrous than any romantic fantasy. The message was from my heart, not my mind: this love is truly special, it's something bigger and more beautiful, cleaner and deeper, than any love I'd known. I wanted to really *be* with Jen. I wanted to discover what it was to feel one belonged with one's lover – one's partner.

# PART TWO:
# PLACE

*home: the place of one's dwelling and nurturing, with its associations*
— **Shorter Oxford English Dictionary**

# 12.

# FOREIGN

AFTER WE'D LOADED Jen's truck and my car with my boxes of books, paintings and rugs, the tables Jen had made from recycled palings and my *wakis*, the weathered wooden chest I'd brought from South Africa, I stared up at my bedroom window and the golden rain tree heavy with yellow flowers. This was goodbye to my friendly house with its verandah view of Mount Chincogan and the friends and neighbours who waved as they walked past. I'd given notice to the philanthropic organisation and rented the house to friends. My home was now my income. I'd sapped it of emotional value.

I wished the farm wasn't so isolated and I didn't want to be a fringe dweller or break my connection with the 'real world'. Yet after participating in the house's birth, I felt strangely knitted to Tywyah. Even if the fire had immortalised the past, I was part of the place's 'now'. It was as if the magical transformation from savage burn site to shape-shifting house had made the space sacred. Tywyah no longer seemed that dusty, dry and grim backwater of my first visit, nor was it a roadblock to our relationship: it was part of it. Now it spoke of healing and resilience and of something I had no notion of: being part of a bigger story of a place in the Australian bush.

From early 2005 my new address would be a dot on the map reached after you turn south off the inland highway, after you pass by paddocks of corn and lurid green oats farmed by people Jen described as the 'squattocracy'; after you travel another twenty-five kilometres and come upon a bushier, rockier area composed of blocks, the smallest of which is a hundred acres. On Google Earth there are dabs of leek green – the open woodland where farmers grow cattle or crops – and splodges and coils of olive green for dams and creeks. Then there's a wad of seaweed green – that's the quilt of state forests and tree plantations bordering the community.

Population: one hundred permanent residents on a generous rough count. No shops, no post office, no mobile phone reception, mail delivered only three times a week and collected from your mail-box if you've hung out a flag. No celebrity tree changers, no fancy houses or iconic tourist attractions. Here lived mostly 'alternates': pioneering nonconformists with do-it-yourself houses, solar power, tank water, vegetable gardens and chickens. Jen and her girlfriend Ash had been among the first to buy a block when the vast cattle station was first subdivided; at the time there'd been two other lesbian couples. Two decades later, Jen's was the only lesbian household, her place referred to as 'the girls up the hill'. Without a local store, the mudbrick hall with the old boiler beside the blackboard was the centre of the community. With no through traffic, the area was the end of the line – a dead end.

If 'far' implies somewhere else is a reference point, the distance between the farm and my coast home – 185 kilometres or two and a half hours' drive – was not nearly as far as the geographical distance I'd once travelled from South Africa to Sydney. But the cultural distance seemed much greater. At the coast there was a movie house and art galleries, live performances and festivals, bookshops and coffee shops, parties and protests. Familiar structures, all. There I was part of a vibrant, creative and diverse community; there I had great friends with whom I had deep and meaningful conversations about emotions and ideas, about social justice in Australia and beyond, about books and being – one or two were even Jewish. There, although I'd sometimes known loneliness, I did not feel 'other'. I had a flock.

Jen too enjoyed some of those things and people – it was also her lesbian community – but none of that was the scaffolding on which she'd built her life. For the most part, her need for social connection was satisfied by occasional visits from or to friends from town, the banter and beers at the hall's fortnightly bar and barbeque, and her friendship with Jack and his bachelor brothers.

Before the fire, other than the Fletchers, I'd rarely seen other locals – to me they'd been 'the big bearded guy' or 'the woman who wears a tie-dyed slip'. But weeks after the fire, although it had been scorching hot and the tin from Jen's house was lodged against the unstable ruins, a group of local men had turned up to help. Standing beside the burned-out horse trailer, an older man and I had stacked the sheets of tin while others pulled it from the ruins. That day those men had ceased to be 'big beards'. I'd learned their names, began to know them as fathers and husbands, as men who'd left jobs in city construction and the police force to live in the bush. Some were gentle dreamers and thinkers, preoccupied with the universe's workings and society's ailments, their houses still unfinished; others were decisive pragmatists, hell-bent on doing things their way and creating homes using their own designs. They seemed unified by one particular thing: beer. They drank it hot or cold, brewed it or bought it, and quantified value according to the price of a carton.

The local women I'd also met during the fire. Over the sink at the community hall, I'd heard how one had escaped an abusive marriage, how another longed for the income of her old city job, how another who prided herself on her gold-plated cutlery swore this was the best place to live and the best community.

On the anniversary of the fire, down at the hall, a man had said to Jen in an alcohol-fuelled drawl, 'Lucky to have her. Saw what she did in the fire. She's a keeper.'

Jen had nodded, I'd thanked him and we'd eased away to talk to someone else. Even if the man had been drunk, I'd felt a surge of belonging: even if I didn't live here, even if my experience and background were very different, I was a part of the community – I had history with people here.

But later that night, when I got up from the plastic picnic table near the barbeque, I'd looked down as that same man's hand groped my breast. I'd stared at him, stunned and silent, and turned on my heel.

When I found Jen, she shook her head and said, 'Stupid old bastard.'

For months to come, I'd waged my silent war against that man: didn't greet him and moved away when he came anywhere near me. But it's easier to be friendly than to freeze someone out and in time I'd decided that in the scheme of my experience of unwanted, complicated sexual attention, the grope was minor – it was a pathetic and public gesture from a very drunk elderly man in a context of remembering, weighty with grief and shock. If anything, the man was to be pitied. Silly old bastard.

That incident had, however, altered how I dressed around the community. Gone were the fitted clothes I wore elsewhere; here I hid my body under loose button-up shirts and opted for sagging old jeans. This very heterosexual male environment was different from the safety and freedom I knew in my lesbian and gay community, different even from the mainstream world I knew. Jen had been right. Here, it was safer not to show too much of one's self.

On that moving day, all of this flooded through me as I handed over my house keys to my friends.

As Jen pulled the last of the rope hitches tight and checked the load, she reminded me again that moving to the farm was my choice. 'You don't have to stay,' she said, as she pulled away from my house. 'The gate's always open.'

# 13.

# FARMER'S WIFE

FOR THE FIRST SIX MONTHS of life on the farm, I straddled two worlds but with a heavily lopsided lean to the stirrup of my old life. Each week I drove the two and a half hours to the coast to rehearse *Pressure Point*, the one-woman play I'd written about attitudes to asylum seekers. But after the production's run in July 2005, seeing friends and doing the shopping became my only reasons to visit town. Now, each morning, I woke to a day free of a job's demands, what many might call 'living the dream'. There was only Jen and farm work, and that childhood fantasy of writing a novel. My bouncy curls drooped to dull 'farm hair'.

One morning when Jen was going fencing, I called out, 'Wait for me, I'm coming too.'

In the back corner of the shed, I scooped leather gloves from the third drawer, loaded the red toolbox onto the tray of the ute, helped load the bundle of steel posts and called 'hup' to the dogs who leapt up to dance across the posts. It was peaceful in the paddock, the autumn sun warm on my back, the magpie choir a perfect soundtrack.

I speared the heavy shovel-like tool into the ground to dig the hole for the wooden post.

'You're making it hard for yourself,' Jen said. She took the tool and again demonstrated how to use it.

The movement looked so fluid and simple when she did it. I tried again; she corrected me again. We'd done this dance countless times before I moved to the farm but now I couldn't laugh at my limitations, and so we didn't flirt and kiss away my inadequacies.

'Just let me have a go,' I said. 'I won't learn unless I do it myself.'

She stepped back with her hands up. 'I'm just showing you an easier way. I don't want you to hurt yourself.'

My eyes smarted. Having chosen to live on the farm, I had to learn to do what Jen did. Why couldn't I get it? When had I, who'd won countless tennis matches, become so physically incompetent? When had I been so useless at anything? I cursed my skew spine and numb arm. Comparisons may be odious but next to Jen I felt wooden, graceless, butter-fingered and stupid. I knew Jen was being helpful and kind, but still I was annoyed by her 'this is the way it's done'.

A city friend with bright lipstick laughed when I described this scene. 'There's no way you'd catch me doing that sort of thing,' she said. 'I'm a princess.'

But I didn't want to bear the label 'princess' or *kugel*, the label I'd been bullied out of as a child. Such labels were attached to women who were spoilt and privileged, lazy and self-indulgent, consumed by materialism and triviality. Like the other labels – the pushy Jew, the racist white, the arrogant South African – and the elements of truth perhaps contained in each, I had to distinguish myself. Prove myself. I had to learn how to do the work my family and culture had disdained as menial and largely left to 'black' people.

What's more, Jen and I were now in this life together. We were making a home together, and with home came responsibilities. I had to – wanted to – do my part. Repeatedly, Jen had told me she had no expectation of me, that it was a bonus having me live on the farm. But how could I watch her do farm work and not help? What then would my role be on the farm – the farmer's wife who had hot scones ready for smoko? And if I had no designated role, what then was my place? Would I ever really belong?

So I persisted. I discovered muscles I didn't know I had. I resorted to painkillers and booked sessions with a physiotherapist in town to deal with my dodgy back. When it came to straining the wire, I watched Jen wield the pipe and pliers. But when I tried, my actions were tentative. I didn't want to cut it too short, strain it too loose – mess up the job. Even if Jen watched patiently, I'd self-consciously surrender the tools, saying, 'You'll do it better and quicker than me.' So, apart from becoming proficient with boltcutters and pliers, apart from cutting thick plain wire and tying it off four times at each steel post, I handed Jen pliers and pipe, spaced out steel posts, unrolled wire and watched her. Without the ability to take initiative, without autonomy or other work that was 'mine', I felt robbed of agency. The role of assistant grew tedious.

Jen's kindness didn't help. I wasn't consoled by 'You can't be good at everything.'

When Jen and Jack worked in the cattle yards, at first I joined them but, apart from playing secretary, there was little for me to do. When they went mustering, I'd eagerly join them too. I'd not ridden horses before meeting Jen but I hoisted myself up onto patient Boxer, slipped my feet into the stirrups and settled into the hard stock saddle. This was what I'd imagined farm life might be.

With Jen on her grey mare Topdeck, Jack on his paint horse Sharni and me on Boxer, we walked through the front gate and down the first stretch of driveway.

'Come on, get into him,' Jen said. 'Who's taking who for a ride?'

I squeezed my calves against his girth and Boxer paused, dropped manure and walked fractionally faster. Jen laughed and shook her head. She tore a twig from a branch and handed it to me. 'Just keep it in your hand so he can see it.'

Boxer walked a little faster, and when I squeezed again we broke into a trot. What pure delight to see the landscape from up high, the rise and fall of the trot, the dogs running beside us. The stuff of story books. When Jen yelled, 'Get out ahead,' the dogs would race out, corralling the cattle and calves into a mob, marshalling them down a fence line or through an open gate to a fresh paddock or into the yards. When she or Jack whistled or called 'get in behind', they'd sheepishly return to their position beside the horses.

Everyone had a function – except me. Sometimes I'd be told to ride in a certain direction and wait in a particular spot. But if Boxer couldn't see the other horses he'd get tetchy. I'd stroke his neck and tell him it was okay, hoping and praying he wouldn't take off. Occasionally we did help – the cattle saw us and stopped. Then I'd feel a brief surge of usefulness. Most often I brought up the rear, squeezing and squeezing Boxer's girth, begging him to 'come on, fellow' to catch up to the others, who'd again had to stop to wait for me. Most often, from Jen's shouted instructions, I seemed more hindrance than help. After a four-hour ride I'd dismount, unstick my legs and stiffly lead Boxer to his stable. Jen would laugh and say, 'Takes a while to get riding fit.'

So when cattle work was going to take all day, I'd stay home where I picked up wheelbarrow-loads of horse and cow manure, and mowed lawns. I weeded the garden but even there I was occasionally scolded for pulling out a seedling. I picked vegetables – I had finally learned not to pull out the whole spinach plant. Sometimes I wandered through the shed but the power tools and timber didn't entice me.

In the garden Jen directed me where to dump the loads of manure, how to dig up and aerate the beds of soil rich from decades of manure and straw, and how deep to plant the bean and bok choy seeds. I was nervous under her gaze, already convinced I should just leave it to her green thumbs. I'd forget to water the seedlings thinking Jen had done it. So when the seeds didn't shoot, Jen took over. My jobs reverted to the unskilled: I weeded, collected manure, mowed and mulched.

When it was too hot to be outside, I pegged the washing on the line and made cursory stabs at housework. I turned on the radio but even its chatter seemed to amplify the silence of the bush. As much as I longed to have the disposition that saw cleaning as a meditation, I'd rather wear a 'Fuck Housework' T-shirt. More and more I felt like the 'wife' – another label I'd never wanted. Even if Jen and I had been critical of the gendered division of labour in heterosexual relationships, to an extent our relationship had assumed a similar division. It was natural, I suppose: Jen was out on the farm, I was around the house.

There was one major problem: Jen was so skilled in this realm too. Apart from her natural talent and training as a home-science teacher, she'd cooked in a restaurant before she'd moved to the farm. What's more, she came from a family of cooks, starting with her mother, who was famous for her marmalade and mustard pickles.

One evening when Jen fished a dusty ballpoint pen from under the couch, she said, 'God can see under the couch, Hayley.' Although playful, her tone was tinged with the scold of the home-science teacher she'd once been.

I flinched. It was true: when she cleaned, the plughole glinted, even the air tasted clean. I teetered on the precipice of that old rabbit hole: I was a spoilt white South African. But after a decade of using mould destroyer and oven cleaner, sugar soap and steel wool, I also knew that on the spectrum of house cleaning I had definite tidiness and grot thresholds. So I shrugged. 'Guilty as charged,' I said. 'It's not as though we live in squalor.'

'No,' she said, 'but you might try cleaning the draining board sometimes.'

Oh, that pious tone. 'Sorry my cleaning's not good enough for you,' I said, swallowing annoyance and turning back to the stove where I was sweating leeks.

In years to come, on a visit back to South Africa, my aunty Sheila suggested another response. She'd asked me to get the tub of *schmaltz* from the fridge – she was teaching me how to make *knei-dlach* for the chicken soup.

'I can't buy *schmaltz* in Casino,' I said. 'I'll have to render down some fat next time our neighbour kills chooks.'

Shaking her gold bracelet, Aunty Sheila said, 'Much easier to go to the shop.'

As I beat the mixture of egg, matzah meal and *schmaltz*, I told her about Jen's cleaning standards – how God sees behind doors and under couches.

Aunty Sheila's advice: 'Just tell her: different God.'


'I don't expect you to do all the housework,' Jen said, leaning on the kitchen bench. 'And I don't expect dinner on the table by seven. Don't cook if you don't want to.'

I speared the pumpkin with the point of the large knife and, using both hands, cleaved through the hard green skin. I knew she didn't 'expect' anything. But in this farm world, the kitchen seemed the most suitable realm and the way I might be able to contribute. I also wanted to extend my repertoire beyond spaghetti bolognaise, roasts and banana cake, a sure way to distinguish myself from my South African past where Ellen had fed our family. It was a way too to distinguish myself from my mother who was only really interested in mind food, and she too was simply following her mother's direction: Granny Hadassah, who'd had a very limited education, insisted my mother 'get out of the kitchen and go study'.

Jen took the knife from me, 'Here, do it this way. You'll waste less.'

I exhaled a breath of annoyance. We'd done this dance in the kitchen before: when I was frying, she'd say, 'Your oil's not hot enough'; if she washed the dishes after I'd cooked, she'd groan and say, 'You are such a messy cook.'

It was all true: when Jen cooked, the schnitzel was crisp, the roast chicken tender with crispy skin, the rump just rare enough, the kitchen ordered.

As with farm work, I both wanted her to leave me alone to try, and to teach me so I wouldn't fail. Unlike with the cleaning, I couldn't shrug off her scolds.

At the dinner table, hawkishly, I watched Jen take a first and then a second sip of the Asian-inspired pumpkin soup. When she said nothing, I asked, 'Is it okay?'

'What's that I'm tasting?'

Busted by her finely tuned tastebuds. I'd substituted an ingredient we didn't have in the pantry or the garden.

I wilted. I'd have got a D in her class and I wanted As. So I adopted my usual approach to learning. I borrowed and bought recipe books, and each morning I'd flick through Stephanie or Delia, Bill or Jamie, select a recipe and set the book on the edge of the kitchen bench. Now my days at the desk or doing farm work were punctuated with kneading, chopping, blending and boiling, and over time I'd become a pretty good recipe cook who delighted in preparing food for friends.

# 14.

# NEW LANGUAGES

TO LIVE SUSTAINABLY and self-sufficiently is humbling; it brings one down to earth in the most satisfying way. Here there were no electric kettles and toasters, no lights left on, no air conditioners or desktop computers, and no vacuum cleaner or hair dryer without firing up the generator. When the solar panels and batteries had been installed, as I'd turned on different switches Jen had checked the meter to see how much power each appliance or light drew. The system was small – only two hundred amp hours a day – and the solar fridge took much of that power. After a grey day, the next morning I'd click the meter to see what the 'soc' – the state of charge – was: whether there was enough power to do a load of washing or to watch a DVD on the laptop that night. Too many grey days and we'd have cold showers or boil a kettle and wash in the laundry tub. Living in cities I'd never given power much thought. Now the simplicity and economy of living off the grid tickled me. Sun in, power out.

It was the same with the water. When it was dry for too long, I watched dams drop and grasses crisp, and our conversation turned to when to start feeding cattle or whether to sell. When it rained, I imagined the water falling on the roof of the shed and house, slipping down the pipes and into the tanks. In the morning I'd check the rain gauge in the vegetable garden and record how many millimetres had fallen. The paper in my printer would grow damp and water in the line would make the phone crackle or go out of order. I wrote stories about countrywomen and the preciousness of rain, and of the ritual of recording it. In our visitors' book was a mud map of the water system: poly pipe that linked the creek, top dam, house, garden, stables and top tank, which gravity-fed down to the house. I learned how to shift levers and gate valves and start the generator to pump up water to the top tank. Each time as the top tank overflowed and I raced over to turn the generator off, I applauded. I'd turn on a tap and marvel as the water miraculously gushed out.

In winter housework included another job: splitting firewood for the stove that heated the house and the 'water jacket' that boosted the solar hot water. After driving in among older trees and regrowth, after finding an appropriate dead tree, after Jen chainsawed the log, after I tossed sawed-up logs onto the truck's tray, after we unloaded those logs beside the chopping block, they had to be split to fit the stove.

'Can you teach me how to chop wood?' I asked one day. I felt cocky: I'd once been a crack tennis player; I had good hand-eye coordination. How different could splitting wood be?

Jen anchored her feet shoulder-width apart, placed her left hand near the handle's top, right hand lower down. 'Aim away from knots or growths, preferably where there are cracks.' She swung in a fluid motion, allowing her hands to move and the axe to fall with its own power.

'Mmm, nice,' I said enjoying the poetry of how her body moved, the leanness of her hips, the firm muscles of her shoulders. Bad feminist.

'Go around the edges if it's too hard,' she said, 'Just keep chipping away.'

I groaned – another bloody lesson in tenacity and patience.

I set myself up, looked down at my boots hip-width apart, feeling the weight of the axe, getting my eye in. I was in character: the countrywoman. I pulled the axe back and swung – to an anticlimax. The point of the axe speared the wood but made barely a dint. I wrestled it free from the log. Again I tried, and again. No thwack, no crack – just a dull thud and a log decorated with a morse code of gashes.

Jen instructed, 'Use the weight of the tool to give you power.'

I tried. Again she demonstrated. I tried again, and again. She demonstrated again. My frustration bubbled up.

'It's the wood; it's not easy to chop,' Jen said. 'Don't give yourself a hard time, I've had a lot of practice. And I like splitting wood. It's a meditation for me.'

For years to come, each winter I'd try. Some years a few logs would split with a satisfying crack; others would seize the blade and leave me aching. Mostly Jen would split all the wood unless a visitor begged to learn and split a few logs before losing interest. As usual my tasks became the unskilled: stack split logs under shelter, fill up wood box on the back verandah and collect kindling from the bush.

Again I chafed at our division of labour. I wanted to be more than the unskilled 'help'. I wanted to crack this hard nut.

Jen's mother, Lola, advised, 'I never learned to chop wood or milk a cow. There are some jobs on the farm you make sure you can't do.'

Still the questions taunted: Was I pulling my weight in this relationship? What was my place on the farm – was I the 'wife'?

When I didn't go with Jen and Jack, when it was too hot to work outside, I retreated to my study, a small sealed-in section of the verandah with windows to the vegetable garden and down the driveway. I may have moved to live with Jen in a place too far from town for a day job but my work life wasn't over. I wanted so much to contribute to the wider world.

I set up a desk and arranged my books on shelves Jen had built, and with the morning sun streaming in, I sat down to write. As a legal researcher, I'd written the stories of migrant and regional women who'd survived domestic violence; as an actor, I'd inhabited characters and written them for the stage. Now I'd animate people's lives in fiction. The girl in me who'd always conquered intellectual challenges thought that here, in a not dissimilar landscape from one of my childhood heroes, Sybylla of *My Brilliant Career*, writing would be my new career – my new sanctuary.

But how did one write a novel?

Each morning as I sat down in front of the blank page I looked up at the painting above my desk; it was by the artist and comedian Mandy Nolan. Against a red background of mountains and moon, an ethereal bride floats. She has long black locks and lashes and wears a wedding dress with a garland of roses around her white veil. 'Virgin in a Strange Land' is scrawled in bold black at the bottom. Perhaps she understood my vulnerability and uncertainty.

I knew nothing about writing fiction but a friend, Jesse, had invited me to join her writing group in town. The other women, all fiction writers, and the writing books recommended 'bum glue' and regularity of writing practice. I copied out a quote from Julia Cameron's *The Right to Write* and stuck it to my wall: 'OK, Universe. You take care of the quality. I'll take care of the quantity.'

Hard work – at a desk – I knew well. It was where I'd always felt most at home. As a child I'd been called a 'swot'. Accurate, really: even aged seven I'd set myself up at a high desk and claim to be doing 'homework'. As a foreign student at law school, my yellow highlighter poised over photocopied cases, I'd studied obsessively, seeing it also as the way to learn about this new country. The solitude of a desk was a sanctuary and salve to loneliness; top marks were proof I existed. Belonged.

At least in this strange new environment there'd be the familiar safety of work: the feel of my feet beneath the desk, the scratch of a pen, the soft clickety-clack of fingers on the keyboard, one word in front of another, the possibility of absolute absorption, the promise of control and ownership – something that would be my 'thing'.

I had no idea back then just how challenging I'd find the life of a writer, how elusive a sanctuary writing would be, and how, if one made publication the mark of approval, one remained dependent on others' opinions. I failed to appreciate too that without other paid work, a creative occupation like writing could easily be sapped of 'fun' and become another 'job', albeit largely unpaid. 'Writer' too could become a label one depended upon for self-worth.

Ignorant of how to progress a plot, I stumbled around writing slice-of-life vignettes. I got up from my desk to make tea, sat down and wrote another page before I got up to hang out washing and wander around the empty house. The writing failed to absorb me for hours. Work had ceased to be my safe home.

I needed something else to do. In the back of the shed, behind the pot of blackened coins that had gone through the fire, I found the box of yellow and blue tile shards and maroon ceramic that I'd scavenged from the burn site. At the library I found books on mosaicking with lists of what tools were needed and a notice advertising a weekend-long mosaic class.

'You don't need a class,' Jen said. 'Just mix up some cement and have a go.'

I didn't. As I stood in the shed staring at the box of bits, I had no idea how to just 'have a go' or 'make it up as you go along'. I wanted a guide or a teacher. As swallows swooped past me I froze as I imagined Jen or visitors looking at the mosaicked stone, commenting on the patterns and the uneven layers, pointing out a tile that was loose. I didn't want to fail at something so permanent and visible. How strange that here where there was so much privacy and freedom, where I could bathe outside or garden topless, I felt self-conscious, watched and adjudicated.

I'd happily 'had a go' at jobs from waitressing to market research, law to lecturing, acting to play-writing, but there at least communication was the medium. Here on the farm everything was manual, a foreign language I struggled to learn.

The next time Frank was killing 'meaties' – the big-footed chickens he kept warm under lights for six to eight weeks – I walked over to help.

I stood back as he grabbed a fluttering bird by its legs, placed its head between two nails on the chopping block and severed it with the axe, sharply, quickly. When the chicken's head fell to the ground, I withered under the stare of the open eye. Frank shoved the chicken into a bag that jiggled like a dying flame. He laughed at my scrunched-up face and the next time, just to show me, he placed the headless chook on the ground and it did run around before he rescued it and put it into a bag.

I watched Frank dunk the bird in a copper of hot water and then slap it down on the steel table in the shade of a spotty gum tree. I gagged at the stench of wet feathers. Gingerly, I touched the chicken. Her feathers were wet, her body still warm. I said my own silent thankyou to her and then, as instructed by Frank, I tugged at the quills. They came away in clumps. I worked carefully – slowly, in Frank's opinion – uncovering and revealing the chicken's pale and goosebumped skin. In the thin morning light, she seemed so naked and vulnerable.

Then Frank made a cut with a worn-down carving knife and scooped out what he called the 'guts'. Puffed up in his role as teacher, he told me about the 'whites' and 'the caw in the throat, the wiver, heart and thing that looks like sausage'. To my surprise, I wasn't grossed out by this digestive tract – there was something strangely beautiful about each organ's shape and function.

'I don't know how I'll go eating chook now,' I said to Frank.

He laughed and said, 'You be awigh.'

That night I wimped out of cooking chicken and, weeks later, after I'd defrosted a chicken, plucked the missed quills, pushed a lemon into the cavity that had once housed the 'guts' and rubbed in the salt and oil, I still couldn't get the live chicken out of my mind. It was unnerving to see an animal that breathed like me now sitting in the roasting tray.

But when the delicious smells filled the house, I too dived into the tender breast and the wing with the crispy skin. Did that mean I was just ethically inconsistent and cruel, or was it because I'd not killed the animal myself?

The next time I went round to help, when Frank placed a chicken on the chopping block, I stepped forward to take the axe – and then stepped back.

'Next time,' Frank said.

But it was the same the next time: I couldn't bring myself to do it.

'You really think you need to do this?' Jen asked.

I nodded. 'Living here – being part of a farm where animals are bred for slaughter – makes me want to take more responsibility for what I put in my mouth.'

So the next time I went over for chook-killing, I said, 'I have to do it today.'

'If you say so,' Hugh, who was helping, said.

There was a different chopping block. Higher than usual. The axe felt heavier in my hand than the one we used to chop wood. With one hand, I awkwardly held the chook, its head between the nails. I silently apologised and thanked the chicken. Then, with my other hand, I swung the axe.

The head didn't drop. The blow wasn't hard or heavy enough.

'No, shit!' I yelped. 'I'm sorry, chookie. Quick, Frankie, help me!'

'Jus go 'gain,' he said, 'I hold 'er.'

Now, with two hands on the axe, I struck again and the chook's head fell to the ground. So quick. I stared at the head with the open eye, at the outline of the chook flailing around in the bloodied feedbag.

I hopped from foot to foot, wanting to take back what I'd done, or disappear. I'd not only murdered and destroyed the chicken's life, I'd done it grossly, badly. I'd butchered that poor bird.

'Gets easier,' Hugh said. 'You did it, that's the main thing. You're thinking about where your food comes from.'

Frank didn't laugh at me as he usually did when I was clumsy at a job. He nodded with solemnity and said, 'Is awigh.'

It wasn't alright. I felt ill. I was no longer even sure why I'd been so compelled to kill the animal, or if I'd ever qualify as a countrywoman.

One hot afternoon we headed down to the creek. Lucy, the young collie with the white stripe across her black rear, stood on the creek bank, dripping cold creek water in stalactite streams. She was naked: her usual ruffle of fur flattened, skin-tight and sleek enough to count her ribs.

'Look at you, you skun rabbit,' Jen said, rubbing her coat dry.

'Skun's not a word,' I said, with a hint of scorn. 'It's skinned rabbit.'

Jen looked up from the dog and smiled. 'No, it's skun.'

'Hang on,' I said, laughing, 'is this one of those jokes? Your Australian humour?'

'No,' she said, 'everyone says skun. As a kid, after we'd been out rabbit-shooting, Dad would ask, "Have you skun those rabbits, Jennifer?"'

'So now you're telling me "skun" can be used as an adjective and as a verb?' My tone might have been playful, I might've cringed inside to hear myself sounding so like my mother, but I couldn't stop myself. Surely the English language was something I did know, something I could rely upon? 'That's not proper English, Jen. The past tense of skin is skinned.'

She started up the truck and over the spluttering motor said, 'Not here in Australia it isn't.'

Checkmate. We both laughed; both shook our heads.

Weeks later, past midnight I woke to the sound of her scrabbling in her bedside table, then the gun being dragged out from under the bed.

'What's happening?' I asked, rolling over towards her.

'Nothing, it's fine. Go back to sleep.'

I didn't. I lay there, wondering what the hell she was doing. The dogs hadn't barked – I'm a light sleeper, I'd have heard them. So it couldn't be the dingo that had mauled the calf in the front paddock. I listened. There was the insistent call of a plover, the boo-book of an owl, frog footsteps on the tin roof. Nothing unusual. I contemplated getting up, and didn't.

An interminable while later I heard the screen door slide open, Jen's bare footsteps on the wooden boards, and then her voice: 'Look, I got the little bastard.'

I clicked on the reading light and propped up on my elbow. There she stood – naked, gun in one hand and a dead rabbit held high in the other.

'Now we can have a lettuce crop,' she said, radiant.

'You shot that rabbit in the dark?'

'No, I held the torch in my mouth.'

'Of course you did.'

As Jen grabbed her pocketknife and headed for the outside sink, she said, 'How about braised bunny for dinner?'

'After you've skinned it.'

Later, when she spooned around my body, she whispered, 'All skun.'

'God, you're tenacious,' I said, smiling, and skin to skin we slipped into sleep.

# 15.

# NIGEL NO-MATES

IF INTIMATE KNOWING and physically participating in a house's construction makes it a home, then this studio-style house was probably home, more so than the grand Johannesburg homes of my childhood, more so than the flats of my peripatetic Sydney years, more so than the house on the hill that had drawn Jen to me. I loved waking with Jen to the morning magpies with the sun slanting against the tops of the gum trees, loved the kookaburras' dusk laughter and the winter nights where I'd watch the orange glow from the wood stove dance across the wall. But despite my desire to be self-contained, despite my attempts at writing fiction, my love of reading and the domestic demands, the hours alone seemed interminable.

When the phone bleated into the silence, I leapt to answer it. With no mobile phone reception, mail only three times a week, no television, slow dial-up internet and no visitors other than Jack or the Jehovah's Witnesses, the landline phone and the radio were the only intrusions from the world beyond. I liked having to call council or make other business calls, and I was deeply grateful to the friends far away who were willing to chat on the phone.

The caller was my mother. Fifteen years since our relationship had ruptured, she pursued, I prickled. Our conversation thrived on books and our connections from our South African past; it foundered on family. Most of my mother's childhood tales starred her father, but the seminal story of her mother, Hadassah, was set at Sapkamma, a sheep farm where my mother lived for her first five years in South Africa's version of the outback, the Little Karoo. In her family memoir, my mother has written of her mother, a woman who'd migrated from Lithuania:

> *Let me tell you how she suffered …*
>
> *She was determined to speak English. Encouraged by my father, she had enrolled in a correspondence school in London and I wish I'd kept two of her neatly written exercises. I remember the essence.*
>
> *In one she wrote of how, on summer afternoons, my father away attending to stock, to bore holes … she would draw the blue curtains of her little lounge room, puff up the cushions, set a tea tray and pretend that visitors would soon be arriving.*

Hadassah is the woman from whom I've inherited an abundance of thick hair and after whom I'm named – in my mother's anglicised, fitting-in kind of way. Hadassah died six months before I was born so I know her only from the black-and-white photograph with the curled edges, her arms folded on a chair back, her tresses tumbling over her shoulders down to the seat.

Now I was haunted by Hadassah's story. When Jen was out fencing, mustering or spraying, I'd glance down the driveway for the first sign of her on horseback. I saw my namesake's life reflected in my own: she and I, both Diaspora Jews, had then moved miles away from family and the familiar, she and I both waited at home for our partners to return from checking stock and fences. She and I were both lonely.

The story of Hadassah's tea party had hovered unspoken between my mother and me when I'd announced I was moving to the farm.

Down the phone line I'd heard her loud gulp. During the long, pained silence that had followed, I'd pictured her in her loft study surrounded by cluttered bookshelves topped with family photographs, at the table where she tutored English to students from Hong Kong and Korea.

We both knew she wholeheartedly disapproved of many of my choices. When I'd left the city a decade earlier to move to the Byron area, she'd repeatedly said that living in the country was 'not right for someone like you, Hayls'. The Byron area with its sea and tree changers was a cosmopolitan metropolis compared to the farm. When I'd quit my job at the university she was disapproving too. She'd taught me to scorn laziness and the privileged who lived a trivial, superficial life and that one should 'whistle while you work'. Now I'd chosen to move to an area without opportunities for work as she and I knew it.

'What have you been doing?' my mother asked.

'Reading, writing, helping Jen, doing farm stuff, the usual,' I said. I didn't want to admit that I found the days on my own empty.

'And are you going to town to see friends on the weekend?'

'No,' I said in a combative tone. She'd been asking the same question all my life. To her, no date on a Saturday night was a tragedy.

I glanced at the wall calendar the stock agent had given us, with its image of a herd of cattle heading for home. Friends had visited one weekend in October but for November the days were blank except for where Jen had circled the fifth and written *5 in 1 injection*. On the twenty-fifth I'd written: *H to town. Writing group. Tropical Fruits Dance?* The twenty-fifth sat in the midst of that blank month like a beacon.

Now, as the silence on the phone with my mother continued, I felt my face grow hot and my anger rise. Again, the push-and-pull ambivalence: I both wanted our compatible connection and to escape her and the family that hovered around her, the isolation that made me feel like a blighted black sheep. I wanted her approval but not her expectations. Particularly, the benefit of 'busy'. My mother's pocket-sized diary had always been jammed with arrangements. Her cardinal rule for living: distract yourself.

So, as I stared at the empty calendar, I said, 'I'm not like you.' Although it would probably have been more truthful to say, 'I don't want to be like you', just as she'd not wanted to be like her foreign mother. Rebellious daughters, both of us.

I'd come to doubt my mother's cardinal rule as I'd come to doubt much of what she now represented. It seemed another term for running away from the wounds that littered one's internal landscape, from one's fears. I wanted to find another way to live, a self-sufficient and authentic way. I'd known this was possible since my years at university in Cape Town, where some of my friends had come from villages and rural properties. Their lives had intrigued me – they seemed to find entertainment sewing patchwork quilts, pressing flowers, cooking and reading. They'd not needed to go out or see other people. At their core they seemed deeply independent. My wise housemate had been like that, as was Jen. She didn't understand how anyone could be bored or lonely and seemed to frown upon the idea. She never was. This kind of freedom and inner sanctity was what I hoped life at Tywyah would instil in me. Like my childhood babushka doll, I'd grow another self, one different from my mother and grandmother, one that was so rich in personal resources as to be truly independent of others and without need of 'distraction'. I'd grow a self that didn't need others or the props of public life.

After my sharp response to my mother, there was a long silence before she launched into a description of the book she'd just read, the pupils she'd taught, what she was cooking for a dinner party, with whom she was playing bridge and what theatre she'd seen. As the conversation wound to its end, she said, 'Darling, it's Rosh Hashanah on Wednesday. Happy new year to you. I just wish you would –'

'Don't, Ma,' I said, swallowing. 'I've tried. Repeatedly. What more do you want of me? Just enjoy your celebration with *your* family.'

I hung up and stared at the phone; I fumed. How could my

mother bury so much? Couldn't she see how her silences and continued relationships constituted tacit acceptance? Where did her loyalty lie? And I wept – for my unkindness to her, for our entangled and embattled love, for how I still culturally valued family, and for my exile from the one I'd grown up in. Telling my oldest stepbrother why I'd exiled myself had led to some special reconnections and meetings, but the bigger silence and lack of resolution persisted. Still I couldn't seem to 'move on'. Even geographical distance, even therapy hadn't helped me to 'let it go'. How I hated and shamed myself for my failure to do so.

Maybe the only way to move on from the pains of the past was to sever the steely tie to my mother altogether. Could I divorce her? And then I thought how she depended upon me, how she'd repeatedly said I was the only person in Australia who understood her. Even if our relationship was conflicted, I couldn't deny the familiarities and compatibilities – the deep love. I too often felt she understood parts of me more than anyone in my Australian life, even more than Jen. She was certainly the only person who provided real continuity between my past and present. Maybe it was inescapable: I couldn't separate from her because I was just like her.

But I didn't want to be. Surely I just needed more contact with my friends or even with people other than Jen. I oriented life around trips to town and phone calls to friends who lived in the city. Like a constant niggle, I felt the call of my community of friends at the coast. Some visited but rarely, and during the weeks on the farm I felt invisible and feared I'd lose connections – I'd become Nigel no-mates. And in the absence of a cohesive family, I needed a flock, didn't I?

I reminded myself my situation was vastly different from Hadassah's. I could get a 'people hit' when I wanted. Jen had been right all those years ago: the farm was too far for dinner. But I had a landline telephone, a car, money to pay for petrol and some of my wonderful friends were only a two and a half–hour drive away. I even had somewhere to stay in town – with timber milled on the farm, we'd built a room in the backyard of my now-rented house. It had felt like insurance: a way of keeping one foot in town life. A way of staying connected to the big world.

Every two to three weeks I'd exchange tatty jeans for 'town clothes', hop into my car, notch up the volume on that day's soundtrack and speed away from the farm.

In town I'd wipe cobwebs from the door and dust from the benches, and put bread and cheese into the empty fridge. Then I'd go down the street to do jobs and gorge on beach walks and cups of tea with friends and my writing group. Real conversations squeezed into the short time. Real conversations to satiate my hunger. But after a couple of days of back-to-back social interactions followed by over-stimulated sleeplessness, I'd long for Jen and our easy togetherness, for our bed, my chores and my desk.

One early evening, Venus already visible as I charged the car up Tywyah's rough road and caught the first glimpse of the bougainvillea and house, I lit up with relief. I changed down to second gear, round-ed the corner and neared the front gate and there were the three dogs, their barks only settling as I got out of the car and they recognised my voice. I swung the gate open and they leapt around me, licking my hand, Lucy hugging my leg with her paws. I looked up at the house and there was Jen standing on the verandah, one arm around a post. Despite my long-ago reluctance to put all my eggs into a lover's basket, now it seemed it was Jen and perhaps the dogs – not friends – that made home.

I hugged Jen tight and exhaled. 'I missed you,' I said. 'I'm over-cooked.'

'You see,' Jen said. 'Every paddock has its own problem.'

# 16.

# WHEN IN ROME

THE MOBILE PHONE BEEPED as it came into range near Casino. Urgent. Call Fletchers.

Frank answered: 'Jack had a stroke. Ambulance has taken him to Lismore.'

Jen and I replayed the last moment we'd seen Jack, standing on the Fletchers' timber verandah, his hand on the blue balustrade. From the front gate Jen had tossed an ear of corn across the yard. Jack, always a fine cricketer, had missed the catch. There'd been laughter and teasing and as Jack bent to pick up the corn, Jen and I had waved and hopped in the truck to drive away to the coast to see friends.

In the men's ward of Lismore's base hospital, Jack suddenly seemed elderly, his hair now whiter against the crisp hospital linen, his broad shoulders shrunken. He couldn't use his left arm and he'd lost his balance. He was bewildered and tearful.

Jen squeezed his hand. 'It's the stroke,' she reassured him. 'They make you cry.'

The doctors told us Jack had had a clot in his brain. We had to wait and see the effects. Each day we visited, bringing a sheepskin for him to lie on or some grapes or biscuits. Some days he lay on top of the bedclothes, some days he sat in a padded chair. Barefoot and dressed in pyjamas not work clothes, Jack seemed almost naked.

'Those feet are terrible, Jack,' Jen said.

The skin on his ankles was pale, porcelain white compared to the tan above his sock line, his toenails were long and curved and his feet were calloused and cracked dry. The next day Jen brought in a tub of lanolin cream, and as she pushed it under Jack's nose, she said, 'You can smell the sheep, can't you?'

He nodded and smiled.

'Will I rub some into your feet?'

He nodded again.

'She's a good nurse for people as well as cows and horses,' I said to Jack, thinking how Jen had unquestioningly attended to every detail when I'd been ill: a wet face washer, sheets straightened, room tidied and aired, chicken soup that would've impressed my Jewish aunts.

I sat on the edge of Jack's bed, watching Jen's hands massaging his chapped feet and marvelling at the friendship they shared. Tweedledum and Tweedledee. When Jen had bought a blue Daihatsu Scat truck, Jack had bought a red one. When Jen got Lucy, the border collie working dog, Jack got her sister Suzie. They spent most days working together in easy companionship. They shared jobs and resources, they looked out for each other and when they worked together in the yards, they didn't bicker or brush up against each other. They got each other. Jen would say, 'How about you do the cutting,' and Jack would reply, 'That'll be alright.'

Yet if Jen and I were different in many ways, so too were she and Jack: she a lesbian, he a bachelor; twenty years separated their ages; he'd had no schooling and she'd been to teachers' college. It was in the realm of work that they were the same: both enjoyed farm work and its challenges, both were physically competent and skilled. A similarity, I'd begun to think, that was crucial to harmonious working relationships in the bush.

Or perhaps it's always challenging to work with one's partner. Maybe work relationships thrive on firm boundaries. Sure, Jen might sometimes tell Jack to talk more clearly or that he was eating too much ice cream and getting a belly, but their relationship didn't cross certain lines: they didn't talk about feelings, had no expectations of each other and weren't physically intimate.

When I'd first hung around with Jen and Jack I'd said to Jen, 'Do you think Jack's just a little bit in love with you?'

'Of course not,' she'd said, her tone tinged with annoyance. 'We're friends – and even if he is, I'm not interested.'

That was plain. Even I, who was quick to jealousy, knew Jack posed no threat to Jen and my intimate relationship.

Yet now, as I watched Jen massage Jack's feet, it seemed the usual boundary was blurring. Infirmity: the ultimate softener of edges.

I'd wanted to visit Jack and Jen had wanted me to come with her, but now I felt a bit like the third wheel. So I did what I do, chatted, asking if Frank had come in and who'd driven him, telling Jack about the patients we'd seen outside smoking.

I lifted the lid on the tray beside his bed. 'Food okay here?' I asked when I saw the plate was wiped clean, the dessert bowl empty.

Jack nodded. 'But not enough.'

Jen and I both laughed.

When I ran out of chatter I pondered how Jack felt having me there – we hadn't developed a relationship independent of Jen. What, I wondered, did he make of me and Jen? I'd railed against Jen's 'no affection' in front of Jack and other locals rule. Yet there'd been that day down at the cattle yards, calves pressed up against each other in the race, Jack prodding them up with a piece of poly pipe, Jen catching them in the head bails, me loading the tag applicator.

'Shari,' Jack had called to me. 'Can you get that dog out of here?'

Shari was the name of Jen's previous long-term girlfriend.

I'd laughed but Jack had blushed and apologised as he'd turned to the race.

Perhaps Jen had been right when she'd said, 'Of course Jack knows. It's just not talked about.' She'd asked me then, 'Anyway, what difference would it make if we were affectionate in front of him?'

I'd shrugged an 'I dunno', wishing I was more like my other friends who'd never come out to their families because they didn't want to upset their mothers. Harmony seemed such a virtuous goal. I just wasn't sure I favoured it over authenticity. To neutralise our relationship – to blend in – seemed to do little more than domesticate the outsider for the dominant majority's comfort. Unity at the cost of individuality and diversity. Worse though, it felt like denial, particularly in a place where Jen had been my only drawcard. I wanted to be free to kiss or put my arm around her at the hall, not feel self-conscious that I, or the combination of Jen and I, might be judged or abused or ogled. I didn't want to be 'careful'. I wanted our commitment to each other publicly acknowledged, affirmed – honoured. Today I wonder if, despite not wanting to be married, I still craved the shelter of a label for our partnership – as if this might help me feel safe and whole, unashamed perhaps.

I looked across at Jack sitting hunched in his chair. Again I told myself, that's Jen's world, not mine. Jack is her dear friend. No tangible or external gain would come from showing or stating our relationship to him. Jack was always warm and welcoming, always kind and respectful towards me. Maybe that was how he acknowledged my place in Jen's life. What's more, it wasn't as though he was a government body or a business refusing to bestow some benefit or right upon us like the laws I'd worked to reform. If anything, there might be a loss for Jen if the relationship were stated: if it embarrassed Jack he might be less comfortable and easy around Jen and me. There was no way I'd risk that. Perhaps there was a difference between a lesbian relationship being denied by others and it remaining unspoken but silently acknowledged. Perhaps, given we lived together in a heterosexual community, there was no way our lesbianism was neutralised, even if it wasn't discussed or paraded.

After we'd kissed Jack goodbye, we walked out of the hospital into the hot summer day. I said to Jen, 'I hope Jack feels okay with me there.'

'Of course he does. He expects you to come with me,' she said. 'Anyway, I want you there. It would feel a bit too weird to rub his feet if you weren't around.'

After some weeks, the doctors told us Jack would be transferred to another hospital for rehabilitation. It was unlikely he'd ever drive or ride a horse again, but we pictured him in the passenger seat beside Jen; or perhaps, like other elderly farmers, he'd spend days on a ride-on lawnmower sculpting the paddock into a bowling green.

Sitting beside his bed, I heard Jack say to Jen, 'I'll come live with you when I come home.'

My eyes widened. Where? In the cabin? In my little study on the verandah? Our house was a one-roomed studio. Is this what Jen would want? And what would that mean – for us, for me? For our freedom to be ourselves in our own home?

As we walked down the flights of stairs, hesitantly I said, 'So, do you reckon Jack should come live with us?'

Jen laughed. 'No, that's not going to happen. Anyway, we don't have the facilities he'll need.'

Later we sat down at the Fletchers' table plotting Jack's return. Maybe Rang could build a ramp for the front verandah, and given there was plumbing to the back room, an accessible shower could be installed. I was selfishly relieved.

Jack didn't come home. He had another stroke, a bleed this time. Barely conscious, surrounded by his family of nieces and nephews, he lay pale and white in the hospital bed, his hands soft and smelling of lanolin cream. Standing at the end of the bed, I could feel his skinny calves through the thin white cotton blanket. At one in the morning, Jen and I kissed Jack's smooth forehead and whispered our goodbyes. An hour later, his niece called to tell us he'd died.

'We weren't even with him,' she said. 'We were downstairs saying goodbye to the others. He shouldn't have died alone.'

But had he waited for them all to leave? Orson Welles wrote, 'We're born alone, we live alone, we die alone. Only through our love and friendship can we create the illusion for the moment that we're not alone.' Perhaps Jack, a man so comfortable with himself, wanted to honour this truth.

Back at the Fletchers' table, Jack's seat in front of the ding-dong clock gaped empty, Frank toyed with his teaspoon, and Jack's twin, Alfie, who'd driven out from Casino, sat with his cheek resting in his hand, his eyes watery and downcast. I set my notebook on the plastic placemat so I could take notes for the eulogy, just as I'd done for the other Fletcher brothers' eulogies: for Norman, who years earlier had been found dead in bed at dawn; for Bruce, who two years earlier, had collapsed against the fridge on New Year's Day. On those occasions, I'd asked the surviving brothers about childhoods and work lives, and Jen had translated the Fletcherese when I looked to her for help. Each time I'd tossed in the question, 'Was there ever anyone special? A partner?' Each time there were gruff headshakes and Jen and I caught each other's eye, wondering about the story behind this bachelorhood.

Jack's eulogy was different. I didn't have to piece together the story of a life only from the brothers. Jen leaned on the plastic tablecloth and talked about how Jack, among others, had taught her to cut down trees, build fences, bale hay and muster. Jack, who'd encourage novices by saying, 'Ah, but today you know more than you did a month ago.' Jack, who'd sit on the wooden bench on the street corner in Casino on his Fridays in town, greeting passers-by with, 'G'day, mate, haven't seen you for a hundred years. Sit down and tell us your story.' Jack, the non-drinker, the larrikin, the yodelling cowboy who liked to sit back in his saddle in the hills, watching the birds and telling stories. Jack, who knew every cow in the herd and would lie in bed imagining and counting them in the different paddocks. The fitting phrase for Jack's tombstone would be 'Always counting cows'.

The large Catholic church in Casino was crammed with people from the district, rural storekeepers and stock agents. In the front pews sat the five surviving Fletcher siblings and their offspring. Jen and I sat beside Frank in his long trousers, only ever worn for funerals. Perched on top of the coffin was a photograph of Jack, his akubra pushed back on his head, his back to a post on our front verandah, his arm stretched out as he held his horse Sharni's reins, his collie Suzie at his feet. As Joan read the eulogy, tears rolled down Jen's cheeks. Her grief felt deeper, sadder even than when her father had died after our first year together.

Surreptitiously, hastily, I squeezed her hand. As the incense and the notes of the last song lingered in the air, together with Frank we followed the coffin out to the hearse. Frank's head was bowed, his expression disorientated. I stood close beside him as people came to shake Jen's hand or kiss her and offer their condolences. Everyone knew this team: Jen and Jack. This relationship that fitted no ordinary – or legal – category.

We were asked to join the family for the reading of the will in the lawyer's offices. Jack had left Jen the block of land next door, a block we drove across to get to our house. No one questioned the bequest. On the farm Jen planted a garden of pansies, primulas, zinnias and daisies, and for the memorial service at the hall where we planted a grey ironbark, a straight and sure tree, she saddled up Sharni and led the riderless horse up the road with Jack's boots strapped to the stirrups backwards.

In the weeks and months after Jack's death, over and again Jen said, 'He was too young; seventy-two's too young.' As I watched Jen ride down the driveway on her grey mare, I ached for her and her loss.

Jack's death had another consequence: Jen now actually needed my help with the seventy cattle she and Jack had run together. At thirty-nine, just a year after moving to the farm, I ceased to be a bystander in the cattle yards. Over the nine years we'd been together, Jen had kitted me out with the clothes of her Australian farm world. That Colly akubra had been the first and for each subsequent birthday present there'd been something else for the 'farm pack': a pocketknife with a cover, knee-high chaps to aid my horseriding, jodhpurs, blue work shirts, sock savers, riding boots.

Now I dressed in workboots and a cotton shirt, strapped a knife to my belt and pulled on my akubra. Standing beside the cattle race, I loaded the red applicator with fly tags drenched in chemicals, and identity tags marked 'Lewis' in black pen. I kept tally of how many steers and heifers, and how many cattle were in the Bush Paddock or Rocky Block.

'You game to give it a try?' Jen asked.

I took a deep breath and nodded. 'Can you just show me again how the lever works?'

With a pounding heart, praying my reflexes would be quick enough, I gripped the iron lever of the crush as Jen pushed a calf up the race, and then as it poked its head through I pulled down the lever to catch the calf's neck in the head bails. Each time I caught one I surged with relief and shuddered; Jen congratulated me.

I climbed up and over the race and balanced my boots on the square-edged wooden rails. The dogs watched our every move, waiting for their favourite delicacy of 'nuts'.

I glanced at my clean white hands. Sure, it was years since I'd traded in the white shirts and suits of my legal profession, but still I grimaced as I lifted and twisted the muddy tails coated with wet or dry manure. But there was no time for revulsion. I didn't want to miss catching a calf or drop a tail; I didn't want a calf to be immobilised in the bails any longer than necessary. Even if I couldn't see what Jen was doing behind the calf, I knew that knife was murderously sharp. I held the tail and my breath as I imagined scenes where I dropped the tail, the calf kicked Jen, the knife flew back cutting her in the face so that she lay on the ground bleeding.

Any concern I'd felt for the calf metamorphosed into concern for Jen.

When drops of bright red blood fell on the dirt I flinched. Again I silently questioned the need for castration. But within minutes the dogs were eating the nuts and I was climbing over the rails to release the calf. The routine and demands of manual labour left little time for inner moral dramas. I maintained my stance: this was Jen's business, not mine. Without Jack, all I could do was help.

There was an eerie emptiness without Jack's red truck tootling up the driveway, without him coming for his second breakfast on Saturday morning when he dropped off bags of horse feed, without him perched on the verandah, dangling his legs as he tucked into a slab of watermelon.

One afternoon I called in at the Fletchers. Defrosting on the draining board was a single T-bone. Tears sprang to my eyes. In the early days of my visits to the Fletchers' house, four T-bone steaks would sit defrosting on that board. After Norman died, there were three. After Bruce died, there were two. Now, after Jack's death, Frank's single T-bone seemed so very sad and lonely.

'Headstone's up now,' Frank said. 'They done good.'

Frank's Friday trip to town was his religion: he went to the supermarket, bottle shop and rural supplier. Now he also visited his brothers, dead and alive.

We'd asked the stonemason to engrave 'Always counting cows' on the tombstone but there was no point asking Frank how it looked. He couldn't read.

On our next trip to town, in the Catholic section of the Casino cemetery, in a row with red and yellow silk flowers in shiny vases, Jen and I stood over Jack's grave and the newly erected headstone.

I bent down to read the engraving: 'Always counting crows.'

# 17.

# A VISIT FROM
# MY MOTHER

MY MOTHER'S FIRST VISIT to the farm a year after we'd moved into the house was carefully orchestrated to coincide with a visitor from South Africa: Liora, my mother's dear friend and the mother of one of my happy families. At last, someone from the past, someone my mother and I both loved and trusted, someone to help us avoid the familial minefields. Now too, for the first time, my past would meet my present – under my roof.

Rain hammered down during the two-hour drive from the airport. It stopped briefly, mercifully, when I turned in at the bottom gate. My mother jumped out to open the gate, telling us that this had been her job on the farm in the Karoo.

Liora laughed and said, 'Like mother, like daughter,' and then, 'Oh, Hayls, what a beautiful place.'

Jen welcomed us at the front gate and hastily, before the next downpour, gave my mother and Liora a tour that included the toilet.

Our toilet was a long-drop (a hole in the ground) with a proper pedestal and seat, a bucket of sawdust with a jam-tin scoop and a morning view of pink and grey galahs and wallabies. When guests arrived, we'd say, 'Please, no plastics or nappies down the hole. They don't break down.' Once that hole was full we moved back to last year's hole, moving the little tin shelter, the podium and the pedestal to sit over it. Before moving we dug out the old hole, filling at least eight wheelbarrow-loads with the compost, and tipped it on the fruit trees as fertiliser. We called the process 'taking care of our own shit'. Sometimes I wondered if this work and the many wheelbarrow-loads of horse and cow manure I picked up were atonement for my South African childhood or the other 'shit' I carry.

Over time I'd come to prefer the loo out the back paddock to flush toilets in boxy little rooms. Lucy, our collie dog, would accompany me, waiting expectantly for the toss of a cardboard toilet roll, and I'd watch kangaroos and cattle in the paddock, magpies and rosellas, the morning sun hitting the trees, the leopard spots of the moulting spotty gum.

But there were cold winter's nights and times when I'd been ill when I longed for a toilet that wasn't a hundred steps from the house.

In the weeks before my mother's visit, I'd panicked. Would my mother and Liora cope with the toilet? Did we need to dig a new hole?

'I haven't got time,' Jen said.

I'd stood beside the toilet, Lucy by my side, debating whether to cancel the visit. The toilet didn't stink like long-drops I'd visited elsewhere, and although you could see the last sawdust sprinkle, it wasn't yet full. On the other hand, I so wanted my mother and Liora to be comfortable, and hadn't at least three relatives admitted they were unlikely to ever visit the farm because of the long-drop toilet? But was I just being uptight about a natural function? Afraid of what others might think of me because of the toilet?

I'd resolved to do it alone – without Jen – or at least get started. I tugged the tin shelter. It didn't move. It was pointless, of course – we usually used a chain attached to the tractor to move it. Who was I kidding? I could dig out the top section but I just didn't have the physical strength to lift out the lower shovelfuls. As I moped slowly back to the house, I cursed how this lifestyle entrenched my dependence on Jen. I couldn't even hire someone to do the job.

Jen of course also wanted my mother and Liora to be comfortable and found time for us to dig a new hole before they arrived. On her time frame.

Now, in the gap before the next downpour, I stood at the toilet beside my mother and Liora, watching Jen.

'The rain means everything rises so you'll have to use newspaper,' she said, placing a broadsheet down the toilet hole. 'Otherwise you get splash-back.'

I flinched with my mother's disbelieving shake of her head. And there again was that tug between worlds. Still I felt responsible and answerable to her – or to the inherited expectations inside me.

But Liora, pluckily dressed in Driza-Bone raincoat and akubra to charge out to the loo, transformed the long-drop from a distasteful embarrassment to an adventure.

The two-day visit passed more easily than the other times Jen and I had spent with my mother. As the rain drummed against the tin roof and tumbled over gutters, Liora, a drama teacher, wanted to know all about my play, and so she, my mother and I sat on the couch peering at the poor recording on the laptop's small screen. We moved from couch to dining table to verandah and then, during the brief respite from rain, to the dirt road for a walk. We laughed, we chatted – about theatre and method acting, about books and ideas, about people we knew, about South Africa. About so much that needed no translation.

'It's exhausting,' Jen said as we climbed into the high bed in the cabin, having left my mother and Liora in the comfort of the house. 'So much talking. I had to go check the weaners just to get a break.'

'Yes,' I said gaily, 'it's tiring but it's so lovely. So much easier with Liora here. More like how it used to be with my mom and me. Companionable, not caustic. Fun. Do you think that beef dish was alright?'

'It was great. Your mother just never eats,' Jen said as she closed her eyes, leaving me to listen to the scratching of a mouse in the corner of the cabin and write the various scripts of my mother and Liora's conversation about how I was now living.

**18.**

# VOLUNTEER
# FIREFIGHTER

AT MY DESK ONE AFTERNOON, draft ten of a short story, the phone rang.

'There's a fire up on the Bulldog,' the captain of the fire brigade said.

'Jen's out on the horse somewhere,' I said. We'd recently completed our basic firefighter training. At the district area's headquarters in Grafton, we'd followed classroom instruction in thick manuals, and after lunch we'd bowled and rolled the long thin hoses, connected hoses with the special Storz tool, piled on top of each other in the truck in case of a 'fire overrun' – as in overrunning the truck. But for the few fires I'd been to, I'd been stuck in the cabin or on the back of the truck, watching, not doing. I'd only ever helped 'mop up' the day after. I doubted I'd remember how to prime the pump or know what to do at a real fire.

'No one's home,' the captain said in his dry way.

'Do you want me to come?'

'Yeah, that'd be good.'

I grabbed a handkerchief and a band for my long hair and drove to the shed where he had the truck ready to go. The personal protective equipment of yellow jacket and pants, helmet, gloves, flash hood (much like a balaclava) and goggles hadn't yet arrived from our district office.

I hoisted myself into the passenger seat and the captain took off, winding up Bulldog Road. I peered through the windscreen as puffy grey smoke swarmed the sky. I'd only ever been up this road once before. Beside me the captain was silent. I opened my mouth and shut it again. My chat would probably seem inane. I barely knew the man, and of course he had more important things to think about.

At a cream-can mailbox, he slowed and turned into a driveway. When we reached the gate, I hopped out to open it. The padlock was locked. Up ahead flames were racing across the dry grass towards the tin shed. Then it would be the house. The captain swerved off the driveway and crashed through the four-strand barbed-wire fence. I gripped the scaredy-cat bar, wide-eyed.

'Oooh shit, captain,' I said. 'I wish it wasn't just you and me.'

'I'll get the truck closer,' he said. 'You get down now.'

My eyes flicked from the truck to the fire raging across the grass. Forwards went the truck, then backwards it beeped.

'Just start her up,' he called out.

Somehow I managed to start the pump, turn the levers in the right direction, press the right buttons, unwind the thick yellow rubber hose from its holder. Somehow I managed to hold myself firm against the force of the water and shoot water at the blaze. Keep pointing and hosing, I told myself. Don't think about what could happen. The fire was creeping closer to a mound of tyres. I tugged at the hose, stepped closer. My arms were aching, my eyes were watering. I coughed and spluttered. Any second those tyres would go up and then that'd be the end of the shed. How was I to rain enough water on them? Was it even possible to extinguish tyres? Don't forget to turn the nozzle 'left for life' if it comes close. If only the captain was able to leave the driver's seat to come and help. Those tyres needed to be kicked away from the shed. And then, just in time, there he was, kicking the tyres into a blackened area. I kept hosing, squeezing my eyes against the sting of the smoke.

'Looks like we got it,' he said.

I nodded. The house, shed and bathhouse, with its walls of mud-brick and recycled glass bottles, were untouched. We watched for spot fires and kicked and raked stray sticks and logs into the blackened area.

'Bell's place is that way,' the captain said. 'If it gets away we're stuffed. Better go fill up at the dam.'

I nodded, clueless about where 'that way' was, wondering how he was going to find that dam. The air was full of smoke, the sky an orange grey. We headed through the bush, the truck flattening eucalypt suckers. While we were filling up, the brigade's other fire truck turned up. The bloke driving crinkled his lip in a sneer and nodded hello. I stood tall, trying to convince myself it was respect I saw in his eyes, not amusement, and hoping the captain wouldn't give me a bad report card.

When I got back to the farm, Jen was home. 'I can tell where you've been,' she said as she hugged me.

'I'm buggered,' I said.

She rubbed at my charcoaled cheek and laughed. 'Might make a farm girl of you yet.'

'I'm not so sure,' I said. 'We put it out but I reckon the captain was wishing I was someone else. I was the last resort.'


Over the next year when Jen and I were actually called to a fire – a rarity given it was a boys' club – I'd dress in the yellow pants and jacket, the hard hat and those heavy boots. We'd hop into Jen's truck to head to the fire shed, lean across to kiss, each delighting in the togetherness of this doing.

At the fire, the men all assumed roles: operating pump, carrying hoses, holding and shooting water, raking leaves and twigs. Jen and

I, the new recruits, were told to 'watch and learn'. A call-out meant hours and hours – sitting in the back of the truck as we drove to distant areas through wild bush and up and down narrow fire trails, waiting for Firecom to give us information, then watching others on the hose. There was often nothing for everyone to do. Sometimes we all waited around to see if the fire sparked up again. There were desultory conversations, another look in the food box for something other than a can of baked beans. Afterwards there was the debrief – a long drinking session punctuated with comments about what had happened on the fire line. After a beer or two, I'd catch Jen's eye: time to go home.

One afternoon on a hazard-reduction burn on a property where Jen agisted cattle, there were two trucks, seven people.

'You stay with the truck,' our neighbour Terry and I were told. 'Keep an ear out for anything over the radio.'

Jen, the only one who knew the paddock, took off with the drip-torch to light the western boundary. Like me, she may have only just qualified but she was a dream to a fire brigade, if the boys would only just see it. She was physically fit and competent, and she knew the country and weather conditions: for more than twenty years she'd been riding this area looking for straying cattle and dealing with bushfire.

The area was thickly forested with spotty gums and red gums, the blady grass was high. I looked up to the sky; smoke had smirched the blue to grey.

'When I think of how I could be at home sorting those sleepers,' Terry said, leaning against the truck. He was building a grand design of a house from railway sleepers. 'This is such a waste of time.'

I nodded my agreement. If I didn't work at my writing, I'd never become a 'writer'. Did I even need to be here? I sighed and scanned the smoky sky, the trees with their portentous twittering leaves. I thought about the short story I'd been working on before we left home, about a young gay boy's coming out. Firefighting seemed like endless waiting. Endless, boring doing nothing.

Slide open, slide shut the side compartments on the truck. Scan the tinned food. Open a bottle of water and take a long glug. Unfold the toolbox first-aid kit. Make a mental note to do a proper stocktake at the next meeting. Jump to listen if the radio crackles – nothing. Ask Terry another question about his building project, about his wife in Brisbane. Wonder where Jen and the others might be.

We'd been warned about the boredom – at our basic firefighter training, the instructor pulled up one compartment of the truck and said, 'We keep folding chairs and a cricket bat in here. For all the waiting around.'

Waiting around of some type seemed intrinsic to manual work in the bush. Sometimes it was necessary, the chance to take a breather when one's puffed. When we'd worked in the cattle yards, when we'd dug holes for fence posts, when we'd built fences, sometimes Jen would lean on the shovel and say, 'Now we have a little meeting, a bit of a toolbox chat. You can't rush this kind of work. You just have to be patient, Hayley.'

When it came to firefighting one waited for a fire to come down from the top of a hill or thick bush, one waited for a decision to be made. What I saw as tedious, time-wasting boredom, others saw as part of the job. It was, as Jen said, often a case of hurry up and wait.

At the next meeting when we were doing the call-out list, I said, 'God, I hate that smoke. I don't know how you all handle it. Reckon I'm just not as tough and fit as you lot. I'll come to training exercises but put me down the bottom of the list for fires.' The brigade had been operating as a boys' club for years. No one – other than Jen – seemed disappointed. I gravitated to the jobs I could do: recruiting volunteers, running meetings, ensuring we complied with the endless bureaucratic red tape, applying for grants, organising fundraisers and making sandwiches. The others elected me president and whenever an issue was raised they'd say, 'Must be time for one of your letters.'

# 19

# ADVENTURES BEYOND
# THE FARM GATE

IN THE EARLY DAYS of my romance with Jen, when I'd suggested we go for a walk, she'd laughed. The only walking she would do was with a horse under her. She warned me not to go too far. 'It's easy to get disorientated and lost close to home if you don't know the Australian bush.'

On those long-ago weekend visits, without a ball of string or Hansel and Gretel breadcrumbs, I'd been cautious – anxious, even. Despite my desire to always vary my route, I'd walked twenty minutes in one direction through the gum trees and then hurried back along the same track. Unlike in the city, I'd had no sense of direction, and who knew what snakes and wild dogs and other feral creatures might be lurking. As I'd retraced my steps I searched for an affirming landmark. Nothing. Everything looked the same: gravel and rocks, scattered crisped leaves and fallen branches, and acres of dull green gum trees. Everything looked parched and dirty, as if the greens had been doused with dust.

Now, every day, after the soupy morning fog lifted, before I concertinaed my body over my desk or tagged along behind Jen, I walked with Lucy, the collie, as my companion. Wearing sunglasses, Rural

Fire Service cap, runners and my uniform of tatty jeans and T-shirt, I walked for an hour over a circuit that went down the rocky dirt and divots of our driveway and across the flat where the plovers stuttered *yip-yip* and corellas shrieked and swooped and spiralled around the large grey gums. I levered my body through barbed-wire fences, trotted along wallaby tracks through the gums, and marched along the green carpet Jen had slashed. I was alive to the changes in light and season, to the summer lemony yellow flower of the cat's claw, to the fireweed anointing the paddocks gold in autumn. I watched spotty gum trunks blister to a speckled mottle like a giraffe's neck or leopard's skin and then to smooth clean emerald that drew my cheek. The grey gum's transformation was slower, first peeling like a banana skin then dangling until its weight fell to the ground. How the natural world soothed and nourished. How I loved this openness and spaciousness.

I no longer feared getting lost or lurking dangerous creatures and could differentiate between myriad shades of Australian outback green, but strangely I seemed compelled to walk the same path, only changing the order: one day I'd set off from the front gate and end at the back gate near the woodpile, the next day the other way. And yet, the walk was always different. One day I'd zing and spring; another, drained and dreary, I'd lug myself around the circuit. Sometimes darkness descended and survival insisted I immediately abseil away from this relative isolation and inner focus back to the career world. I wondered if it was as much my mercurial internal landscape as the universe's changeableness that altered what I saw. The landscape seemed always to feel unknown and full of mystery, the unexpected seemed to occur over and over, day after day. Was this, I wondered, a result of my outsider status? How would a Bundjalung artist paint the area I walked? Would the dams and watercourses, the paths and tracks multiply? What of the songlines? How someone with this land in their veins would read this place was as indecipherable to me as the scents that drew and delayed Lucy.

On the public road, my ears pricked: was that an approaching car? Who would it be, would they stop? I missed the kind of spontaneous encounters with a stranger or acquaintance that are part of urban or even small-town living. Now those 'incidental encounters', as social researcher Hugh Mackay terms them in his book *The Art of Belonging*, those moments when one smiles or says 'g'day' to another person without having to fully engage, seemed priceless. This area offered no venues for such encounters – no post office, library or railway station; no café or bookshop; no playing field or dog-walking park; and I wasn't a parent who'd meet others at the school bus stop.

One winter's morning, as I sat on the back step lacing up my runners, I was seized by panic: what was this farm life doing to me? I valued and needed safety but I'd always loved adventure and the unfamiliar. Whether in conversation with a stranger on a train or in an unknown landscape, I'd always delighted in discovery, slipping down unknown laneways, deviating and disobeying maps, and resolving doubt by adhering to a simple guide: 'Just go left.' After our first holiday when Jen had said, 'The best thing about travelling is coming home', I'd scoffed and doubted our romance would survive. Now I wondered if my choice to walk the same path – to make Tywyah home – indicated that farm life was neutralising my adventurous zeal and curiosity, or was it simply revealing how truly boring, lazy and unadventurous the real me was? Was I growing a new babushka doll skin, or sinking deeper into the self that was the tiniest, most vulnerable core doll?

I scanned the 'what's on' sections of local papers wondering how to explore the district beyond our small, end of the road community. I was too young for carpet bowls at the hall, I didn't like alcohol enough to become part of the hall crew who packed the fridge on Thursday evenings and went for 'clean up' on Saturday morning, and I'd never learned a musical instrument so Sunday jam sessions were out.

One afternoon, I drove the forty minutes to a neighbouring village. Slowly I walked around its small gallery. I examined all eight paintings once, then again, then sat for a while wondering if anyone else would come in. No one did. I had a coffee with my notebook as companion – and drove home. During a two-hour outing I'd had a two-minute conversation with the man who'd made me instant coffee. How did one meet like-minded people – make friends – in a new place?

Another morning I made a special trip the ninety kilometres to Casino. Instead of our regular stops – the supermarket, the vet, Pete's Plants and the rural supplier – I headed for the art deco building with 'The School of Arts' etched into the stone masthead. On the first floor I found the Historical Society – closed – and a book exchange with shelves of chunky novels displaying raised glossy titles. But when I eavesdropped on other borrowers' conversations there were no entry points, so I bought the newspaper and sat in Kibbles Bakery watching the overweight teenage girls pushing prams, the farmers in akubras, and the elderly women in pastel florals. Women who reminded me of *tannies*, the Afrikaans aunties, women of a certain age in rural South Africa. My mother's family might've once lived on farms but that was before my time. I'd been unfamiliar with country people, assuming they all spoke Afrikaans and were racist towards blacks and Jews. As I translated those prejudices to Australia, I felt lonelier and lonelier, more and more out of place.

For a Lions Club fundraiser on Mother's Day, we drove down the road and through the gate of Keith's Art and Stone Sculpture Park, up past the calf scratching her shoulder against a gigantic red chair. Keith made hay feeders and cattle crushes but his passion was using the detritus of farm machinery, discarded metals and volcanic rock to sculpt characters and shapes both modern and medieval.

In the winter sun Jen and I walked the mown track where old chains had become tin men, and blades and coils, rusted rakes and plough discs had become abstract sculptures. A helmeted figure standing sentry was a metal basket over a head of rocks on a dead tree stump.

We paused to greet the farmer from whom we bought corn, which we mixed with minerals and salt and cement to make lick blocks for the cattle during the winter months. He shook his head and gesturing to one of the sculptures said, somewhat tongue in cheek, 'That bit comes out of a header. Should take all this stuff to the tip.'

In the amphitheatre, seated on a chair fashioned from two flat rocks, I listened to locals belting out hard rock and watched as kangaroos paused before hopping away. Over and again my eyes returned to the bright blue rollerskate balanced artistically on a rock ledge.

Lunch of roast pork or beef, eaten at trestle tables in a cleared section of the large work shed, was jollied up by raffles and auctions and cans of cold beer. People now recognised me as Jen's friend, perhaps even as her partner. I made conversation with the stock agent, the woman who ran the preschool, the farmer from whom we'd bought corn, and a woman from the Country Women's Association. The conversations usually petered out after I'd asked a few questions. No one asked me anything.

As I drove home, I felt morose. Here in the bush, conversations seemed so impersonal. They centred on the physical, not the intellectual: local events, weather, animals, local gossip. Stuff of this local rural world. Stuff of which I knew little. Where were the conversations about books and art and social justice, and about how people went about this crazy thing called life? Where were the conversations that catapulted from the parochial out into the wider world?

'Everyone's pleasant and friendly,' I said to Jen, 'but it doesn't seem like there's anyone for me to be friends with out here. No one I seem to really connect with or who really sparks my interest. I just can't see myself going off to join those ladies from the CWA.'

'But I saw you chatting to heaps of people. Everyone likes you,' Jen said. 'You make people feel special and interesting.'

I frowned. Sure, I was interested in people different from myself;

sure, I could chat to pretty much anyone. But was it enough to be the curious outsider – to talk to people only about what interested them? Did I want to make my home where my interests were so different – and invisible?

As Jen got out of the car to open the gate, I wondered if I was just culturally incompatible with the local community. Perhaps I'd never fit in here.

'It's like I'm from another planet,' I said. 'Maybe it's the Jewish or South African thing, or the lesbian or city girl, or the law background or the bookish and theatre stuff or the childlessness. Or that I'm not much of a drinker and here alcohol's the local currency.'

'It's not like you're marrying anyone,' Jen said. 'They're just your neighbours.'

# 20

# ATTACHED TO LUCKY

STANDING AT THE STOVE, I heard the swing of the feed-shed gate, then Jen's boots dropping against the timber deck.

'No luck,' she said as she came inside. 'I hope it's not another one in trouble.'

She'd left early in the day, ridden the paddock up and down searching for the eighteenth Brangus cow. It had been a week of calving problems. Two nights in a row, just before dark, Jen had found a cow who needed help calving. The first night our burly neighbour, freshly showered, wet hair combed back and a little sozzled, had given us a hand. On the second night I stood up against Jen, anchoring her as she leaned back and pulled out the calf, a slick viscous black body, barely breathing. Jen laid him down gently, put her hand into his mouth to clear his airways, then rubbed his chest to stimulate him. Moments later he was on his feet and having his first drink, his mother licking him clean. My jeans were spattered with manure and urine, Jen's jeans and shirt were bloody and mucky, and for days her hands carried the smell of that birth.

The following day she went off again to ride the paddock before the fire brigade meeting. I was waiting for her, fire brigade paperwork, banana muffins and rice salad ready to go, when she'd rung from the Fletchers to say, 'Bring an ice-cream container or something with a lid and meet me down at the bottom gate.'

As she'd ridden the paddock again she'd heard a calf moan from
a neighbour's property. If the little calf – later named Lucky – hadn't
cried out at just that moment she wouldn't have found him beside
the body of his dead mother, in the shade of a spotty gum tree.

We stood beside the dead cow. Still, cold, blood-soaked, she lay
amid the blady grass. Flies hovered around her and around the calf
bed, a pink mass of muscle, tissue and blood, chunks already gouged
out by the watching crows.

'I wonder when she died,' I said, disturbed as always by the loneliness of death.

'Probably last night while I was riding around looking for her.
She's prolapsed and probably bled to death.'

I waved my free hand about as flies settled on her eyes. In my
other hand was the blue ice-cream container. I had no idea what it
was for.

Jen knelt beside the cow. 'Look at this,' she said, pointing to the
shiny teats. 'If they're shiny she must've been up after she gave birth
and given him a bit of a lick clean and then he'd have had a drink.'

I watched her squeeze the cow's teats. 'You can't milk her,' I said.
'She's dead.'

'And she's still got colostrum,' Jen said. 'Hold the container here
to catch it.'

I squatted beside the recently dead cow, swatting flies as creamy
yellow colostrum like thick custard spurted into the container.

We lifted the calf onto the tray of the ute and when I climbed up
beside him, he nuzzled into me. He moaned, he mewled. His lashes
top and bottom were longer than the falsies I'd worn to an ABBA
fancy-dress party. His fur was black-brown, soft and curly, unlike dog
or cat fur, unlike a toy teddy. It took me back to my early childhood,
to my mother's calf-skin coat, the individual hairs coarse but the
overall effect so warm and glossy as I held it to my cheek. In 1970s
Johannesburg, on cold nights, oblivious to the cruelty it represented,

my mother would wear it out – that or the mink she was given by my father when I was born – and when she came home she'd drape the coat over me and I'd snuggle into its silky warmth.

At the Fletchers', we fed Lucky by sticking our milky fingers into his mouth and encouraging him to suck. When we left him with Frank in the picket-fenced yard to go to the fire brigade meeting he cried out.

'He's taken a liking to me,' I said.

Jen laughed.

As we drove to the fire shed, I said, 'We have to save him.'

'Yeah, I know.' She sighed and rubbed her eyes. 'Sometimes I'd rather find them dead than like this. It'd be easier.'

'Surely we can get milk from Frank's cows to feed him,' I said.

'If he's got enough,' Jen said. 'It's just all the effort and all the expense, and then if the calf makes it, he'll go to market and sell for less than he's cost us.'

I hated the thought of Lucky at the meatworks, and I was no vegetarian or card-carrying ethicist. I'd lasted less than four years after swamping my housemates in too many soybeans and glugging back endless iron tonics until finally the doctor had prescribed iron shots and a return to meat. I'd eagerly obeyed. Of course I knew, in more than an intellectual way, that livestock farming is about death: live animals become dead animals. What's more, I'd first registered this – witnessed from a safe distance – as a child.

When I was eleven, for reasons I didn't then understand, my father – a bridge-playing, overweight intellectual who'd always lived in the city and never done a day's manual work – sold his insurance business and bought a farm. On Sundays, he'd collect me from my mother's house for our weekly visit. We'd drive away from Johannesburg's jumble of houses and into the *bushveld*, green in the summer months and blackened from burns in the winter. The cream leather seats of the Jaguar were comfortable and for the hour's drive we'd do the *Sunday Times* crossword and my dad's cheeks would trumpet in and out as he bum-bum-bummed along with the classical station. He'd quiz me about my role in the school play, about tennis squad, about the friends whose families were emigrating to Israel or London or California. Then he'd challenge me with mental arithmetic until we spotted the first sign to Broederstroom. Eventually we turned into a gateway with an arch of steel lettering that read Sangiro, the name of a South African writer.

The days were languid and we flicked away flies as we strolled down to see the pigs. My dad, the Jewish pig farmer, his ubiquitous Havana cigar between his fingers, pointed out how pigs kept their food and sleeping quarters clean and that they'd worked out how to use the new nozzles to drink.

'See,' he'd say, 'George Orwell was right in *Animal Farm*.' Then he'd lean over the low brick wall and rub the nose of a boar and say, 'Good boy, good chap.'

We'd walk from football field–sized chicken shed to shed, examining the charts that hung from clipboards recording mortality rates and mineral-enriched grains. I'd watch the fluffy little chickens scurry and peck and drink from the red feeders that dangled from the roof. Over the orchestra of twittering, my father met my questions with explanations about 'day-olds' and how much space, sunshine, mineral-enriched grain and quiet the chickens needed to grow. He explained these were free-range chickens with ample room to move in the sheds, not caged. This was how chickens were grown in South Africa. Back then, before the provenance of food became controversial and the definition more accurate, I knew no different and didn't think to imagine another way.

In later years, the next stop on my father's rounds was the newly constructed abattoir where black-skinned women in white uniforms and black gumboots stood at long shiny benches plucking and packing the dead chickens. When I think of the abattoir now, my strongest memory is of the *shh* sound of the jet of water as a woman hosed the cement floor. My gaze didn't linger on the plucked chickens hung on hooks, legs pointing upwards, and I certainly have no memory of watching those chickens being killed. Perhaps that was the one section of the abattoir I didn't enter or perhaps my adult ambivalence has blotted the memory. But I do remember lunch at the farm manager's house, the day of my first abattoir visit.

I'd looked forward to the lunch Oom Piet's wife, Tannie Barbara, was making: according to my dad, her *melktert* and mashed pumpkin were delicious.

Tannie Barbara handed me a plate of roast chicken with sweetened pumpkin. I said, '*Dankie*, Tannie,' and set it down on the lacy cloth.

Across the table my dad was tucking into the chicken, his loose jaws cycling up and down. After the rounds of the abattoir, I hesitated.

Oom Piet said something in Afrikaans. I didn't quite catch it. Tannie Barbara laughed and said to my father, 'You better change the order of the tour.'

I swallowed and wished we'd brought sandwiches for lunch.

My dad looked up. 'Don't be silly, my pud,' he said, 'that's where chicken comes from. You know it doesn't just turn up on the plate.'

I stared at the chicken wing before me as I listened to their laughter and chatter and the sawing of cutlery on china. That, I realise now, was a pivotal moment. If I'd been the kind of child who was secure enough to need little external validation, I'd have pushed the chicken to the side and eaten only the pumpkin. As a young adult, I'd probably have found others who shared my views and, bolstered by a community of shared beliefs, I'd have become a militant vegetarian, joining protests against chicken farming and campaigning for law reform. Many times I've imagined how such a personality – unquestioningly and unashamedly certain of one's rightness – might've spared me the doubt and confusion I've often felt.

But back then, these thoughts didn't cross my mind: I was a good girl, keen on affirmation not disapproval, and sensitive to teasing. I gritted my teeth. I glowered defensively: I wasn't stupid; I wasn't a baby. Of course I knew roast chicken had once been live chicken. I picked up my fork. I would distance this meal from the fluffy, fragile little chickens I'd heard chirping hours before, from the carcasses I'd seen hanging in the abattoir. I would prove to them I was not a silly little girl.

Decades later, as I stood beside Jen looking down at the newborn calf, it struck me that with Jen I'd witnessed the other side of farming: caring for the orphaned and the sick; giving the little pony Billy daily physio on his injured leg; checking on Yuppie, the dog with epilepsy, every few hours through the night; delivering a calf that was a breech birth; shoving a prolapse back in; milking out a cow with mastitis so a calf could latch on to drink. Caring for animals was integral to life on the farm. It was perhaps what made the place home for Jen. Something that, despite my affection for the dogs and other animals, was not stitched through my being.

Frank insisted we try to foster the calf on another cow. Jen was doubtful but she mustered an Angus cow with prominent hipbones and a huge bag of milk and slowly, without any cattle dogs, we pushed the cow and her calf up to the yards. The cow had no name; she was simply 'Number 62'.

We put her up the race and pushed Lucky up behind her. Bingo. He sucked straight away, and she let him. When he'd had his fill, we ushered them through the race and into a yard where rusty tin was tied with wire to the rails for a calf enclosure. The cow showed no interest in Lucky but she tolerated him and she had ample milk. How accommodating she was: one little black calf on either side, sucking, occasionally butting her udder with their heads.

Lucky was unsteady and slow. For the first week he stayed in the little tin shelter on a bed of hay and I'd hold and stroke him while Jen took his temperature or gave him his shot. His rear was tanned and leathery from so many shots – Tetravet, penicillin, another antibiotic when that didn't work – each time a thick needle rammed into muscle on his hindquarters. Our solar fridge thermometer was promoted to calf diagnostics, pushed up Lucky's anus morning and night to check if his temperature was down from the too-high forty-one degrees.

The symptoms were consistent with 'joint ill'. I wasn't sure if this was a scientific term but that's what Jen called it because that's what Jack would've called it. Joint ill fitted. When Lucky moved, his legs were stiff. He didn't gambol about like the other poddy calves. Every small step was jerky, hesitant, painstaking. At times he stood frozen, not even moving when I bookended my body through the wooden rails of the cattle yard.

When I googled 'joint ill' I discovered it was a veterinary term, not a Jack term. It was also known as 'navel ill' and occurred as a result of infection entering via the umbilical cord at or soon after birth. The bacteria settles in the joints.

Every morning I walked over to see Lucky. As I stretched through the rails of the yard, Number 62 looked up at me. She was on a diet of hay, molasses (lollies for cows) and corn, and sometimes we locked up the calves and let her out to eat grass. After a few weeks, Number 62 seemed a little protective, concerned about what we were doing to Lucky, and then Lucky too got up and moved away from me.


'You can't sell him,' I told Jen as we leaned on the rails watching him. 'Keep him as the next bull. Then it'll really be a happy ending and it'll make practical sense – you'll save money and you won't have to buy another Mr Z.'

Jen wasn't so sure Lucky would even pull through.

When he was seven weeks old, we moved him and his foster family to the horse paddock in front of our house. We'd done all we could for him: multiple calls to the vet, driven the hour and fifteen minutes to get yet another antibiotic from town, my closest friend in Sydney had him on the prayer list at her Buddhist centre, and my homeopath friend from the coast gave us Rhus tox to squirt in his mouth.

On a perfect shining morning, I walked through the horse paddock over to the Hills hoist. Number 62 and her calf looked up. Lucky barely stirred.

Lucky made it through. Six months later when he was about 180 kilograms, Jen said he had to go. Number 62 was ready to calve again. We separated Lucky from Number 62, pushed him up the race, and Jen pierced an identification button in his ear. A few days later, along with the other calves, I watched him walk up the loading ramp onto the truck bound for the saleyards. Now he should be renamed 'Not So Lucky'.

I felt a wrenching ache. 'It's terrible, Jen. How can we do this?'

'The cattle here have a good life,' she said. 'You'll get used to it. It's the old girls I find harder. I've known them for so long.'

As I watched the truck pull away, I wondered if Lucky would live to see the end of the week. I knew he wouldn't be turned into a calfskin coat like the one in a cloth bag buried at the back of my mother's cupboard. I knew we wouldn't be eating him. Jen hadn't consigned him straight to the meatworks to become this year's 'beast in the freezer', cut by the butcher according to our order into chuck, eye fillet, mince, blade, T-bone, scotch or rump. Only when the 'vendor detail report' arrived in the mail after the sale would I know if Lucky had been given a temporary reprieve of his death penalty and gone to graze on a richer paddock somewhere not too far away.

The next day as I pegged white sheets in the bright sunshine, the air ached with the cries of the cows whose calves had been sent to the saleyards. For days the mothers would mill around the yards, searching, sniffing, calling, coming back to where they last saw their babies. They'd bellow, they'd keen, they'd wail. And then after a few days, they'd wander away to graze.

How strange this life was. Every morning I'd walk through

paddocks speckled with cows and shiny-coated playful calves. I'd say 'morning, girls' and when the cows continued grazing, seemingly unperturbed by my presence, I'd delight in the possibility that they knew me. I'd help Jen as she inoculated, ear-tagged and castrated calves. Then for dinner we'd eat homegrown beef.

As we sat down to a winter dinner of rump steak with homegrown steamed cauliflower and broccoli and pumpkin mash, I said, 'I'm not so sure "the cattle have a good life" is sufficient justification for cattle farming, even if I set aside my issue with castration and carting cattle to town.'

'Well then, don't eat that rump,' Jen said. 'Go right ahead and become a vegetarian.'

'But even if I stopped eating meat, I'd still be participating in cattle farming. Just by living here I'm indirectly participating.' I told her about J.M. Coetzee's book *Elizabeth Costello*, where the parallel is drawn between meat-eaters and those who said nothing as the Nazis murdered millions of people.

'So should we sell all the cattle and then you can support me completely?' Jen said between mouthfuls.

From abstract ethics to hard reality. A familiar dynamic: me in the ivory tower of ideas; Jen on the ground, bringing me back to earth. This was Jen's only income source. This was Jen's autonomy and lifestyle.

'The industrialisation of food's the major problem,' Jen said. 'Not us eating homegrown beef. The only problem I see there is that we should be eating the offal, the cheeks and the tongue, and using the hide.'

When we'd first gone to the butcher to collect the boxes of meat that had once been the 'body' we sent in for slaughter, I discovered that the abattoirs didn't give us every part of the animal – they sold the 'unwanted' parts to the Asian market at a healthy profit.

'Anyway, you can't do anything else with this block,' Jen said. 'It's too poor and rocky for crops. At least by grazing cattle we're converting the grass – which humans can't digest anyway – directly to protein. We're helping feed the population real food by producing meat.'

'Oh god, even that term "producing meat" is a problem,' I said. 'It completely distances us from the reality that we're breeding live animals – sentient beings – to be killed. It's all euphemisms. It obscures the reality that this is a form of slavery.'

Jen sighed. 'I see the parallel with slavery, the way the cattle are lined up in pens at the saleyards then auctioned; we get rid of anyone who becomes dangerous in the yards, and we breed domesticity into the herd. And yes, of course they're sentient beings, each with a different personality. You see that with the old girls. I'd even have to say they have emotion, or at least they feel pain and they take care of their calves. But you could say the dogs are slaves too ...'

'Except we love and pet them. And we don't eat them,' I said.

'Even if we've made slaves of cattle, if I had to choose between an animal and a human, I know what I'd choose. At least we take care of the cattle as kindly as we can. There are others who don't treat their cattle as we do here,' she said, taking another mouthful of steak.

'That sounds much like how white South Africans treated black domestic workers under apartheid,' I said. 'I can just hear my parents using those same words. But what about the actual killing? Paul McCartney reckons that "If slaughterhouses had glass walls, everyone would be vegetarian."'

Jen shrugged. 'I've killed and butchered sheep and chicken and kangaroo and rabbit, and then eaten what I've killed. Speaking of which, you going to eat that rump?' she asked, her fork raised.

'Maybe,' I said. 'I haven't decided yet.'

'Well, don't let it get cold.'

I sliced the meat and took a forkful. Tender, tasty. 'Shit, shit, shit,' I said.

Jen laughed.

'Don't,' I said. 'I don't know how to do this. I feel gutless. Like I've got zero moral courage. The arguments against eating meat make sense so why can't I take that step? Am I just too lazy to be a healthy vego, or am I an addict?'

One Saturday morning the phone rang. It was a woman from a neighbouring village.

'We heard you have cattle. Would you sell straight from the paddock?' she asked. She'd recently read Michael Pollen's *The Omnivore's Dilemma* and was trying to find a more ethical way to eat meat.

I pounced on the idea. 'I'll call you back after I've discussed it with my partner,' I said.

'Paddock to plate' would save the cattle the stress of the trip to town, the saleyards and the abattoir.

It would also mean the cattle could be killed without knowing what was coming. Even if 'happy meat' was an oxymoron, this would at least be kinder.

Jen said no. Our solar power couldn't run the necessary refrigeration, and it would be costly to get a butcher from town to come out and cut up the animals. She couldn't butcher a calf – she could only do rabbit and roo and sheep.

I asked around if anyone knew a local butcher and did a rough costing, factoring in running the refrigeration off Frank's mains power. Maybe hard numbers would tempt Jen.

'It won't work, Hayley,' Jen insisted. 'It's not just about resources. This country's too poor. Cattle from here need to be "finished off" before they're eaten. That's why restockers buy them. What if someone down the road buys a calf and the meat's tough? Remember last year? The beast we put in the freezer was really tough.'

I did. I had to slow-cook everything and still it was disappointing.

'There's no getting away from selling the cattle through the saleyards – and given where we live, that means they have to travel.'

'God,' I said, frustrated, 'you just won't try anything new.'

'I've been doing this for years, Hayley, and watching how others do it. This is just how it is out here. You have to know and work to the conditions and area.'

# 21.

# THE PINK GUMBOOTS

AS THE SUN TIPPED the tops of the spotty gum trees and a Hereford cow tore at thick clumps of grass outside the bedroom window, Jen placed a bulky parcel on the bed.

'Happy fortieth, gorgeous,' she said.

I ripped off the red wrapping and there they lay: the brightest, Barbie-pinkest gumboots.

'Something for the farm pack,' Jen said, smiling somewhat bashfully. 'Now up. I'm going to saddle the horses.'

'What, no breakfast in bed?' I called after her as I slipped my feet into the gumboots. Was my story really in *this* footwear? I turned my foot in then out, staring at the clunky boots. Were these my ruby or golden slippers?

Two months after I turned forty, the local community hall turned ten. Twelve children filed up on to the low wooden stage in front of the regulars' board. During the weekly straight-off-the-school-bus drama class that I'd been running, they'd skipped around the hall, laughing, pointing, touching the mudbricks, hugging the timber posts, saying, 'Do you remember when …?' Now they clustered around the three microphones, clutching sheets of paper. Laughter and voices floated in from the smokers' tables outside.

'Just start,' I whispered from the side of the stage. 'Really loudly.'

They chorused, 'We've grown up with the hall, it's ten now.'

'Speak up. I can't hear,' someone called out.

'Oi,' the bearded bloke behind the bar shouted to the stragglers outside, 'shut up.'

'Into the mikes,' I mouthed and mimed to the children.

Finally, the crowd hushed, and then down the line the children went. 'I'm fifteen, I'm eleven, I'm thirteen, I'm ...'

> *You've grown older*
> *We've got taller*
> *Only the playground's*
> *Got smaller.*
> *When it used to rain*
> *We jumped naked in puddles*
> *When you were building*
> *We slid down mounds of dirt*

I looked across the hall at Jen in her button-up blue work shirt and jeans, leaning against a post, smiling. I felt the warmth that swarms through me whenever I look at her, and then I thought, as I'd often done, that if it wasn't for her I'd never have chosen to live at Tywyah, miles from a university or library, from job opportunities or theatres, miles from the scaffolding I'd believed life depended upon.

Jen caught my eye, smiled and winked. The poem was no literary masterpiece and a second rehearsal would've been good, but everyone seemed to be enjoying it.

During the week, as I'd stitched the children's words together, I'd been struck by how, for these kids, this place was home, habitat, refuge, perhaps even identity. It was where they were born, home-schooled until they were old enough for the long bus ride to school, and where they zithered in and out of each other's homes, the hall and the creek. They knew the meaning of home and belonging, deep inside their being – no thinking about it, no longing for it.

As a child, I too had assumed this belonging: to South Africa, to my blended family, to the culture and traditions of Diaspora Jews and our urbanised, educated community. I'd lived in Australia for eighteen years now – estranged from most of my immediate family – but when had I truly known 'home'? When I turned the key to my Sydney flat, swiped a security card at the tribunal or university where I worked, danced to 'We are Family' at the Mardi Gras party, bashed the pool volleyball at my house near Bangalow? I'd hoped each of those incarnations might be 'home' and yet they'd lasted five years at most. Was it even possible to belong somewhere different – geographically and culturally – from where you and your ancestors were born?

'Is this place home for you, more than Tycannah?' I'd asked Jen after I'd read her the poem. She'd told me once that when she couldn't fall asleep she'd count the dams on Tycannah, the sheep station of her youth.

She'd shrugged. 'I've been here for twenty-five years. I like what I do here; I like living here – especially with you. So yeah, it's home.'

Standing in the community hall, I looked from the kids to the blokes with big beards, to the women wearing elasticised workboots or sensible flats. I might've only lived here full-time for eighteen months but after nine years with Jen I knew all the hall regulars. Perhaps this isolated rural place was where I'd find the sense of home that I so longed for, that sense of home that Jen and these children seemed to exude and take for granted.

# 22.

# NOT JUST A
# SLEEPING PARTNER

JUST A FEW MONTHS LATER, in February 2007, Jen's much-loved mother, Lola, who was reasonably fit despite her Parkinson's disease, was planting seedlings in her patch of backyard when a stroke struck her down. It paralysed her left side.

Those first days and nights beside her bed in a Gold Coast hospital, we didn't know if she'd survive. The doctor said it was unlikely: the bleed was vast. I held a fragile, tearful Jen tight. All the family was summoned to say their final goodbyes. In the hallway I comforted tearful grandchildren and great-grandchildren after they'd said their goodbye to Nana.

Jen and I were the last to go in. Lola looked at us and said, 'You're in the happiest relationship of all my three daughters.'

I couldn't believe what I'd just heard. Was Lola now prizing our lesbian relationship over the heterosexual relationships of her other two daughters? I'd been with Jen for years, and yet it had always seemed the other sisters' husbands or de facto male partners were more truly 'part of the family'. Certainly, Lola and I had found some compatibility around lovely clothes and walks around the block after long Christmas lunches. I'd sat with her as she'd shown me how to quilt and I rang her for recipes. She'd even read the women's stories in my domestic violence report. But Jen was key to our interactions. I was convinced I was still perceived as the outsider – exotic with my South African Jewish background, different with my academic background, and not as much fun with my relatively limited interest in alcohol and television. Jen and I had agreed introducing our mothers would be too challenging for everyone, and when my mother sent Lola a Christmas card, Lola had seemed surprised and a little embarrassed.

'It's good you're there on the farm with Jen,' Lola said. She worried Jen might hurt herself. 'Promise me you'll look after her.'

Her blue eyes were a desperate entreaty. I squeezed her hand and said I would.

Lola didn't die. As the days elongated into weeks, she gained more movement and function. I drowned the long days in the hospital room in sudoku and crosswords, traipsed up and down from the parking meter and the cafeteria to the sixth floor, talked to bureaucrats about aged care and the entitlements available under the veterans' affairs gold card given to Lola as the wife of a prisoner of war. In the wee hours of the morning I read Lola's blockbuster novel *The Valley* out loud to her. Some days, along with Jen and her sister Kay, I visited prospective high-care nursing homes for Lola to move into. There we squeezed past wheelchairs in dimly lit common rooms that reeked of urine, indignity and loneliness.

After Jack's death just a year earlier, it was another period of grief for Jen. Watching her feed her mother and massage her feet, my heart ached for them both. Week after week on the Gold Coast stacked up with a monotonous routine: breakfast, short walk, day at the hospital, back to the house, cook dinner, watch television with Kay and her husband. Jen didn't want to leave her mother to return to the farm. She didn't want to be four hours' drive away. I didn't know how long I could keep doing this but I was afraid of spending time alone on the farm. I wondered too what form our life would take now. How much time would I spend on my own out there? Would I survive life in the bush with a partner preoccupied with caring for a sick parent who lived hours away?

One morning before we went into the hospital, Frank rang. 'The tree people want to talk to you,' he said.

The 'tree people' – a corporation that had turned a vast cattle property into a tree plantation – offered Jen a lease to agist cattle.

Months earlier we'd gone to a forum 'Too Many Trees' in the bowling club of Bonalbo, a village an hour's drive away. We'd sat on red plastic chairs in a row of blue jeans and scuffed workboots. Scientists had railed against the recently established plantations' monoculture and insecticides, their effect on the water table and land degradation. The tree plantations were unpopular with the locals too. 'There's more wild dogs since the plantation in our area,' one check-shirted farmer said. Someone else chimed in, 'They got more space to breed.' There was a chorus of complaints: 'We don't have the roads' and 'Who's going to fix the potholes? They take months as it is now.' One of the women at the table laden with slices and cakes and a giant teapot said, 'And what about the community? We'll lose a few families every time they buy up the land.' Someone else grumbled about the way they were inflating land values. 'Makes it unaffordable for the ordinary bloke to buy a place.'

Now, amid all the grief, to me the opportunity to agist cattle on the plantation was the evening star. Another new beginning – another baby. Jen's response was characteristically cautious; mine excitable. My businessman father had gone from selling furniture to insurance to chickens, and although I'd always been uncomfortable with how he'd turned chickens into numbers, that day I did the same.

On the way to the hospital, I began to calculate. I fired questions at Jen and keyed numbers into my phone calculator. 'How much would one cow cost? How much would we sell a calf for? After what time period? What are the costs?' Jen reeled off estimates for what we'd need to buy.

'What about labour?' I asked.

She laughed. 'As if I'd factor that in. It's not like we'll be hiring anyone.'

It was an extraordinary eight to ten per cent interest on any investment, at the very worst. In the lift up to Lola's hospital room, in the lift down to the parking meter, in the lunchtime sandwich queue, I thought about the possibilities and implications.

Even though we now lived together on the farm, we still largely kept our finances separate, maintaining sole ownership of our properties.

'I should pay you rent,' I'd said to Jen before we'd moved back to the farm.

'Why? I didn't pay you rent when I lived in town,' she said, 'And anyway, you've paid for half of the new place and you pay for food and everything we do away from here.'

'But I'm more than happy to pay for that – and I can. What's more, if I didn't live here with you, I'd need a decent paying job.'

'And I don't want to feel dependent on you,' Jen had said. 'I might not make much but I've always managed to live within my means.'

It had taken countless conversations over cups of tea and beers at the bath fire to work out a financial arrangement. But we both knew I still held the power to decide what I did with my money, and Jen still felt partially financially dependent on me.

So when the offer came through to lease this thousand acres of extra land, all I could think was: if I gave Jen the money to buy cattle she'd be able to make more of a living from the farm. A viable cattle business seemed another way to even out our financial differential – to increase Jen's financial independence.

That evening as we walked along the broadwater, flushing ourselves of the hospital's smells and sadness, and watching children shriek in and out of the water, I hazarded my suggestion. Jen said nothing. I watched a pelican catch a chip tossed by a small child.

'Only way it could work,' Jen said, 'is if we go into business together.'

'Okay, so I'll be the sleeping partner.'

'No,' Jen said. 'I already need your help in the yards. With more cattle I'll need you more.'

'But you'll still be doing way more of the work.'

'And you'll be carrying the financial risk,' she said. 'If we go into drought again or the price of beef drops you can lose badly. I've known someone to get a bill from the saleyards. This is the real stock market.' She shook her head. 'I don't know. With Mum's stroke the timing couldn't have been worse.'

'Or better,' I said. 'It's an opportunity – for us. Something for us together. Something that might help me feel more part of the farm.'

Months later, after Lola had moved into a nursing home, we went in to see the stock agent in Casino. He was tall, fair and blue-eyed – a handsome, confident country bloke. A charmer. While he and Jen discussed why breeders not steers were a better idea for the farm, my eyes roamed around the office decorated with calendars picturing drovers and cattle. Not a book in sight. When I'd invested in the other stock market I'd sat in glassed sky-rises with spectacular city-scape views and shelves with leather-bound tax reports and guides. There, although I'd staked my claim against mining and tobacco, I'd had a limited understanding of the complex machine that translated figures on a spreadsheet into money in a bank account. Now the language of the 'real stock market' seemed equally incomprehensible.

Afterwards as we climbed into the truck, I said, 'He seems nice. I'm sure he'll do right by us.'

Jen laughed. 'No, he won't. He'll look after himself, which means looking after the seller so he gets his commission. Mum used to say you'd have to wash the bullshit off the walls of the pub after the stock and station agents had been in.'

I laughed, fleetingly aware that just as I ceded power over money to financial advisors, here again I was placing my trust in an older man with 'knowledge' as if he were my father who 'knew'.

The cattle venture made us a team – Jen with the knowledge, me with the chequebook and curiosity. Now our relationship would have another glue: a shared business. Soon we'd have shared money, and perhaps I'd feel I had a real role and tangible purpose on the farm, other than farmer's 'wife'.

'Shopping' for cattle was an exotic adventure. Dressed in akubras and loose button-up shirts, we visited a farm two hours away to look at a line of Gelbvieh heifers we subsequently bought. In the couple's kitchen during the obligatory cup of tea as we pored over their spreadsheet of the cows, I covered my holey sock with the other foot – we'd left our shoes outside, as you do in the country. This was the most intimate country life had ever seemed.

At the Casino livestock exchange our boots clinked against the metal steps. We peered at the red and blue tags on the heifers' tails as their hooves clicked against the concrete underfoot and the cowboys whistled and called, 'Yard up.' I nodded to the other farmers; the older blokes were dressed in pressed trousers and akubra hats, the younger in jeans and checked shirts and caps. There were one or two women – one bought poddy calves and raised them, another wore a cap with *Tres Chic* in glittery letters.

To the seesawing song of the auctioneer, my eyes bounced around the crowd, searching for the nods and almost imperceptible finger movements – including Jen's – until the auctioneer's stock-whip-as-gavel struck against the iron rail, and the woman beside him made notes on her clipboard.

Lunch of rissoles and gravy or white-bread sandwiches was at half past eleven. The canteen with its formica tables and pink plastic mats had walls decorated with different brands; some seemed like squiggles, others arrows or diamonds or infinity symbols. There were only women in the kitchen and at most of the tables were men, young and old, their caps over their knees or their akubras on the tables beside them, an indentation left around their hairline. Deep laughter and booming voices joined the groans of the air conditioner.

Every fortnight Jen would leave the farm to go up and be with her mother on the Gold Coast for a week or ten days. In the fortnight she was home, I'd join her in the paddocks. We'd sit back in our saddles and just be with the cattle we'd recently bought, familiarising them with the horses and the dogs. Although I enjoyed the rides on Boxer, the sun and air, the trees and birds, just as I'd needed puzzles to amuse me in a hospital room, after a while in the paddock my mind searched out some other purpose. I took to guessing at cow friendships or love affairs and monitoring what I saw as the triangles under the cattle's hips to see when they'd fit Jen's 'fat cattle are happy cattle' motto. Before long, my mind was jumping away to short-story plots and titles. I tried to learn the differences in breed. We had bought what Jen called a 'Heinz variety': there were Gelbviehs, Brahmans, Brangus, Angus and Herefords, one hundred and eighty of them. Too many for me to really come to know as individuals. Instead, strangely, it was the five bulls I came to know and care about.

In the cattle yards my confidence and skills expanded a little, as did my lexicon, which now included statements like: Walk out, girls. Yard up. Up the gully. Hup hup hup. Shshshsh. Up you go. Steady, girls. Out, dogs. Walk up, girl. Please, ladies, please. Up you go, little fellas.

Conditions were often treacherous. The gate across the race was stiff and I had to plant my feet and use all my strength to slide it closed. The cowpats were slippery when you were watching cows, not your feet, and the yards were either dusty or churned up and gluggy with mud after rain. If we waited for the summer scorch and humidity to go out of the day there was limited light, so we had to hurry to finish the job. The castration, even the tagging and inoculation, seemed so harsh, so violent. Everywhere were flies and noise. Cattle bellowed and moaned. Dogs barked. Jen yelled instructions.

My initiative was often met with a curt, 'It won't work, you'll need me too. Just wait.'

Jen was right, of course. As soon as she joined me in the yard, the cattle worked. Not only was it easier to move cattle with two people, she was quicker, surer, fitter – and unafraid.

As we drove home in the dark, tired and manure-spattered, silently I'd curse Jen, the physicality and harshness of the work, my tentativeness and fearfulness. Sometimes I'd say, 'This would be so much easier for you if Jack was still alive.'

And yet I felt an odd joy when we worked side by side in the yards, the grunt and realness, the earthy physicality of being among the bellowing and barking and dust under the big sky. I even got a kick out of coming home tired, ditching the filthy sweaty clothes and making dinner, amused to find myself playing the role of 'good farmer's wife'.

At the annual Fletcher Christmas party at the hall, over a table of pavlova and trifles, I asked two of the local women how it was, working with their husbands in the yards. One admitted she'd stopped doing it. 'It's better that way,' she said, 'fewer arguments.'

The other hesitated. I leaned in closer, hoping she might reveal something personal, a rare moment in this community where people so rarely verbalised emotional undercurrents. But then a windshield seemed to come up and all she said was, 'I ignore him, or give back as good as I get.'


One sticky hot February day, as Jen kicked off her boots, she announced, 'Angel's dead.'

Angel was our Brahman bull. He'd come to us in spring, when Jen had extended the trellis to support the bumper broad bean crop, and the paddocks had been so rich in green pick that the cows hadn't trundled after the truck bellowing, 'Feed me, feed me.' Angel had a hump higher than my eyeline, a tan-brown hide, a wobbly black-and-white spotted dewlap, a stunted horn and droopy Brahman ears. We named him Elvis at first because our great-nephew had just won our fire brigade fundraiser's talent competition with his rendition of 'Blue Suede Shoes'. It seemed right for this grand and regal bull that instantly claimed his harem of Hereford cows, hovering and super-vising, patrolling and corralling. He was king.

Months later we'd renamed him Angel because of the quiet way he walked up the race, poking his head through the bails, presenting his ears for fly tags or opening his mouth for the drench tube. He didn't snot and snort; he didn't assert his territoriality like the Angus bulls. Angel was above all that, different somehow.

That day, after Jen had found Angel dead with a shattered lower leg, we slumped on the couch, stunned.

'It doesn't make sense,' I said. 'He was fine when we drenched them before the floods.'

Jen sighed. 'Maybe he got his foot stuck in a rabbit hole or be-tween two rocks. Or maybe those bloody neighbours shot their high-powered rifle.'

It had rained for twenty-three days in January. The causeway had been knee-deep in water, the driveway a bracelet of divots and ditch-es, the paddocks too swampy to even ride a horse across. We hadn't seen Angel and his herd for three weeks.

Out loud I wondered if anything could have been done to save him if he'd been found earlier. If he'd suffered for long. To die alone was still the ultimate representation of loneliness, my deepest fear.

That evening I clung to the truck's scaredy-cat bar as Jen drove, tyres hissing along washed-out dirt roads and sodden tracks. We bumped up and down across the river paddock and then left the ute parked on a hill. In our gumboots we waded through thigh-high sticky grass, watching out for wet manure and snakes.

Near a barbed-wire fence, Jen pointed out an area where thick clumps of blady grass had been flattened in circles. There were six of these rounds, side by side. I imagined Angel pivoting his large bulk, thrashing about, swinging himself around from grass bed to grass bed. Was he trying to get up? Trying to get to water? Further down the paddock I peered at another Venn diagram where Angel had set-tled and rotated. A crow quark-quarked from a nearby spotty gum. If Angel had known he was going to die, would he, as cattle usually do, have withdrawn from the others? If it had been an accident, would the cows have witnessed him thrashing around, would they have witnessed his death?

Further down the paddock, closer to the gully, we found Angel: a backbone with vertebrae the size of my hand; a skull with its de-formed horn. The jaw, as long as my forearm, lay separate from the rest of his body. There were his hinge joints at the hips and knees. One leg – the broken one, the cause of his death – was missing, prob-ably carried away by wild dogs. His hide was draped over his upper body like a cloak, spattered with the white paint of bird droppings. There was no flesh left. He had been sucked dry, eaten from the inside out and the outside in – a feast for maggots, flies, beetles, moths, wasps, wild dogs and goannas, maybe even foxes.

Silly and sentimental though it was, I told Angel that we missed him, that other farmers like Rusty and the cowboy Roland had been saddened by his death. I told him I was sorry if he had suffered.

As Jen knelt down to take his yellow ID tag, I stopped her.

'It's perfectly good,' she said. 'We can reuse it.'

'No.' I was adamant. 'Leave it there, like the dog tag of the fallen soldier.'

# 23

# SEXUALITY AS A ROADBLOCK

FROM MY DESK, I watched a pair of wrens peck at their image in the window. Lucy lay asleep just outside the study door, her chest floating up and down, her legs twitching as she chased dream rabbits. Inside I had a pot of soup on the stove, and a date a month away circled on the calendar when friends were coming out for a visit. Beautiful. Peaceful. So lucky. If only I'd found sanctuary in the writing or could be content with farm work and fire brigade, or just 'being' on the farm.

Two years of farm life had shown me that if I was to settle here, I had to 'do something', paid or unpaid, that contributed to a better, fairer world. Although I'd had a few short stories published and a profile on Keith, the local artist with the sculpture park, the writing hadn't become that yet. Using my skills to help other people was certainly core to my values but it had also been the way I'd found 'my people' and my place when I'd migrated to Sydney and when I'd moved to the north coast.

A neighbouring town had a pub, post office, police station, preschool, primary school and highway shop that sold overpriced fuel and groceries. Nearby was a village where most of the local

Aboriginal community lived. Some still called it 'the mish', others called it by its Aboriginal placename. In years to come I'd hear a deeply generous man, a local elder, explain where the town had got its name: 'When the European fellas came along, my folks didn't know much English and these folks didn't know much language. But they had a talk and a greeting. My folks said, "This is our place, we're from here," but the European fellas couldn't say it that way. I guess they couldn't hear.' Living in the area, I'd been startled by the strength of the separation between the Aboriginal and non-Aboriginal communities. At hall nights I'd heard stories about the conflicts that raged on the school bus between the kids from the different communities. Although a couple of the neighbours had connections with people from 'the mish', they rarely came to our hall nights, and the only time I drove into the village was when I'd given a hitchhiker a ride or had a job interviewing Indigenous artists for a book. The barriers seemed as marked and impassable as the South Africa of my childhood. Australian apartheid. Apart-hood.

The places where the different communities seemed to come together were the preschool and primary school. Perhaps I could volunteer there.

My first day at the primary school, the teacher sent me to sit outside under the silky oak tree and, one by one, the children came to practise their reading. Some of the girls were studious and competitive, others wanted to play with my hair. One of the boys was jumpy; he flicked the page up and down and didn't seem to recognise any letters. Later I discovered he had foetal alcohol syndrome and was happier dancing than staring at a page. I had no idea how to teach a child to read, and when words like king and queen, vase and zebra were met with a wide-eyed 'what's that?', I wondered about shared languages and what chances these rural kids had in Australia's education system. During recess I was comforted to see how all the kids seemed to play together. Reconciliation seemed achievable.

When I came home with an outbreak of nits, Jen said, 'Why're you doing this? Schools are terrible places.'

'I like kids,' I said, 'and maybe I've got something to offer.'

I washed all the bedding, drowned my hair in conditioner, combed out the offending lice, and from then on leaned back when the kids came up close.

During lunch breaks I joined the teachers in the staffroom. I hung back around the urn, listening to their conversations about weddings and babies. There were no spare chairs at the square table and no entry points to the conversations. I longed for the bell.

The year before I'd run a drama class at the mudbrick community hall for the twelve local children until a friendship rupture between two of the girls had frayed their tight little community. Maybe a drama group at the school would be less vulnerable to small community dynamics; maybe an opportunity for creative play would cut across the cultural boundaries. How hard could it be? At the end of the year I knocked on the busy principal's office door. Would she allow me to run a lunchtime drama group?

Certainly. But she couldn't guarantee any children would turn up.

They did. Some Thursdays we'd walk across hot coals or sink knee-deep in soft sand; sometimes we were frogs; sometimes we'd build the Harbour Bridge or a sailing ship with our bodies, or watch a football match or a horror film. Sometimes they'd role-play scenarios. Mostly we laughed. Week after week they came back.

'Hey, Hairy Hayley!' someone called out one week as I walked through the school gate, its posts stencilled with turtles and goannas.

I turned in the direction of the voice. Katia, one of the older Aboriginal girls, stood beside a wooden lunch table under the wispy silky oak trees, hands on her hips, chin tilted up. She'd come to drama group for the first three weeks, taken over the sound system and played her own CD, answered for the younger Aboriginal students and when we'd danced in a circle – moving first our eyes, then adding ears, then tongues – she'd roughly elbowed a smaller girl out of her way. I'd watched others step aside, wilt under her glare. I'd not known how to deal with such behaviour and hadn't been sorry when she'd stopped coming.

Katia was staring at me, as were nine other Aboriginal kids, all different ages.

One of the games we played in drama group was a memory game where you introduced your name with an action and an adjective beginning with the same sound as your name. Now all the kids at this small rural school, not just those who came to drama group, called me Hairy Hayley.

I called back, 'Hi, Cool Katia.'

'Come over 'ere,' she said, gesturing to me.

I walked over to her table.

'How you doing?' I asked, sitting on the bench beside her.

'Have you got a boyfriend?' Katia said.

I wasn't prepared for this question. It's a loaded one when you're a lesbian in an environment where you feel foreign and unsure of yourself and the place's unwritten rules.

The options flashed before me. I could say: 'No, I've got a girlfriend.' But that didn't seem appropriate for the primary-school playground. I could say: 'It's none of your business.' But I wanted to connect with these kids, and to do it truthfully.

'No,' I said, trying to convince myself that I was just answering the question I'd been asked.

Katia said, 'Tallie says you've got a girlfriend.'

Tallie was a girl who also lived in our area. We saw her most Friday nights at the local community hall. She'd hung out with us at the annual cricket match, helped us draw witches and spiders to decorate the hall for a fire brigade fundraiser, and the previous year we'd given her brother a job helping us pull out fireweed and stuffing it into old feedbags.

I was rattled. Katia and the nine other kids were staring at me. I was comfortable with my lesbianism – unlike the other labels I was ambivalent about. I knew it wasn't a criminal offence to be a lesbian. Even the federal government had recently recognised our relationships for the purposes of social security and tax. Jen had said it made her feel a little easier about being out in this rural community. Never before had I had second thoughts about coming out. But as the branches of the silky oak swayed above me, and a posse of children stared at me, 'lesbian' flashed neon.

My heart hammered. What's education department policy on discussing this kind of thing? What's this school's policy in a rural area where sexuality still seemed problematised? Would the teacher on playground duty march over and order me off the school grounds for saying the L-word? Would the headmistress summon me to her office and say, 'Thank you for your time but we'll no longer be requiring your assistance with drama group'?

I felt mocked, vulnerable and caged. I imagined judgement and denigration. But I wouldn't lie – I couldn't lie.

'That's right,' I said to Katia. 'I do.'

'So does that mean you're a les-be-n?' Katia asked, lingering over each syllable.

'Yes,' I said. 'I'm a lesbian.'

My fingers reddened as I clutched my bottle of water; my palms sweated. Around me the sounds of chatter faded, everything telescoping onto my interaction with Katia. How long was it since someone had spoken? Should I have said something else? The children were watching me, waiting.

'True?' Katia said. Her mouth widened into a sideshow-alley laugh, and suddenly I was one of the kids in the playground and she was pointing her finger, shaming me.

At last Katia looked away. I considered getting up and running to the safety of the classroom. But Katia wasn't finished. She turned to the crowd of kids.

'Ask 'er,' she said. 'Come on, ask 'er.'

From the other side of the table, a boy of about ten said, 'Are you a les-be-n?'

'Yes,' I said. 'I am.'

And then another young girl asked me, and another young boy. Every single child at that table asked me if I was a 'les-be-n', each one let their lips and tongue linger over each syllable.

None of the other children came over to join in the questioning. It was just these ten kids. And they all had to hear it from my mouth. I wondered how long they'd been planning this inquisition. I imagined their conversations in the playground, at the morning line-up, as rumour of my sexuality had spread. Like smug hunters with traps set, they'd been waiting for me to turn up for drama group.

As I answered 'yes' and then 'yes' again to each of those children's questions, I started to wonder if this would seal the fate of drama group. Maybe none of them would come: they wouldn't want to play with the 'les-be-n'. I also realised that if the school rumour mill worked swiftly, it wouldn't be long before the whole school knew I was a lesbian.

Drama group was finished. Kaput. I could see myself putting the CD in the player, pushing the tables and chairs to the side to clear a space, then waiting, reading and re-reading the nouns and adjectives printed on orange cardboard pinned to the walls. I'd spend the forty minutes alone waiting for participants, with kids' laughter and voices outside. When the bell rang, I'd push the tables back in place and scurry, shamed, to my car.

Then it occurred to me that if drama group was kaput, there wasn't much to lose. Sitting on the wooden bench, mentally staging future events as Katia and company gazed at me with real interest, I was struck by the thought that these kids wanted to know who I was. This might be the first time they'd met a real, live, out lesbian.

So I said to Katia, 'You know, I'm not ashamed to be a lesbian.'

She laughed, her spittle spraying my cheeks. Then she turned to the others and they too laughed on command. They were almost sneering at me.

I had to swallow that lump in my throat, still my hammering

heart and stay on this bench; I had to turn this inquisition into a conversation.

'How old are you, Katia?' I asked.

'Twelve.'

I said, 'I've been with my partner for twelve years. That means we've been together as long as you've been on this earth.'

She looked at me wide-eyed, then said to the crowd, 'She's been a les-be-n for twelve years.'

'Oh, no,' I said. 'Longer than that. I've been with Jen for that long. I've been a lesbian for about twenty years.'

Katia looked stricken. Was she shocked that I was that old? Or because I'd admitted to the affliction of long-term lesbianism? Perhaps such lasting deviance showed I was beyond redemption.

But Katia was smart; she'd claimed the name 'Cool Katia' for good reason. She recovered herself and asked, 'So her name's Jen?'

'Yes.' I paused. 'You know, it's not a secret. Everyone who knows us knows we're together. We're not so different from the other adult couples you know, like your mum and dad and aunties and uncles, who're in love and in committed long-term relationships.'

Oops – I'd used another L-word.

'You in love?' Cool Katia was giggling now. So was the rest of the audience.

'Yes,' I said.

'Next week, you bring in a photograph. I want to see what she looks like.'

'Haven't you met a lesbian before?' I said to the assembled group.

Katia and a few others shook their heads.

'No way,' Katia said. And then, taking the upper hand again, she said, 'So do you have s-e-x?'

I couldn't answer that question. That would surely be considered a breach by the principal. And the next question would probably be 'How do you do it?', and as a rule I never answer that question. Although perhaps if I had, I'd have had packed classes and avoided the problematic second-guessing that's associated with foreignness. I felt my back straighten and I shook my head. I might want to relate truthfully to these kids, but this was rude, not just cheeky.

I looked at my watch and said, 'Drama group starts in five minutes.'

As I slipped Angelique Kidjo into the CD player, I chewed the side of my mouth and scanned my class plan. Just focus on the activities. Would anyone come play this week? Katia hadn't said anything negative, even if she'd looked stricken. Maybe I was being foolishly fearful, assuming the kids would be operating on some negative stereotype. I sighed: here I went again, second-guessing others as if it might keep me safe. I consoled myself with the thought that it had been an interesting experiment that had got me out into the community a little – ironically, in more than one way. Twenty-five students had come the first week. Chaos. After that it settled down to ten to twelve students from kindergarten to year six, mainly girls, both Aboriginal and non-Aboriginal. And although there was a different group each week, there were always the same five eager regulars.

Just as I was ready to pack up my books and CD, Katia strode into the classroom, six of her posse in tow, and then the five regulars slunk in, wide-eyed at the new batch of participants.

As we played piano, then guitar, then flute, then saxophone with our fingers and mouths, I felt Katia's eyes on me, everyone's eyes on me. Were they thinking *is this how a lesbian moves?*

I swallowed hard and said, 'Play drums,' and kept my gaze away from Katia.

When we played the name game and it came around to six-year-old Louise, I held my breath. Would Katia intervene and say, 'Call 'er Lesbian Louise'?

She didn't. Someone suggested 'Lovely Louise' and my shoulders relaxed.

When we sat in the circle to play the birthday-present game, I read the rules from my book. Under Katia's gaze I couldn't trust my memory. While the game moved around the circle I worked on my light and cool persona; I made sure I treated everyone the same. Even if Katia was testing me, even if she was here to play 'let's watch the freak more closely', she wouldn't be able to fault me.

That day, I gave my greatest performance – and then I bolted for my car. I felt ruffled, sick, uneasy. And I was baffled. Not by Katia's questions; I admired her guts, admired her for asking. I knew how I'd often defined myself by demographics, and how the use of a label – to define one's self or another – can be as much about the construction of one's own values and identity. So why had a bunch of children brought me undone? In the past I'd confidently confronted and challenged homophobic comments or behaviours. I was an out and proud lesbian; I favoured discussion over silencing. So why the fear? Was it because this time it hadn't been my choice to come out? Was it because I had too much investment in this volunteer job, which seemed the only non-manual opportunity to do something useful? Had Katia seen deep inside me, touched a nerve of shame? Did I still have some deep-rooted sense that the way I lived was 'wrong', that my lesbianism damages those around me, that it means I'm 'bad'? Internalised homophobia? Self-hatred? Had this come to the fore because I felt like such an outsider in the Australian bush and Jen had warned me to be careful?

When I got back to the farm, I bush-bashed across the paddock after the tractor. I had to tell Jen what had happened, immediately. She'd thought my drama group ill-advised. 'Why would you choose to go into a school and teach kids and not even get paid for it?' she'd said.

For two years in the 1970s she'd taught home science at a large public school in western Sydney. She was part of a lesbian teachers' group formed when a lesbian maths teacher was advised to resign from a private school after the media printed a photograph of her, complete with seventies afro and a feminist slogan T-shirt, being dragged into a police wagon at the first Mardi Gras march.

Jen halted when she saw the car bumping across the paddock. She jumped down from the tractor and took off her earmuffs.

'What happened?' she asked. 'Are you okay?'

Over the tractor's hum she shook her head as I told her the story and said, 'Bloody kids. They're all the same. Now do you understand what I mean?'

As I leaned against the tractor in the strained winter sun, I said, 'It wasn't a total disaster. Katia and her crew came to class. That says something.'

'What does it say? That they want to check out the lezzo?' Jen said.

'Yeah, maybe, but maybe they'll see me as cool now – isn't lesbianism the latest thing?'

'For kids out here?' Jen said. 'Doubt it.'

'Maybe Katia thinks I'm more acceptable now 'cos I'm from a group that also cops discrimination. Maybe there's some subconscious minority-group identification going on. Maybe it can be the beginning of some real connection, of some open-hearted curiosity. I don't know. All I know is, Katia came to class.'

'Just wait for next week,' Jen said, winking. 'You'll see, they'll chant "lezzo, lezzo" when you walk in, not "Hairy Hayley".'


The following week as I walked through the gates, it felt as if every single child was watching me. Should I have worn a dress? Should I change my walk? Stride more; wiggle more. What, I wondered, were these children concluding from watching me?

I was relieved when I heard someone call out, 'Hi, Hairy Hayley!'

Saskia and Tina, two of the Aboriginal girls who often came to drama group, were sitting apart from the others.

'We're on bench,' Tina explained. They'd been punished. 'We have to eat here.'

Saskia said, 'What's your partner's name again?'

'Jen.' So the news was all round the school.

Tina's jaw dropped; her hands and sandwich froze mid-air.

'Tina didn't know about you,' Saskia said to me, conspiratorially. 'She wouldn't believe me.'

Tina didn't come to class that day.

But Katia came. She monopolised the sound system. She directed the other kids. She answered for the little ones. Her gaze silenced and withered a year-two boy.

Was this just who she, an individual, was? Or who she'd become? Perhaps because she'd witnessed violence, itself a result of racism and generations of oppression and trauma? Or was Katia seizing the upper hand in the one place she could, and in the only way she knew? Katia was perhaps acting the bully just as she was also a survivor of injustice. Duality, multidimensionality.

All I knew was that I hadn't projected authority: I'd not disciplined Katia, and for that there was a consequence for the other kids, and for me. I could attribute my inaction to my inexperience with children. But I knew too it was because I, a white South African, still felt afraid of being labelled 'racist'. Perhaps my insecurity and inaction had facilitated Katia's behaviour. I don't know.

There was only one thing I was sure of: during lunch in the back section of the year five and six classroom, twelve students, including Katia, followed my directions and made their bodies into cups and saucers, into knives and forks; they performed the roles of mothers, teachers, lost dogs. They gave themselves a round of applause at the end of the class.

And no one mentioned the L-word. Not even Katia.

We got through to the end of the year. As I walked into the school grounds for the last class carrying a large bundle under my arm, Katia asked, 'What's that you got?'

I said, 'We're playing pass the parcel in drama class.'

'Cool,' Katia said.

'Yeah, but you don't get stuff in this game – you have to do stuff,' I said.

Thirty students crowded into the classroom that day. One or two refused to do the activities and left as the parcel bumped around the circle.

The next year I was almost relieved when the principal suggested I help with the school's entry into a national story-sharing arts festival. This was a chance to learn how teachers handled this diverse body of kids and to perhaps have colleagues again.

On the day of the first meeting outside the classroom, the teachers were hurried and unfriendly. I wondered if this was an unwanted additional load or whether they were homophobic. No doubt they'd heard I was a 'les-be-n'.

When they told me we were entering in the story-dance category, I said, 'I'm not sure I'll be any help. I love to dance but I don't know a thing about choreography.'

They shrugged. They'd both done jazz ballet. 'You can help with the story,' they said.

In response to my questions like 'who's the main character' and 'what does she want', the students created a story about the new girl, Betty, who's tormented by Peta, the school bully. I was intrigued that this was the topic they'd chosen. Just as I was intrigued after some research by how bullying was a major issue in countless schools Australia-wide despite the Education Department's anti-bullying policies and excellent leadership at schools such as this one.

The next week when I arrived, the door to the classroom was closed. I peered through the window. The class was in full swing. I crept inside.

'Oh, hello,' one of the teachers said. 'We started earlier so we can finish early. Show Hayley what we've done.'

I watched Betty sashay onto the stage into a circle of other kids clapping, hip-shaking and pelvis-thrusting. The kids seemed to be enjoying themselves but those movements seemed inappropriately sexual; or was I, who had no kids of my own and was unfamiliar with contemporary youth culture, being prudish? Were my sensitivities heightened because here in the bush I was uncertain about how my own sexuality might be received?

As the weeks rolled on and I stood by watching, I felt like the useless and ineffectual outsider. I'd assumed I could offer these kids something. But this had nothing to do with creative play – it was simply about performance. What had I been thinking? I had no skill or training for this kind of work or student body. I wasn't even a parent. I longed for escape. I considered not going back to the school – after all, this was a voluntary job. But I didn't want to be irresponsible and unreliable. And how would I explain myself? Could I say I was no use? That I was too different? That I didn't belong?

Until the dance was videoed and sent off to the competition, I turned up each week, standing back, offering rare comments on the clarity of the story, smiling and clapping. When, during the last class, Katia, who'd left the school, sauntered in and gibed at me from the back of the hall in front of the teachers, I turned my back on her as I shrivelled smaller.

Weeks later a parcel arrived: a box of Quality Street chocolates with a thankyou note, a picture of all the children and the certificate from the competition. Even as I unwound the shiny wrapping and bit into a caramel-centred chocolate, I knew I wouldn't be going back to teach drama the next year.

# 24.

# COUNTRYWOMAN

EVERY FORTNIGHT JEN DROVE the four hours to the Gold Coast to spend a week with her mother. In the months after the stroke it had been every ten days. 'I want to,' she said when asked, 'and it gives Kay a break.' Jen's oldest sister Kay went to the nursing home every day after work, with home-cooked food and clothes she'd washed and ironed.

It flummoxed me that apart from my hour as volunteer drama teacher at the school, and my once-a-month meeting with my coastal writing group, I now spent my days alone in this middle-of-nowhere place while Jen was out in the world, connecting with people, becoming part of a nursing-home community. I could of course go with her, and I had regularly. So much so that most people at the nursing home recognised me and thought I was Lola's daughter.

But on my last visit the routine had felt unbearably oppressive. Sign in, douse hands, greet Mary and look at her photographs again, greet Lola, get pills from the nurse, walk ahead of Lola's wheelchair to open doors, unlock car, place slide sheet on seat, tip wheelchair, fold up wheelchair and put it in boot. At the mall, follow wheelchair into movie theatre, then to restaurant, then to disabled toilet. Dig out the incontinence pad, read cleaning notice and count tiles on wall and floor. Then reverse the process and stare at television gameshows, get Lola's clothes out, hang on doorhandle, put dirty clothes in that bag, get bowl of warm water, fill up water carafe, make up protein drink, place tissue under Lola's hand. Go back to sister Kay's house, recount day, stare at television, fall into bed before doing it all again the next day.

I so wanted to be helpful and supportive, caring and patient. I marvelled at Lola's courage, Jen's competence and capacity to care, and at such physical intimacy, something I'd never known even with my own mother. I was awed by Jen and her sisters' extraordinarily selfless love and care, but after a day I was bored bored bored. I counted the hours until we could get out of there, until Jen might come walk on the beach, or go out to dinner or a movie with me. When she refused, or when the conversation was of nothing but the nursing home, I glowered.

'You just can't stand it when my attention's not on you, Hayley,' Jen scolded as we drove away from the nursing home. 'You're jealous of my mother. It's unbelievable.'

I cringed. 'It's not that,' I said. 'You just get so preoccupied and obsessed. I wind up feeling completely invisible – and you feel un-recognisable.'

'That's not true, Hayley,' Jen said, setting her jaw. 'I'm always there for you. My mother needs me. Don't make me choose.' After a pause, she added, 'You don't have to come. In a way it's easier for me when you're not there.'

'Don't you want me there?' I asked, shrinking into rejection, afraid of all the time I'd wind up alone on the farm. I was torn, years off appreciating how much a desire to be supportive and belong can submerge one's own needs and interests.

Jen shook her head. 'All I'm saying, Hayley, is that you don't have to come. I'm not telling you I don't want you.'

Alone on the farm I watered seedlings as instructed, with the hayfork filled wheelbarrows with horse and cow manure, weeded, mowed – and I wrote and read. In the mornings I unchained the dogs; in the evenings, I fed and chained them. In the mornings I stabled the horses, mixed up their feeds and filled their drinking troughs. On winter mornings my pink fingers stung as they thawed under the hot tap; on summer mornings the horses called me out of bed. In the evenings I stabled the horses and doled out biscuits of hay.

Most days I saw and heard no human voices other than the radio, an occasional phone call from my mother or a friend, or when Jen rang to tell me what movie she and her mum had seen, which resident had complained about the food, and about her new nurse friends. The aloneness was overwhelming, frightening.

When I walked each morning, as I passed the red-browed finches that gathered near the mailbox, I hoped this might be one of those rare days when a neighbour drove past and stopped for a through-the-car-window conversation, which sometimes in their intimacy resembled conversations I'd had with strangers on city trains. The colonel's widow once blotted her mascara as she told me she was overwhelmed by the physical responsibility of the property, and the fisherman admitted retirement had brought visits from the 'black dog' which only fishing alleviated.

As I tossed a ball into a gully of water for Lucy, I considered jumping in the car and heading to town. A friend now lived in the room in the Mullumbimby backyard but there were other friends with spare rooms who seemed happy to have me stay for a night or two.

No, I told myself. Stay on the farm. In town you'll feel like an extra in the drama of others' lives and wonder what the hell you're doing with your own. Stay and work on the short story about the woman in the wheelchair who longs to travel beyond her country home. You'll enjoy yourself more than all the socialising. And then those castigating voices started: it doesn't matter that you shovel manure rather than get manicures, you don't want others to label you as that privileged white South African who lives according to the 'do what you love' mantra. You have to get published. It's the only way to be a 'writer'. The only way to prove your worth.

I walked on, conscious suddenly of the percussion of my body, how my walk moved with the tempo of my beating heart. How slowly I truly flowed. It struck me that all alone, without concern about finding my way, I was able to listen more carefully to the rhythm of my limbs and breath. In moments, in those gaps and pauses before my mind's net scooped up yet another proposition, I was emptied out. Spaciousness seemed to spread through the landscape of my being.

After a few days I'd go to Frank's with the bucket of scraps for his chickens. Sometimes I'd find him meandering in his gumboots from pen to pen collecting the eggs. Sometimes he was sitting on the verandah and I'd lean on the faded blue post and ask, 'So what's news?' and 'Did you have a good day in town?'

I was still not completely fluent in Fletcherese but now I had no qualms asking him to repeat what he'd said until I got the gist – or pretended to. Without Jen, our conversations trickled out. Frank never invited me to stay for a beer, and I didn't take a pew on the verandah.

In choosing not to be at the nursing home with Jen, I wanted to learn self-containment. I wanted to overcome my perennial fear of loneliness. But was this isolated life what I wanted for myself?

Curiosity accompanied the fear of aloneness. I watched and noted my responses. Sometimes I felt lost and frightened, as if I were disappearing. Sometimes I longed for escape. Mostly I feared I had been forgotten by busy friends geographically far away. But, to my surprise, during the daylight hours I noticed a new kind of freedom and ease. It felt remarkably like joy. Unobserved and unhurried, I kept myself company. I didn't have to be anything for anyone else. I could choose what I did and where my head went. What a revelation: aloneness could be pleasurable. It needn't equate to rejection or being 'unlikeable'. I wondered if this was what was meant by happy solitude or psychological fulfilment, and then I felt a surge of achievement: I'd hatched out of the familial cast and found true independence.

At night that delight disappeared. I heard a rustle in the orange jessamine outside the bedroom window, then a bang or creak or scurry. Was it human or animal? Mouse or rat or some unfamiliar bush animal? My body was rigid, on guard. There were thuds on the tin roof. The hum of a motor. Then one of the dogs barked. This was it: an intruder – a man or a group of men – was coming to get me. Would I be able to say no this time? No one would know. The house was up a long curved driveway, way off the road. It was a fishbowl without curtains and it didn't lock. Frank was a mile away, a seven-minute drive if I only had two gates to open.

I clutched my body tight in bed, debating whether to ring a neighbour. But if I turned on the light to make a call the intruders would see me. My eyes pinned open, my every muscle tense. Jen was never scared on her own, so why was I? Was this another legacy of my childhood? Even before my parent's divorce, as a small child in a house with burglar bars and security gates, I'd tiptoed down the carpeted passage and squeezed in beside my mother. I was afraid of the dark, and of the bogeyman Ellen had told me about.

'Just leave a light on,' a friend suggested. One night I did. But then I worried I was draining our battery power, and anyway the intruder would be able to see me in bed, or at least know I was in the house. What would I do if he attacked – bite, kick, freeze? Screaming would be no use. There were no neighbours to hear.

I got up to turn off the light. It was a male intruder I feared, not the dark.

I lay in bed thinking of John Bonhominie, a swarthy Italian with molasses eyes, always trailed by a swarm of local women. He'd lived on a property ten kilometres from our front gate, along a dirt road that council had forgotten. Some months before at the hall, I'd heard that he'd been found dead outside his back door, his black kelpie beside him, guarding against wild dogs and predators.

'He was all bloated and blown up,' I'd been told across the bar counter. 'Cops reckon he must've been there a couple of days. In this heat.' The cause of death was unknown.

Would that be what happened to me? Just as I'd done in my early months in Sydney, now too I imagined myself as another lonely death, this time a rural version, not a newspapers-piled-up-outside urban version.

Rational thought returned only when the sky eventually lightened, the sun poked through the gums and the horses whinnied for breakfast. Of course Jen would call and if I didn't answer for twenty-four hours she'd ring Frank to go check on me. Truth was, even if many of the neighbours were recluses or even hermits, they seemed more aware than city folk that something tragic could easily happen, more willing to step in and offer physical help rather than rely on public services. I just had to trust that isolation and distance didn't necessarily make me more vulnerable.

So, after a sleepless night, I'd drag myself into the light of another spacious day. Again I'd find myself unafraid, happy in this aloneness, happy at my desk, happy moving to the rhythm of my own body and mind.


One afternoon through the trees, just across the gully: a glow of red, flames a metre high. I scrabbled through the cobwebbed shed searching for a hessian sack and a rake-hoe and scurried down the hill towards the smoke. A log smouldered beside a blackened diamond but up ahead was more smoke, winding up from a bed of sawdust where, six years earlier, we'd milled the timber for the house. The dogs scrambled through the bush, slapping themselves down in the ash. A flock of choughs squawked and coughed as I walked towards a flaming log as thick as two bodies clasped together. With the rake I pushed back twigs and tinderbox leaves from the burned area, making a ribbon of dirt. Oh god, would this do?

I sucked at a bloody scratch on my thumb and looked around. There was no wind and there was a big blackened patch. Jen always said as long as you lit up close on dark you were usually right. I could even hear her say, 'It'll be alright, the wind will drop and the evening damp will put it out.'

What if I made the wrong decision? How would I deal with an out-of-control fire then? I thought of the Rural Fire Service magnet on our fridge: 'Leave early if you're going to leave.' I toyed with the idea of calling one of the blokes in the brigade, but I didn't want to be silly or play 'the girl'. I didn't want to overreact either and disturb someone unnecessarily. With the rake-hoe I scratched at the dirt, dragging away more fuel. When is enough enough?

By nightfall I was back at the house, pacing the verandah. In the deepening dark, through the forest of gums, I could see a faint red glow. Gradually it softened until it was no more than the tiny red light on an alarm-system sensor. Grateful for a 'book', I pulled out the thick blue manual from our basic firefighter training and ticked off everything I'd done. Now I had to wait and watch to see what the weather did.

Past eleven, there was no sign of the glow. Outside the air was still. I climbed into bed and lay there, ears pricked. Had I done enough? And well enough? In the dark, my panic rose.

I woke disoriented to a ringing phone. Midnight.

'Hayley?' It was Karen, our neighbour. 'Fair bit of smoke's coming our way. Rob's on his way over to check.'

I pulled jeans over flannelette pyjamas and screamed down the road in my car. The forest of ironbark and spotty gums up on the hill was alight. A wall of orange and red floated in smoky black sky, its roar filling the night.

Headlights wavered through the smoke. Rob and I stood beside our cars in the brisk night air, watching the front.

'Always looks bigger at night,' he said. 'It's okay.'

'Are you sure?' I wondered how many beers he'd had. 'Should I call someone to bring the truck?'

'I don't think you need to, but you might get a few calls,' he said laughing. 'Anyone up on the ridge will see this. I'll come over and check it in the morning.'

I apologised profusely, thanked him repeatedly and watched him crease his long body into his car and drive away, grateful for the way people in the bush helped each other with such willing generosity. I stared at the flames stretching a football field's length where earlier there had been just a few burned-out diamonds. An orange glow twisted through the trees. But Rob had said there was nothing to worry about.

Back home, I put another log on the fire, set the kettle on the stove, tried to read the local paper. The whirr of wind down the chimney was the approaching front, then an aeroplane in the distance was the fire. Outside, the air was close with smoke. If the fire approached now, it'd be too late to leave.

Dawn came finally, minus-two degrees on the verandah, the mulch on the flower garden powdered with frost. With the dogs in tow, I walked across the gully and up to the ridgeline. Trees had collapsed and lay on top of each other, their mouths gaping smoke, surrounded by talcum-powder blackened dirt with frost sewn into it. Fairy floss tufts of burned grass melted to ash as I trod on them. I kicked at a limb that was still burning and pulled it into a black area, the sawdust smoking. Rob joined me and we pulled and pushed at limbs and tufts of grass, swept back leaves and sticks.

Later Jen rang. 'That'd be the sawdust from when we milled the timber for the house,' she said. 'Just make sure you've hoed round the edges and there's nothing left to burn near it. You might've saved another house.'

'With Rob's help,' I said, any new sense of competence only

slightly tarnished by embarrassment that I'd been so freaked out by it.

Another week, there was a fetid, rotten smell to the water from the tap. 'Might be something dead in the tank,' Jen had said as she packed for her week away. 'You'll just have to deal with it yourself or go to town. I have to get going. I told Mum I'd be up there by lunch. Take the strainer off the top tank and look inside.'

As I waved her goodbye at the front gate I muttered, 'Shit, shit, shit.' I was no good with dead things. I'd grown up in a family squeamish about death. Dead animals, even our pets, were 'dealt with' by the vet or by Million, who worked for us. Dead or close to death, I wouldn't touch it. It was hard enough to even look at it.

But if I didn't deal with whatever was dead in the water tank, I'd have no water for drinking, cooking or washing. For a week. For a second I contemplated going to friends in town. Or I could bathe in the creek and fill up some of the white drums Jen used for water when nursing a cow. A twenty-litre bucket would be all I could lift. It wouldn't get me far.

Or maybe I could do this. I'd now had countless experiences with blood and urine, guts and tissue. I drove up the paddock to the tank stand, stood the ladder on the truck's tray and climbed up: the strainer had been dislodged. I drained the tank of water and peered inside. The dim beam of the torch lit up the remaining small puddle of water and a dead frog, its legs dismembered. Jen could climb in and out of that tank – she'd once cemented it from the inside – but I didn't have the upper-body strength to lift myself out. I looked down at the dogs. They'd be no help if I got stuck inside the tank, and there'd be no visitors unless the Jehovah's Witnesses turned up.

With a net fashioned from a pillowslip attached to a stick, I concentrated hard on frog-fishing and cursed loudly. A wet pillowslip did not a net make and the smell of dead frog and contaminated water was nauseating. But what to do? Give in? Scurry to town? Call a neighbour? But who? There was no one I felt that comfortable with.

When something stuck in the wet pillowslip, I pulled it up and flicked it onto the boards of the platform: unrecognisable, perhaps a frog's leg. Gross, I thought, not 'poor little frog'. Again and again I fished: more unrecognisable body parts. Be patient, I told myself. Finally, I convinced myself that the bits made up a whole frog. I hallelujahed and the dogs ran circles around the tank. And later, after I'd pumped water to fill the tank, came my second trophy: clean water gushing out of the tap.

Perhaps, when left alone, when Jen wasn't around to just easily 'do it', I wasn't so useless after all.

# PART THREE:
# COMMUNITY

*And one of the questions I want to answer now, for myself, is what*
*makes a place feel like home. I know that it is not so simple as living*
*where people speak your language and look like you and have lost what*
*you have lost, but there is a kind of comfort in that, too.*
— Eula Biss, ***Notes from No Man's Land***

# 25

# BORED FARMER'S WIFE

OVER THE FOUR YEARS Lola was in the nursing home, life developed a pattern: Jen would be home for three weeks then away for a week with her mother. When she came home, I welcomed her with kisses and clean sheets. I sprawled on the bed, watching as she emptied the bag of her mum's incontinence nappies and the little plastic bags that had contained the lunchtime pills. I listened to tales of the other residents and the staff, outings to the movies and the RSL club.

One afternoon Jen found a Hereford cow down. 'She's probably got three-day sickness,' she said as we loaded drums of water onto the truck.

Morning and night Jen ministered to the cow: lucerne hay and molasses, a bucket of water. When the cow didn't want to eat, Jen handfed her, tipping the bucket to get her to drink. I hovered, watching, helping where I could.

At home, Jen was tired and flat and didn't say much. With all the time away, she was stretched and busy. She had little time or headspace for anything but farming. Her conversation was of what might be ailing the cow, or of the nursing home or the neighbours. When she regaled me with descriptions about which herd of cattle were in which paddock, I'd lose the thread as my mind wandered off to the book I was reading or the story I was writing.

'Sorry, I'm boring you,' she'd say when she realised I wasn't really listening.

I winced, chastising myself: how could I weary of her concern for an animal's life, for her passion for her livestock? Her extraordinary capacity to care – for her mother and for sick animals – was so admirable. My concerns – writing stories about people's hopes and challenges – seemed so insignificant in comparison.

Where she'd always been interested in what I was writing or reading or learning, and brought her sharp mind and experience to our discussions, now those conversations too trickled out. I wondered how other couples connected if their passions and interests were different. Out in the bush we had no friends or family to infuse our connection; mostly it was just she and I. A relationship hothouse.

'I can't believe your tenacity and patience,' I said one day as we climbed into the truck after giving the cow fresh hay. 'Lucky animals having you and not me.'

Jen shrugged. 'Yup, tenacious is what I've always been called.'

'We are so the odd couple,' I said. 'You physical and tenacious, me heady and easily bored.'

'Yes,' Jen said, looking straight ahead. 'But if you have a job to do or if you're interested in something – if it's an intellectual thing – you're unbelievably hardworking and persistent.'

Despite how we kept talking and acknowledging our differences, despite the warmth and love we still felt for each other, the sexual spark, I felt strangely lonely. How was this possible with Jen beside me? Maybe I hadn't truly found happy solitude. Maybe that giddy feeling I'd experienced during the weeks alone was simply a sense of usefulness or accomplishment: I'd conquered the challenge of staying alone on the farm.

One evening at dusk, when the pretty-face wallabies were nibbling grass closer to the house, I went to feed the horses. I glanced down the driveway for the familiar shape of rider and horse lilting up the paddock and the dogs, tongues dangling. Where was Jen? She'd gone mustering midmorning. She should be home by now. Facts and stats swarmed: a 'widow-maker' is a branch that tumbles to the ground unexpectedly. Being a jockey is considered more dangerous than being a boxer, skydiver, motorbike racer or pilot. When Jen mustered, sometimes she rode flat out across paddocks, under tree branches, over barbed-wire. Risks perhaps equal to a jockey.

'Stop being silly,' I told myself. She'd rarely come off a horse in fifty years. I considered driving the battered 4WD with the dim lights and poor brakes up and down the corridors of trees searching until I'd find Jen injured in a ditch.

I went inside to cook dinner. Was this thinking just a consequence of being the stay-at-home partner? When I'd recently read *Persuasion* I'd underlined a passage where Anne says to Captain Harville:

> *We certainly do not forget you as soon as you forget us. It is, perhaps, our fate rather than our merit. We cannot help ourselves. We live at home, quiet, confined, and our feelings prey upon us. You are forced on exertion. You have always a profession, pursuits, business of some sort or other, to take you back into the world immediately, and continual occupation and change soon weaken impressions.*

Was I Anne? Was Jen my Harville? But when had I, an independent woman who'd once had a legal career, become a character in a Jane Austen novel? How had my life shrunk so much that I'd become a bored farmer's wife, looking to my partner to fill me up?

As I stirred the risotto and inhaled the scent of mushrooms and wine, I heard the clink of the gate's latch and looked out the window. I could just make out Jen and Topdeck and the panting dogs.

'That's a relief,' I said when she slid open the door, 'to see you home safe.'

'Sorry, it got dark suddenly,' she laughed. 'Needed headlights on the horse. I had a couple over at Frank's. It was Oxford Street – Rob was there and then Haze and Les came for milk, and Frank kept handing me another beer.'

As she headed for the bathroom, I turned down the risotto. I would've been welcomed at Frank's but I didn't really want the beers or accompanying conversations. It was my choice to stay home alone.

'How about we go away for a weekend?' I suggested at the dinner table.

Jen sighed. 'I'm spending that much time away with Mum, I can never catch up around here.'

'It's just, it'd be nice to do something together, away from here,' I said, wondering if away from the farm and the Gold Coast we might connect again as we once had, that this awful loneliness would pass.

'Don't pressure me, Hayley,' she snapped. 'I don't make demands on you when you're busy with your work.'

I nodded. It was true. 'But don't you want to do something different? Go somewhere new together?'

'What for?' she said, as she gathered a forkful of risotto.

'Don't you ever get bored, Jen?'

She shrugged dismissively. 'No, there's always something to do. You need to learn how to just be, Hayley.'

I shrank with shame. If I was the hero in a story and was being tested, I was definitely failing. I lacked the virtue required for rural life. How selfish and self-indulgent to complain of boredom when one lived in such a beautiful place with so few responsibilities and the freedom to write. Surely one could only be bored by something imposed, such as the monotony of an assembly line.

I went through the motions of working in the cattle yards, feeding horses and dogs, cooking, collecting kindling and lighting fires, sitting at my desk scribbling my heart onto the page. I stared at the gum trees and the paddocks of grass, listened to the magpie's warble, felt the autumn sun on my cheek, cuddled Lucy, slept wrapped around Jen. I was 'living the dream': I had a partner who said she loved me, I lived in a beautiful landscape and I had Virginia Woolf's necessaries: a room of my own and perhaps close to the equivalent of her 'five hundred a year'. Still, I was miserable.

Maybe I wasn't cut out for the inwardly focused life of a writer in a middle-of-nowhere place. This was a 'job' short on satisfaction, on reward, on a sense of belonging to a group one connected with regularly.

Maybe the silent and stoic bush had a dehumanising and alienating quality for someone like me. Here I seemed to feel more and more displaced, more and more invisible. I decided I needed a role in the outside world; I needed the ordinariness of regular connection with human beings other than Jen.

'The gate's open,' Jen reminded me.

# 26

# JEALOUS GIRL

TO THE SOUND OF WAVES CRASHING, Jen and I walked hand in hand along a path lit by tea lights in brown paper bags. We'd driven to town for a party.

'I've got nothing to talk about,' Jen said. 'Other than death, strokes and fire.' It was months since she'd been anywhere but the farm or the nursing home. It was months too since we'd gone out together.

'I'm not sure I've got much to say either,' I said, taking a deep breath. 'But it's lovely to be invited and you do look drop-dead gorgeous.' The dress code for this fiftieth birthday party was formal, and Jen was dapper in tails and high white collar.

We stood on the edge of the gathering, searching out familiar faces in the light of flaming torches and braziers. We were offered canapés, directed to the bar and then to the living room for the concert. The birthday girl was a composer and pianist who'd composed the music for my play years before. Now the grand piano had been pushed to one end of the room and chairs and couches set out for the audience.

The strains of 'Calling All Angels' lifted the room. From where I was sitting I couldn't see the singer but that voice, that song shot me back more than a decade to the era when we'd played Jane Siberry's album over and over in our share house near the beach, back to the weekend I'd first visited Jen's farm for her birthday party.

'Sounds just like Jane Siberry,' I whispered to a friend.

She smiled. 'It is Jane Siberry. Except now she calls herself Issa.'

After the concert, as we filed out of the living room, Jen whispered, 'What are we doing at a party with the beautiful people?'

'Some of them are our friends,' I said, aware too how I also attached that label to this crowd. 'Look, there's Miche and Fiona, and Roe and Trace and Mags and Andi and Jesse.'

Sometime later when I came off the dance floor, I looked for Jen. She was standing near a brazier in animated conversation with a woman in high black boots. Jen introduced us and told me the woman from Sydney was a film producer. The woman, who towered over me, promptly turned back to Jen and asked another farm question, and then another. I listened to Jen narrate her 'moving to the empty block of land' tale, and that she rode horses and farmed beef cattle. The woman was captivated. I knew exactly how she felt: this was the Jen I'd fallen for too, the woman whose life had been so unfamiliar and exotic.

Don't feel threatened, I told myself as I pulled my jacket tight against the cold. Don't be jealous.

I listened a little longer from the sidelines as conversation and electricity bounced between Jen and the woman and then I slipped away unnoticed.

Trust her, I told myself. It means nothing.

I retreated to the dance floor — usually my safe zone — but I couldn't get inside the rhythm. My movements were wooden, my feet heavy. I looked down at my black boots against the square of red carpet. That carpet, once my bedroom carpet, had found a home with this household when I'd moved to the farm. Now that old life, that old bedroom seemed so distant and unreachable.

When the crowd thinned and the hosts kicked off their heels and turned up the lights, I found Jen and the woman still outside beside the brazier, talking and laughing, heads close together.

I touched Jen's arm and said, 'It's time to go.'

'Already?'

Reluctantly, she agreed. The pathway's candles had gone out. As I steadied her walk to the car, as I drove back to where we were staying, Jen talked and talked about the woman in the high black boots: her job in film, her humour, her horses.

In bed, Jen fell asleep instantly. I lay beside her listening to her light snore, thinking how this was not the first time we'd faced this scenario. But as far as I knew, Jen hadn't broken our agreement and kissed the woman. So what was my problem? I should be happy for her: with that woman hanging on her every word she'd shone again, as I'd not seen for all the years of strokes and death, of hospitals and nursing homes. She'd had a good time and she certainly needed that.

I rolled over and looked at her sleeping face in the moonlight. Perhaps that sense of safety and stability – home – that I thought I'd found in this partnership had been illusory. Once upon a time we'd sparkled together, as she and that woman had. Perhaps now that I wasn't the law lecturer or the girl with the house in town, perhaps now that I lived in her world where I wasn't shining at anything, I'd lost my allure. Perhaps domesticity, familiarity and too many losses had snuffed out that spark. After all these years, our time together may have run its course.

Again, I balance-sheeted the relationship and catalogued our differences. Again, I wished I was someone other than who I was, and decided Jen would be better off with a woman from another world or someone more physical and at home in the bush. Or maybe she needed someone lighter and more playful, someone less internal and complex. Someone not quick to jealousy.

'I think you'd be happier with someone like that woman,' I said when Jen woke.

'Oh, Hayley,' she said, shaking her head. Then she laughed as she added, 'Anyway, she's straight.'

'That's comforting,' I said, pulling the covers up to my chin, longing for reassurance that she wanted no one but me, wishing we didn't have such different conceptions and needs of social interaction and safety. For years to come I'd struggle to understand that Jen's social persona – flirtatious, playful and charming – had nothing to do with her love for me. On a night like that she simply needed to hang out with someone who didn't know her, someone who wouldn't talk to her about bushfires or strokes. She wanted a day off from being herself, validation perhaps of who she was, just as I looked for it in intellectual conversation.

We sat in bed, silently, sipping tea.

After a while, through a tight jaw Jen said, 'I just don't understand why you can't trust me,' and then she began to cry. 'It really, really hurts me. I have no doubt or question – ever – about my love for you or this relationship.'

Of course Jen was right. I was jealous. I had 'trust issues' that went way back. But how does one, as an adult, learn to trust when even a mother's love has disappointed? I wanted to trust Jen, I wanted our love and bond to be sure and strong and lasting, but could any bond ever be so? And if I did trust her and then she broke that trust, would I shatter and vanish into tiny pieces? That word: *trust*. From the Middle English *traust* meaning shelter, protection. Like a home perhaps. But can a person ever be another's shelter?

On a trip to town, at Dragonfly Café I ran into Valerie. I'd met her years earlier when I'd played a witch in a production of *Macbeth* – she'd been the voice coach. Back then she was red-faced, stern and a bit overweight. Now the woman who stood beside the café table was slim and smiley. She was no longer a voice coach; she was a receptionist.

'Never been happier,' she said. 'No more diagnosing people's voices and patterns, no more tiptoeing around their egos. No more dealing with my own ego,' she said, rolling her eyes. 'Now all I do is answer phones, type and file. Marvellous.'

I bought the thin local paper and scanned the jobs vacant. Perhaps I should stop writing and 'do a Valerie'? I circled an ad for a paralegal and one for a telephone marketer. Back home, as I pinned the adverts to the corkboard in my study, my eyes caught a scrap of faded pink paper stuck to my filing-cabinet drawer. On it was a quote I'd written down when I'd read *Heart of Darkness*. It was Marlow who said:

> *I don't like work – no man does – but I like what is in the work – the chance to find yourself. Your own reality – for yourself, not for others – what no other man can ever know. They can only see the mere show, and never can tell what it really means.*

Had Valerie 'found herself' in her work as a receptionist, or was her work now simply a footnote to the rest of her life?

I crumpled up the job advertisements. I was too young for work to be a footnote to my life. I wanted work that was meaningful – not just a 'job' – Marlow's kind of work, although I didn't yet understand the real meaning of his words, the independence to which he alluded. All I could think was that such work would mean moving, as most of my good friends had done, to a city, and that would mean ending the relationship with Jen.

So said my family mythology. On a long-ago childhood visit to my mother's family sheep farm, Uncle Norman had driven us to the small town of Uitenhage. We'd parked outside a house with a curved window: 1 Frost Street. The family home from the time my mother was six – for everyone except her father.

As we gazed up at the house, my mother had told me how early every morning she'd hear the phone ring and then her mother, who'd suffered from tinnitus and what was later diagnosed as Parkinson's, would say, 'Yes, a little bit, Judah,' and then, 'No, the ringing's still there.' On Saturday evening, after the Shabbat had ended, having driven the rough corrugated roads in the dark, her father would arrive to spend a single night with his wife and children. On

Sunday he'd return to Wolwefontein where he lived at the hotel. As my mother spoke of her parents' one-night-a-week relationship, I heard her sadness.

What was a relationship if not life and time shared? When Jen and I had lived separately during our first five years, our lives had begun to diverge and our relationship had gasped for air. Now I wondered what we, with our many differences, would share if I left the farm. What would it be to live without her? Would our relationship even survive?

One afternoon I looked up from the computer, noticing for the first time that the bride in the painting 'Virgin in a Strange Land' above my desk seemed to have no arms. No agency. That's what had happened to me. So determined had I been to discover what it was to be tethered to a place, to be safe, I'd become subsumed into Jen's life. Farmer's wife was a role I'd never signed up for, particularly in a world where the law didn't even allow me to marry my love. I felt like a hollowed-out husk of a cicada, clinging to Jen, wanting her to give my life meaning and interest.

Perhaps a change of scene would give me the space to work out how to accept my circumstances or to take the risk of losing Jen and get a meaningful job in a city – if anyone would employ me after my years away from the conventional workforce.

'I think I'll go to Sam in Spain for three months,' I said to Jen. 'She wants me to come stay.' Sam and I had been close friends since university in Cape Town.

Jen shook her head. 'You're doing it again, Hayley: all because things aren't perfect you decide everything's bad.'

'But I'm miserable, Jen.'

'Running away doesn't fix things,' she said. 'You take yourself with you wherever you go.'

I bristled. 'I know doing a geographical's not going to fix everything,' I said. What I didn't know was whether I wanted to escape the relationship with Jen, Tywyah, or myself and the family past that still so tormented me.

'What about us?' Jen said. 'Are you going to throw away a relationship that's good 99.9 per cent of the time?'

# 27.

# LOVE APPLES

INSTEAD OF RUNNING AWAY to Sam in Spain, I went outside, pulled on leather gloves and loaded firewood. One afternoon as I was weeding the beds around the house, the fork hit something hard. When I dug down I found a chunk of compressed glass, the consequence of that hungry fire. Everywhere on the farm spectres of the past were embedded. As I rubbed dirt from the glass I wondered if this was what kept me 'hanging on', why severing my tie to Tywyah seemed so difficult. Sure, I'd fallen in love with a good-humoured, wise, kind and sexy woman, but perhaps I'd also fallen in love with Jen's stability and continuity. She, who held herself firm and clear amid my swirling and swinging. She, who knew what she wanted and where she belonged. But was hanging on self-destructive? Simone Weil wrote in her pre-war notebook, 'I believe in the value of suffering in so far as one makes every (legitimate) effort to avoid it.' How was I to find that balance? If I didn't want to be ridiculously masochistic, what 'effort', I wondered, should I – could I – legitimately make?

In the hiatus between the summer humidity and the winter frosts, cherry tomato bushes flourished in the garden. They grew unbidden and self-seeded, spread by the king parrots that had perched on the barbed-wire fence and, with tomato in claw, pecked out seeds and discarded flesh. True to seed – and to the scarlet pimpernel of their botanical name, *Lycopersicon pimpinellifolium* – those crimson bite-sized tomatoes were everywhere I looked. They crept across the vegetable beds, sprawled where lime and mandarin trees grew, and poked out from among the pumpkin vine's broad leaves.

They were nothing like the demanding plum variety or the Roma, the Grosse Lisse or the Black Russian, nothing like the Oxheart or Big Beef varieties that Jen grew during summer. Those varieties were deep-red and juicy with few seeds, so large that a single globe occupied my open palm. Those tomatoes Jen watered, staked and netted. To save them from fruit fly and king parrots, she picked them early and set them on the windowsill to ripen. They were her treasures and her trophies.

In contrast, the ubiquitous cherry tomato had become my preoccupation. It was all carefree resilience and feral independence. I loved its self-sufficiency and self-containment, its reliability and dependability, its independence of spirit. No care or careful consideration was needed to produce this perfect petite fruit. Tough and bolshie, proudly bucking and confounding classification, it said 'take me as I am'.

I plucked a tomato from its bush and slipped it into my mouth. Seeds and juice slipped and swarmed over my tongue and down my throat. If I was the demanding and difficult Roma or Oxheart that Jen cared for, was she the independent, resilient and juicy cherry?

In previous seasons, when the tiny globes turned scarlet, I'd fill my cap or the basket of my upturned T-shirt and carry the crop inside for salads, sauces, salsas or soups. When I rubbed garlic and then tomato onto freshly baked bread and drizzled it with olive oil, I was with Sam in Spain. Those tomatoes gave me a napolitana or bolognaise, a Jerusalem shakshuka or a nostalgic South African clump of stodgy *mielie pap* dunked into a tomato and onion gravy. Perhaps food would allow me to travel the world – from Tywyah.'

'You'll never have to buy another tin of tomatoes,' Jen had told me when she'd first introduced me to the art of bottling tomatoes, making mustard pickles, chilli jam and relish.

'But what about bacteria and botulism?' I'd asked as I matched bottles and lids from the box under the bench.

'Something in my past, either Mum or home-science teaching,' Jen said as she stood over the stove, a tea towel slung over her shoulder, 'tells me it's okay to bottle fruit, not vegetables. It's food science. Tomato has a high acid content. As long as you bottle hot tomato sauce in hot jars and create a vacuum seal to expel the air, bacteria won't survive.'

I nodded, and then I prayed I'd remember this lesson, prayed my 'good student' wouldn't again go into hiding when Jen was the teacher.

'Anyway,' Jen said, 'you'll know if there's been fermentation when you take off the lid and hear the *phhtt* of gas.'

For me, who'd once rejoiced at the shiny skin of a cucumber wrapped in plastic, this practice at first seemed bizarre. Over the years I'd come to delight in it and redefined it as one of my responsibilities. Bottling was now *my* job.

Each season I picked tomatoes, tumbled them into the sink, washed off dirt, plucked stems, scooped handfuls into a saucepan, mashed and simmered. Poured bubbling sauce into heated glass jars. Listened to the sizzle. Instantly screwed on lids. Set jars on the windowsill. Waited for the satisfying pop of safety buttons, and then labelled and placed the jars on the pantry's top shelf beside the chilli jam, pickled gherkins and cucumbers.

I'd thought it was a simple task until dinner one night: a bolognaise.

After a few mouthfuls Jen frowned. She tapped her tongue on the roof of her mouth and scrunched up her cheeks. 'You'll have to get rid of the seeds,' she said. 'They make the sauce bitter.'

'Bloody hell,' I said. 'That's worse than a needle in a haystack.'

When next I had a pot of tomatoes on the stove, with a small sieve and a wooden spoon she demonstrated how to fish out the seeds.

It was finicky and frustrating. I rolled my eyes and moaned. I rubbed my stiffened back and gritted my teeth.

'Just enjoy the process,' she said.

I didn't. It was time-consuming and tedious. I bought a food mill that only required scooping and handle-turning but, although it fixed the seed problem, too much of the flesh was lost. I rebelled against Jen's decree, straining only some of the seeds and waiting, silent and watchful, to see if my disobedience would be discovered.

Eventually Jen invented a new method: pick, wash and then dump tomatoes into lettuce dryer, squash and massage until seeds and juice squirt and ooze. Then spin and twirl until juice and seeds escape dryer's basket, leaving pulp captured. Strain seeds from the liquid and cook up juice and pulp. Voila, a delicious thick and chunky sauce.

Over time, Jen willingly left the tomato processing to me. In years to come, from the couch she'd say, 'With all the gas used, maybe it's more environmentally friendly to buy cans.'

She had a point. Two kilograms of cherry tomatoes produced just a few jars and took a couple of hours to produce. But I couldn't stop. Whenever their blushing abundance teased me from under the lime tree or through the verandah boards, I hurried to pick and process before they wrinkled and shrivelled.

Over the years, as I'd stood mashing and stirring, I'd wonder why I persisted with this task. I was certainly no culinary perfectionist or footprint-obsessed greenie counting every food mile or tin can sent to the recycling depot.

There was a chance bottling was simply nostalgia and sentimentality in action, a clinging to the past, preserving the taste and memory of that juicy flesh swarming one's mouth. On the farm, tomatoes were the last of the seasonal warmth; as the zucchini bushes shrivelled and the last of the eggplant dangled seedy, only the cherry tomato crop still exploded. Sometimes I'd imagine the nodding approval of Ellen and Dora, the women who ran the kitchen of my childhood Johannesburg home, who'd taught me not to waste food. With so much abundance, to buy a tin of tomatoes was to cheat. Mostly, I'd reach a simpler conclusion: in the semi-sustainable world of Tywyah, the sentries of bottled tomatoes were proof I'd found my place.

Now, during that season of sadness and uncertainty, as I picked tomatoes, the question 'What am I doing here with this woman?' screamed and wailed. As always, my mother was there, shaking her head from bushes and benchtops, saying, 'It's not right for someone like you, Hayls.' For these four years I'd tried to make Tywyah 'home'. Even if I accepted our relationship was built on a tension between the familiar and the mysterious, why was I choosing to stay? The question was deafening.

I crushed the tomatoes with my hands, their seeds squirted and scattered, and the juice spilled out. The rich warmth scented the kitchen. I watched the level of the sauce gradually drop, leaving a red rim along the pot's sides, a reminder of what there'd been to begin with. And what had there been? I thought about the lyrics of the song 'Wild Thing' that I'd performed in bridles and leather all those years ago on my first visit to Tywyah. Had I stayed to test the depths of this love? Or because of our many years of passion? Or because I wanted an iron-clad certainty that Jen, that this relationship, was 'the one' for me?

With the ladle and little green jug, I filled the hot jars with sizzling sauce and stacked them on the windowsill. How I loved that magical alchemy and transformation. I felt the settledness inside me, a feeling I couldn't substantiate with rational explanation. Pure heart, not mind. Maybe there were some things one would never 'know', maybe certainty wasn't always possible.

The jars popped and I reached up to stow them on the top shelf.

Bottling: an investment in a future one can't foresee but one can at least trust the provenance, ingredients and method. Perhaps this was what a long-term partnership bestowed too. Was this why one didn't run away? In the staying was a chance to learn about yourself from another person. A chance to live with love, an elemental love that one's heart knows to be true even if one usually relied on intellect as the mode of knowing. A chance to be accompanied and enriched and anchored by someone worth trusting, into the unknowable future. A chance to know safety.

Like those tomatoes now blended together, I couldn't rationally cordon or determine my love for Jen – or cherrypick the parts of her that suited my disposition. Skun or skinned, country or city, Jewish or non-Jewish, Australian or migrant, middle class or self-made peasant, intellectual or physical: all superficial differences, really. We could still understand each other. We had the language of love.

Perhaps, again, I had to steady my impatient self. Put up, adapt, accept, stand firm – *vasbyt*, as we used to say in South Africa. Don't bolt. I'd been with Jen through the catastrophic bushfire and then the recovery, lived on the farm through drought and flood. Perhaps partnerships could be just as resilient as landscapes. What I didn't know was whether I was resilient enough to find happiness in this isolated place.

# 28.

# FIND A FRIEND

'MAGIC SHOW, Saturday 2 pm' was chalked on the blackboard beside the old boiler out the front of the community hall. A show! Live performance! I was keen; Jen reluctantly agreed to come. We said hello to the adults drinking and smoking at the picnic table outside and took our seats behind the row of leg-swinging children. With dramatic flourish, the magician, dressed in tails and top hat, marched onto the low wooden stage.

Jen whispered to me, 'Is she family?'

'Reckon so,' I said, even more delighted we'd come down to the hall. What a novelty: another lesbian at the hall. The handkerchief and card tricks instantly improved. As the kids' jaws dropped, Jen and I clapped and laughed.

Later, over a ute's bonnet, beers in hand, we were introduced to the magician from Melbourne. She'd come to visit her friend who'd recently moved to the area.

'Come over for drinks,' the magician said to us after the show.

We wound our way up the hill to a house on the ridge; apart from the Fletchers', I'd rarely been into any other homes.

Rugged up against the cold night air, I squeezed onto the verandah where conversation ranged from composting toilets to solar power and homeschooling children. The magician's friend was articulate and bright and I, who'd had much less to drink than anyone else, thought we'd hit it off. Maybe we could be friends.

The magician's words to me as we left were: 'Look after my friend, please. She's a princess.'

I wonder now if that 'princess' label drew me to the new arrival. Perhaps rural life was also a long way from what she knew and dreamed of. 'Be careful,' Jen warned. 'Don't get involved. She knows we're here.'

I volunteered to help when she decided to homeschool her eldest child, and spent a few mornings playing with letters and numbers with a delightfully chatty little girl. But the homeschooling didn't last and, despite a few chats, our friendship didn't grow beyond the superficiality of the fortnightly bar and barbeque.

I was baffled. Was I unlikeable, a horrible person? Maybe those siblings who hated me were right. Or was it the culture of this environment? Did people here prefer to give of themselves physically and practically rather than personally and emotionally? As far as I knew, neighbourhood conflict, even when it was physical violence, seemed to be skated over, despair and disappointment drowned in alcohol rather than debriefed. Maybe candour and honesty complicated relationships in small rural communities where geography made you depend on neighbours. Certainly there was a generosity to the community: people willingly helped each other out with jobs without conscious expectation of return. What's more, during fires and floods when creeks and rivers broke banks and bridges, we were often completely isolated. If fences made good neighbours, perhaps boundaries and privacies were similarly crucial in the country. Or perhaps others had deeper friendships and there were just too many gulfs between the young heterosexual mum and me, a childless forty-something serious-minded lesbian.

Surely I'd be able to find common ground with some of the other locals, perhaps those who were more my and Jen's age group? I got out my recipe books and invited two of the women for dinner and a game of Scrabble.

'Thanks, a night off cooking,' one of them said as I placed a platter of roasted vegetables on the table. 'You should've seen their faces when I said I was coming here. They couldn't believe they had to fend for themselves.'

'This is just so nice,' the other woman said, looking around. 'I'm sick of living in a house that's unfinished, with a bucket for a toilet. It was okay when we first built and the kids were little and we were homeschooling, but now.' She sighed.

'See,' Jen said, 'takes a woman to get the job done.'

'A certain kind of woman,' I added, knowing I couldn't do what Jen did, wondering too if some of these men also lacked her skills and resourcefulness. Certainly, none of the South African men I knew would've been able to build homes from bush materials on such tight budgets.

'Nah,' said one of the guests as she served herself fresh garden peas, 'not even that will make me jump the fence.'

As I cleared the table and swirled honey through yoghurt for dessert, I felt that awkward self-conscious clenching inside, as I did whenever money seemed the root of someone's struggle. But then it struck me that money had played only one part in the creation of our house: mostly it was Jen's skills and smarts, another privilege or 'advantage' perhaps but one that, unlike financial advantage, stood proud and respected. It might not be 'fair' but there would always be some people who'd have more than others: more love, more stability, more skills, more ability, more intelligence, more diligence – more money.

Comparisons, I knew, were odious and differences simply part of human relationships, but I wondered then when they became roadblocks to real friendships. With my long-term friends – those that seemed more like my touchstone than my family did – at times I felt my limitations keenly, at other times my advantages. But in the friendships that had lasted, there was an honest acknowledgment and acceptance of difference, a cohesion created over time from candour and intimacy.

I looked at our dinner guests and wondered what it would take to develop that sort of intimacy with them. Should I have a go at a conversation about equality and fairness and how to live with difference? Or would revealing more about myself simply highlight the gulfs and make me suspect?

Our guest's voice broke my reverie. 'You two are so lucky,' she said as she took a swig of wine. 'You have such a great relationship.'

I looked up from the bench where I was spooning blueberries and strawberries on top of yoghurt. No, this was not the place for my preoccupations and anxieties. If I wanted to belong, it was better to remain silent, to downplay the differences. And was our guest right about our relationship? Did I just want and expect too much from Jen, particularly at a time when she was dealing with what might be her beloved mother's last years?

# 29

# ANOTHER WRITER

NESSIE, I HOPED, might be friend material. One winter's morning, armed with warm banana muffins wrapped in a tea towel, I drove over to visit, turning in at the gate just before the 'Nessie Bell Bridge' sign.

Now eighty-four, Nessie had lived all her life in this area, first with her parents way out beyond our place, and then, for the last sixty years, with her husband, Lionel, in a weatherboard house close to the road. In between mothering four children and countless animals, mustering and milking, and breeding working dogs, Nessie had written bush ballads in rhyming couplets. Here was someone with whom I might share a passion for creative writing and literature.

I'd met Lionel and Nessie at the hall one Friday night. At the bar when Jen had introduced me to Lionel, he'd stretched out his hand to shake mine.

'Don't,' Jen had said.

Confused, I'd retracted my hand. She and Jack had laughed and shook their heads at Lionel – his favourite trick, they explained, was to grip the proffered hand and mash the fingers. Nessie was sitting at one of the trestle tables. She wore a red beret at a jaunty angle and rested both her hands on top of her walking stick. She had one glass eye and glaucoma, and relied on familiarity, her black lacquered walking stick and Lionel or her black labrador to get around. When Jen told Nessie I also wrote, Nessie asked if I'd read her book of poetry. I apologised; I hadn't.

'It got burned in the fire,' Jen said. 'We'll have to get another copy.'

'May I come over for a visit one day?' I asked Nessie.

'That will be alright.'

When I arrived at their house, Nessie and an unshaven Lionel were sitting at the formica table in the bright front room. I kicked off my workboots and stepped onto the linoleum. Lionel poured me a cup of tea and pushed the sugar bowl towards me – 'bugar', he called it – and then waved to any cars that passed on the road.

Nessie had been preparing for my visit. She'd found a copy of her book, *Down Through the Years*. She'd published it herself in 2001, assisted by her cousin Isabel who'd self-published a number of books about the area's history.

'How awesome, Nessie, you've written a book,' I said as I looked at the yellow cover illustrated with a line drawing of horses grazing beneath a large gum. 'This is my dream. To publish a book of creative writing, not law.'

She sat back in her chair with a self-satisfied smile.

I flicked past the plastic cover and read out the table of contents: 'The West Wind', 'Concerning a House Cow', 'Rodeo Day', 'Alone'. I flicked to the page with 'Life on the Land' and read out:

> *I think to live upon the land you need a stubborn streak,*
> *A heart as big as all outside, it's no place for the weak.*
> *A sense of humour, that's for sure, to see the funny side,*
> *Of situations, rather grim, that touch of fear to hide.*

I looked up at Nessie. Her eyes were dreamy, a sweet smile on her lips.

'I'm not sure I have all that in me, Nessie,' I said. 'Reckon there's quite a difference between city and country folk.'

She nodded but said nothing. Clearly, she wanted me to keep reading.

> *Down deep our hearts must always hold a strong love of the soil,*
> *A feeling of belonging, and the strength for daily toil.*
> *Respect for all the living things that help to form our life,*
> *Companionship is working shoulder to shoulder with the wife.*

I laughed. 'My mother likes to say she married my stepfather "for life but not for lunch". That's not how it is in the country, is it?' I said, addressing both Nessie and Lionel. 'Out here you've really got to be okay about spending almost all your time with your partner.'

They nodded and then Lionel broke into tales about mustering, about how in the old days it'd take days to drive cattle all the way to Lismore for the sale. He didn't mention Nessie, although Jen had told me she'd always worked with him.

Nessie listened silently, her eyes staring ahead.

When I could I looked back to the book and read out more of the titles: 'Hard Times', 'The Goondiwindi Grey', 'Boy in the Bush', 'The Man and his Packhorse', 'A Day at the Show', 'The Cattlemens Lament'.

'It's everything about life out here: faithful animals, droughts and floods, the bank on your back. And this one: "My Mother Never Worked". Will I read it out?'

She smiled a yes.

> *"You know my Mother never worked, she only kept the house",*
> *I hear these words and wish to hide just like a little mouse.*
> *Then thinking back upon the years that span my empty life,*
> *There comes to mind the many jobs allotted to the wife.*

'You're the original feminist,' I said, looking at Nessie, and then read on about raising children, milking cows, feeding animals,

227

drawing water, making clothes, growing vegetables, stitching up animals, preserving surplus vegetables, driving to town.

Lionel broke in then with a story about his time in the army during the Second World War. When I twisted the conversation back to Nessie, Lionel left us. Nessie gave me a cheeky victorious smile.

'I've not written any poetry,' I said to Nessie. 'I did write law books and a play but now I'm writing short stories. They're sort of made-up rather than directly about my life like your poems.'

Nessie smiled and nodded. 'I've written lots of poems,' she said, getting up. She walked slowly, unsteadily, to a table at the other side of the room. It was loaded with a stack of old exercise books.

Clearly, she had no interest in my writing.

The pages of the books were filled with her curly cursive and in among the leaves I found faded bills and circulars with handwritten poems, as well as thin sheets of paper typewritten with whited-out corrections. I flicked through, reading titles and a few lines.

'Do you think there's enough there for another book?' Nessie asked.

Evidently, Nessie also thought I was there to help her produce another book. How could I not?

'Looks like it,' I said. 'You've been very busy.'

As I drove away with the bundle of exercise books, Nessie, her black labrador beside her, waved and smiled.

At home as I typed Nessie's poems I was swamped by the rhyming metre, a form and style I found numbing and repetitive. Although it wasn't what I'd been educated to regard as 'real literature' and I missed the surprise and discovery of poetry with varied forms, I didn't want to dismiss it for reasons that sounded so 'snobbish'. What's more, I was touched by the heart and intrigued by the content: the poems told the story of a country childhood, of life as a stockwoman, housewife, mother, wife, grandmother, active community and Country Women's Association member, friend and animal lover. They described a woman anchored to her family and community, to the work of the bush, to her landscape. She really knew home. I was fascinated too by how the poems about cattle work were in a man's voice. To me the work she did cast her as a true feminist and yet she silenced herself in her poetry, surely the one place where she could truly express herself. This was a powerful kind of silencing.

I was struck too by how Nessie adhered to the rule 'write what you know', a rule I'd heard at school, from my English teacher mother and read in countless books on writing. And yet, just as I'd loved studying method acting, drawing on my well of feelings and experience as I stepped into the high heels of another character on stage, so too climbing inside another's voice and skin was what had attracted me to writing fiction. I looked up at a line I'd snipped from a Sebastian Faulks interview and stuck on the study wall: 'DON'T write about what you know.' It was this advice I'd been following but in years to come, when I'd read Henry David Thoreau's *Walden* about his experience of building and living in a log cabin on the shore of Walden Pond, I'd again think of Nessie and wonder if back then I should've heeded her unspoken advice.

On my visits I'd show Nessie the sheets of paper and, because she could no longer see enough to read, I'd read the poems aloud.

Always she'd ask, 'Do you think it's good enough for the book?'

When I said yes, she'd say, 'I suppose it tells a story.'

Our process took years of irregular meetings. One week she wasn't well, another week Lionel wasn't. Then Lionel was admitted to hospital and Nessie, with her compromised vision and unsteady walk, was alone in the weatherboard house with the bathroom down the back steps and along a cement pathway. She told me she wasn't afraid on her own – and she didn't want to leave. Carol, who lived across the road, struck a deal with Nessie: 'If I don't see the roller door of your garage up in the morning, I'm coming over to check on you.'

But months later, after an ulcer on her leg became infected, Nessie's children, who all lived far away, made the tough decision: it was time to move into a nursing home close to her son and daughter-in-law. Lionel was in the hospital wing at one end of the building and Nessie's room was in the nursing home wing at the other end. Friday night hall was abuzz with local outrage: that's so sad for everyone. How could they move Nessie from her home? It was the first time she'd lived without a dog as companion. It was the first time in eighty-seven years Nessie had lived away from the area.

Now to visit Nessie I had to drive an hour and a half each way along an unfamiliar, potholed winding road through a forest of ghostly white gums to another small country town where there was nothing but a nursing home, pub and store with a takeaway and post office.

'Well, don't go if you're over it,' Jen said.

I ached for Nessie though, transplanted as she was to this very different 'home' from a place she'd known since birth, and I had to finish what I'd begun – Nessie must have her book. I, perhaps more than anyone around her, understood how much it mattered to her; and in some ways Nessie was my model for how writing made life in the bush more bearable. What's more, in this country life I seemed to do so little for others. I wanted – needed – to be useful, to help someone other than Jen. I now wonder too if perhaps I was discovering something about 'connection' in the bush, how one develops friendships with people over time even if those connections don't really feed one the way one expects.

'It's a lovely view of the mountains,' I said to Nessie, aware this was probably lost on her. 'And your roses,' I said stepping out onto the patio, 'their scent is so sweet.'

Nessie nodded but didn't smile. She asked if I'd seen her dog.

When I asked if she'd like to work on the book, she said, 'Maybe next time.'

So I read out a few poems and she sat back in her chair with her eyes closed.

Within a year Lionel was dead and Nessie was more infirm. She was moved to a room beside the dining room on the hospital side of the building. When I arrived for a visit, I'd kiss her soft cheek and say loudly, 'It's the girl with the poetry.' I don't think I ever heard her say my name.

Some days we sat in Nessie's windowless little room, and as the kitchen staff clanked cutlery and crockery and the staff chivvied residents to 'come along now', I sat on the edge of her bed and read out her poems. She listened with closed eyes and a little smile on her lips. When I finished, she'd open her eyes and nod, and tell me the story behind the poem. I'd note down what she said on the bottom of the page, hoping to capture her voice, hoping her descendants might care to read it one day.

30.

# GRAND DESIGNS

NESSIE MIGHT'VE BEEN WILLING to self-publish her poetry, I might've spent many hours helping her make that happen, but for my own creative work, I wanted something different: I wanted the big world's approval. A published book, I hoped, would justify the career choices I'd made and the time I'd spent 'unemployed' on the farm. A book would allow me a seat at the 'real' writers' table. A book would prove I was valid and worthwhile, a responsible human being who contributed to society.

A publisher who'd read my short stories after I'd won a residential mentorship in 2008 had advised, 'If you want to publish a book, write a novel.' So when one of my short stories – about an eighteen-year-old who, suffocated by her own mother's expectations, leaves her twin babies when they're six months old – seemed to ooze beyond its confines, I decided it contained the germ of a novel.

'Just keep writing,' my coastal writing group advised.

One grey morning, when I was working on that first draft, I was out walking with Lucy. My mind zigzagged over the point-of-view choice I was making for my novel: Lexie, one of the twins, as narrator imagines and reconstructs her mother's life as preparation for a role in a production of Caryl Churchill's *Top Girls*. As my eyes scanned the kangaroos sprawled out in the thin winter sun, their ears twitching intermittently, I wondered if I was being insanely ambitious.

Just then, my neighbour Terry brought his grey truck to a stop beside me. He'd recently moved down to the hundred-acre bush block he and his wife, Shelley, had bought in 1998, eleven years earlier. They'd named it Buggabeindown and installed a caravan, tables and plastic chairs, a bench with a gas cooker and a sink that drained into a bucket. At Easter and Christmas they'd drive down from their home in Brisbane with an entourage of friends for one long party. They'd slow-cook legs of lamb and whole chickens in large cast-iron camp ovens over an open fire; they'd clamber onto the back of the truck and hoon down to the river; and they'd party to the siren songs of summer cicadas, watched only by wallabies and kangaroos.

Over the years Terry, a carpenter by trade, had erected a four-bay shed with water tanks, drawn and lodged plans with council and had a bulldozer clear spotty gum trees for the building site. Their plan had always been that at some point Terry would stop fitting out shops and move down to live in the caravan while he built the house which Shell, an award-winning interior designer, would then decorate. Now that time had come.

Through the truck window I noticed Terry was unshaven and his eyes glistened bloodshot.

'You okay?' I asked.

He shook his head. 'Didn't get any sleep. It's these steel columns. Kept wondering if the railway sleepers will slot into them, and how far apart I'll need to set them. And if the sleepers will be in good enough nick for the walls. Round and round. All bloody night long.'

'Can you ask other builders how they did it?' I asked.

He shook his head. 'There's no other houses built like this, not that I know of, anyways.'

I walked on after Terry took off down the road to get his flagon of fresh milk from Frank. There was a sudden lightness to my walk: of course, I was very different from Terry, but designing and building a unique dream house seemed much like writing a novel. Both were grand designs, both began with a seemingly simple vision. Obsession – with its attendant sleepless nights – was the subtext of both our grand designs. We'd both caught the bug; our projects had taken us by the throat and wouldn't let go. There was perhaps something deeply invasive and potentially fatal about our ambitious projects.

Over the next couple of months, as the word count on my novel grew, I'd hear the distant whine of power tools; Terry had told me he was cleaning up the steel columns, sanding surface rust, priming, painting, drilling. The sounds comforted me; Terry too was working on his project.

I'd invite Terry round for dinner – grill extra sausages, mash twice the potatoes and caramelise double the red onions. He'd arrive with his towel for a hot shower, carrying his little esky of beer cans. When I asked how the work was going, he'd detail that day's challenges. He and Jen would discuss milling timber from our property for the rafters and joists, and cementing in the steel uprights and the fifty-seven piers; they'd bemoan the challenges of recycled materials and ground so rocky a jackhammer and crowbar were needed to dig a hole. I'd listen, saying little.

Eventually I'd inject the conversation with my kind of adrenaline: extrapolating from the physical details of house-building to the self-motivation, solitariness and anxiety of uncertainty common to both our projects. The first time I suggested the parallels between our processes, an amused 'you're a bit strange' smile floated across Terry's face. But as the months wore on, after dinner Terry would clasp his hands on the placemat in front of him and say, 'So, how's the writing?' Apart from Jen, he became the person out in the land of manual and farm work who seemed to appreciate that for me work referred to what I did in my study rather than the cattle yards or vegetable garden. Friendship can perhaps be found in the most unexpected places.

That year was relentlessly wet. It rained the afternoon Terry dug his footings – and for what seemed like the next seven months straight. I relished the rain; it excused me from picking up manure and weeding and even cattle work. As the rain trammelled the bush, I pressed on writing scenes. I was following E.L Doctorow's advice about how writing a novel is 'like driving a car at night: you never see further than your headlights, but you can make the whole trip that way'. When the ending to the novel eluded me, I wrote a forty-thousand-word novella from the mother's point of view twenty years after she'd left the twins. Still I couldn't find a satisfying ending.

With summer, the dry days finally arrived and Terry finished digging the footings. He dug trenches, laid PVC pipe for the waste system and cemented in his steel columns. I made banana and walnut muffins and went next door when I heard the grind of the cement trucks. All the local men were there, wearing shorts and knee-high black gumboots and sporting shovels. Wet cement tumbled in a mound onto the black plastic, reo and mesh, then it was shovelled, spread and butter-smoothed. Bare-chested, the men wept sweat. By early afternoon all that pipe, all those trenches, all Terry's back-breaking and mind-bending preparation had disappeared. Now there were only a few initials and the date scratched into a vast cement slab. Like a novel, all the preparation was invisible.

'Now Shell will be able to see some real progress,' I said to Terry.

He shrugged. He wasn't even sure she'd be down for Christmas.

'What about the usual crowd?' I asked.

'They've been asking why it's taking so long, saying I'll never finish it.' Terry kicked a stone with his boot. 'I don't care if I never see them again.'

I didn't press the parallels that day; I didn't ask Terry if he too doubted himself and his project. The white flag of surrender had ghosted across my mind too.

Jen had even said, 'If it's so hard, why don't you just quit?'

I couldn't. If I did I'd be a loser, spineless, gutless, a wimp. And hadn't I heard countless writers say a novel takes time and patience and many drafts? And this story had to be written; it itched and pinched and prodded me incessantly. No, I had to follow through this obsession. Beside the red P-plate above my desk I stuck up a birthday card from my writing group friend Jesse: 'Never never never give up', a simplified version of Winston Churchill's quote.

So in 2010 I enrolled in an online class on novel writing. When I was told the novel needed more drama, I added a genetic disease, killed off Lexie's father and amputated her stepmother's right arm. I got to the end of the first draft and punched the pages into a ring-binder. Two of my writing group friends read it – all 233 pages. Their feedback was kind: they ticked sections and told me what they liked – and that it wasn't working yet. Self-punishing thoughts taunted me: I wasn't cut out to be a writer; I shouldn't have left my job as a legal academic; shouldn't have moved to Tywyah. I needed a job where I was doing something useful for others, and where connection with others structured and affirmed my work. As the grumble of Terry's tractor wafted through the bush, the novel files on my computer sat untouched.

In November of that year, for twenty-four hours we sat beside Jen's mother's bed in her room at the nursing home with the green and pink candy-coloured hallways. Lola was eighty-two. For four long years she'd lived with the disabilities and disappointments caused by the stroke.

Jen stroked her mother's thin grey hair, she cradled her head and slid it gently against the pale-blue satin pillow, she dabbed her forehead with a damp washer, she moistened her dry lips, she rubbed moisturiser into her skin. Jen's sister Joan sat beside the bed, her head buried in the sheets, her arms folded over her mother's legs. I checked the clock again, praying Jen's oldest sister Kay would return soon. Kay, a nurse, would know how to ease Lola's pain.

When Lola's quiet cries of pain intensified, I held her hand, set in a claw since the stroke. She wasn't fully conscious, the time between her gulps for air stretched longer. Still, her pulse was strong and fast.

The room smelt of overripe mango. The air conditioner hummed, the buzzer sounded in the corridor outside.

I'd sat with dying cats and dogs and horses, seen and felt the sudden contrast between life and death. But this was the first time I'd sat with a person dying. Until now death had only ever been announced by a shocking phone call. How intimate such witness seemed.

Again I was aware of how, although Lola still felt so foreign and unfamiliar to me, we'd shared a strange intimacy over the last thirteen years. The countless times I'd helped Jen with Lola's personal care, and even the years before the stroke when she, so game and fit for a woman her age, had skinny-dipped with us in the creek on the farm. I remembered how, after one Christmas lunch, she, Kay and I had gone walking and seen the koala up in the tree; the conversations we'd had about the younger generation, how I'd defended while Lola had disapproved. I thought too of her advice on all things domestic and how she'd taught me about 'Lena', the cup against which one leaned wet plates before drying them with a tea towel. There'd been the day she'd taken me to her favourite boutique just before I started work for the philanthropic organisation, the day she and I had gone to buy curtains for my house.

Up on the wall beside the firefighters' calendar with its muscled men was the photograph of Lola and her three girls and their partners in our straw hats at the Outback Spectacular. Every item in this little room had been so carefully chosen to make Lola feel at home, everywhere the signs of love and of a family that had included me. And yet, over the years I'd been with Jen, I'd continued to feel like an outsider.

'I know everything about your family but no one's interested in me,' I'd repeatedly said to Jen. 'They never ask me a single question.'

'Not everyone is skilled at conversation like you,' Jen would say.

I thought of how Lola had read my domestic violence report, listened to one of my stories on the radio and come to see my play. How I'd been touched by her interest – but anxious when she'd not said anything afterwards. That time Jen had said, 'Mum might not know how to give feedback.' Inevitable cultural differences, rather than affection, were perhaps what had kept me from finding 'home' with this family.

Now, as I sat watching Lola's life come to its end, as I thought of my boredom and bubbling irritability during the four years we'd spent hours together in this room, I wished I'd been a better person, more patient, more pliable, less demanding. I wished too that I'd been able to more gracefully accept that I had a role and place in this family. Perhaps that might've filled my family hole – an abyss still, despite a reconciliation with my eldest stepbrother and his delightful family, despite cousins scattered across the globe. The pains of the past such a distraction from the opportunity of the present.

I looked across at Jen, holding a damp face washer to Lola's forehead. I asked that old Jewish God of mine to end Lola's suffering. Then I switched to a more familiar loving kindness Buddhist mantra: may Lola have physical peace, may she have emotional peace.

Lola's breath began to change. Then it came in irregular gasps. Black gunk oozed from her lips. Gently, Jen wiped it away.

The nursing-home manager came in and knelt at the end of the bed, holding Lola's feet as tears streamed down her cheeks. She, like every member of staff in the home, had come to love and respect Lola.

Finally, Kay returned and strode down the candy-coloured passage to the nurse's station. Half an hour later, the registered nurse told us, 'Doctor's approved this for pain.'

She pulled back the sheet and revealed Lola's legs, still supple-skinned despite her age, still toned despite the paralysis from the stroke.

The needle pierced Lola's papery skin; the morphine slipped from the plastic syringe. Gradually, Lola's distress settled. In time, Lola's life drained away.

Jen wept and wept. I hugged her close.

# 31.

# FAILURE

THE NEXT YEAR, 2011, was wet too. When Shell came down in early spring for a weekend of rest after she'd had major surgery, I went over for a visit. We stood together looking at the house slab, at the pink string line that marked the verandahs, at the king's view of paddocks, at the rise and fall of the dirt road and the blue mountains looming in the distance.

'I hope the verandahs will be big enough,' she said, concern dulling her usual sparkling voice. 'It's the only way I'll survive those stinking summers. The heat here's torture.'

I agreed about the heat and reassured her: the pink string line indicated their place would be of Olympian proportions. I told her how our house had shapeshifted at every stage of construction. Small when pegged out, larger after the stumps and bearers and joists, then smaller with stud walls, large again with the rafters and battens, and then smaller again when the walls were clad.

'I'm not sure how I'll go,' she said. 'I bring tribes of people when I come down because it's boring without them. I'm a people person.'

Silently I wondered – as Jen and I had many times – if Shell would handle living out here, and if her and Terry's relationship would survive.

'And are you okay living out here all the time?' She waved her arm around, her bracelet of bling catching the light. 'You're not too bored and lonely?'

I told her I missed my friends but my writing made it bearable – I wasn't there only for Jen. So badly did I want to believe I'd found my home with Jen that I refused to admit to anyone in the area that when I wasn't working I was indeed 'bored and lonely'.

'I'm not sure what work I'll be able to do from here,' Shell said, shrugging. She turned back to the building site. 'Well, I'm definitely not moving down until I've got a comfortable house. Look at this.' She thrust out her arms; the undersides were red and blotchy. 'That's from the caravan. Last trip I got an infection in some of the stitch lines from the op. I'm not a well person. I can't face another weekend in the dirt and this mould-covered caravan, and showering out of a bucket is fun for a lark but after fifteen years it sucks.' She sighed. 'I wish it wasn't taking him so bloody long to build. He's too anal. Who cares if the sleepers aren't the same stain or thickness?'

Days after I'd waved goodbye to Shell, with her movie-star sunglasses and the car speakers blasting Sonny and Cher, I was still thinking of what she'd said about Terry's perfectionism. I wondered if I too had got lost in the details with my novel.

Over at Terry's one winter's morning, I watched as the two central ridge beams were installed. A year before, Terry had felled the bloodwood tree, then milled the seven-metre-long beams with his chainsaw, seasoned and dressed them. Pink when first cut, once seasoned the wood was a beautiful rich red. Each beam weighed nine hundred kilograms. Terry had done his research and planning; now it was time for the execution.

I stood oohing and aahing as a chain over the teeth of the excavator's bucket lifted and then lowered each beam onto the uprights where Terry and another carpenter stood on high scaffolding. After some jiggling, prodding, pushing and chainsawing, they then coach-bolted the beams into place. The structure of Terry's house was finally set. We all stood back, marvelling at its royal dimensions, and the local fire captain christened it 'the Parthenon'.

How I envied Terry that day. How concrete and vivid manual work was: a job's done when it's done, whereas a writer can always add another comma and subtract another paragraph. It occurred to me too that where Terry's structure was assured, mine was not. Maybe this was my problem: I hadn't planned the story's structure.

So I read Robert McKee's *Story* and Christopher Vogler's *The Hero's Journey* and began a second draft of the novel. Ever diligent and disciplined, I applied *The Hero's Journey* to my story. Again, with rules to follow, I was absorbed in my project. Instead of my usual high word count, I drew charts according to the thirteen steps outlined in *The Hero's Journey*. The plan eased the self-doubt and provided confidence, direction and companionship. It suggested I knew where I was headed.

On one of our roadside through-the-truck-window chats, I told Terry about *The Hero's Journey* and how we were both on such a journey. We'd answered a call to adventure and our obstacles – weather and materials in his case, plot points and self-doubt in mine – were simply ordeals we had to endure. That if-you-say-so look floated across his stubbly face as he drove back home to sort, stack and insert sleepers into steel columns.

For Shell's Christmas cocktail hour, amid the scaffolding of Terry's building site, I settled into a camping chair expecting the lightness and laughter Shell always brought with her. The roof and walls of smoky-grey sleepers were up but the doors and windows were yet to be installed.

'Are you happy with how it's coming along?' I asked Shell.

She tossed her sheen of waist-length hair over the back of her chair and told me she hated the cement floor. 'I wanted it darker, not grey.' She shrugged and said, 'He wouldn't listen; he never does what I suggest, even after he asks what I'd like.'

I had some idea what that felt like. After my mother's visit to the farm, I'd insisted we had to get a proper composting loo closer to the house, or a flush loo. Jen's response was practical: where would we put it?

We'd walked around the yard. No spot was right – too close to the house, a blot in the back garden, too difficult to get a bobcat in to dig the trenches required, no local plumber to even pay to do the job for us.

And then my urgent wish had again subsided. We didn't have visitors very often – certainly not my mother – and I loved the 'loo with a view'.

At other times I'd suggested a 'luxury', like a blind to shield the bedroom window from the hot western sun or a shower screen to replace the curtain. None of these suggestions were realised either. What to me often looked like recalcitrance, excessive frugality or Jen's resistance to 'calling the man' was usually Jen identifying potential limitations to the suggested changes, or ways to do things more cheaply. Mostly I conceded. Those 'things' mattered little to me. I liked the frankness of farm life and that the contrast made overnight stays in friends' houses luxurious, simply because there were indoor toilets, no sandflies and ticks, and mod cons like mobile phone reception and fast internet.

I rushed to mentally differentiate my experience from Shell's: Jen discussed everything with me and sometimes did as I suggested. A few times she'd even accepted my money for a farm cost, but only if it was a human need like water tanks. We were both clear: even if the farm was my home, the house and the farm itself were Jen's. It had always been simpler to operate this way: Jen made all the decisions.

Later, I raised my beer bottle and said, 'Well, Terry, I take my hat off to you. I quit my novel but you're still going. How long's it been?'

'Three years on the twenty-sixth of January since I dug the first footing.'

'More like five years,' said Shell, her voice tired and heavy. 'You were doing the plans and sourcing the sleepers before you dug the footings.'

I tried to generalise and include Jen in the conversation. 'So when does one say one started a building project?'

Shell was categorical. 'When he wasn't earning.'

Terry stared down at the cement. 'I was still earning when I was doing the planning.' He looked straight at Shell. 'Why don't you just say it was when we first bought the block?'

I chimed in to douse the argument. 'I've been trying to work out how long I spent on the novel. Is it the time actually spent writing, or the whole period even though I worked on other stuff? Or when I first wrote the short story it was based on?'

'It's when you start on the foundations,' Terry said.

Shell turned away from him and back towards me. 'So why did you quit?'

'A publisher told me to go back to the drawing board and work out plot development,' I said, thinking about the rainbow of folders that I'd shoved into a large plastic box and stowed in the shed between the tool board and sawhorses. I took a deep breath and looked at Shell. 'I just couldn't do it,' I said. My ears rang with the word 'failure'.

'I might just add,' Jen said, 'that the publisher also said it was really good writing with heaps of potential.'

I shrugged and tore at the label on my beer bottle.

'You shouldn't care what someone else says,' Terry said, shaking his head.

'If only,' I said.

Silence seeped between us.

Getting up to take a cracker and hunk of cheddar from Shell's Christmas platter, I joked that it's meant to take ten thousand hours to learn how to do something well. 'Maybe next time round – if there is one – I'll actually complete a book,' I said.

A month later, when the summer cicadas screamed mercilessly,

Terry drove up to our front gate. His blue-green eyes were red and sunken and his hair seemed to have greyed since Christmas. Before he even told us that Shell had asked for a divorce, I'd guessed. I knew Shell had grown to hate everything to do with the house. It may have started as their joint dream but it had become Terry's dream – and she was the collateral damage. Now she'd had the guts, the sense of self, to extricate herself. This was not where she wanted to make her home.

Jen and I listened to Terry, we fed and consoled him, we did figures about the value of their assets and the potential cost of legal proceedings, and then watched him climb into his grey truck and rattle down our rutted driveway towards his silent building site.

# PART FOUR:
# HAUNTINGS

*Haunt: from Old English* hāmettan *provide with a home, house;*
*Old Norse* heimta *get home, recover*
**– The Oxford Dictionary of English Etymology**

# 32.

# THE WORLD
# OUT THERE

'CAN I GET EGGS, PLEASE?' I asked Frank, who, as always around five in the afternoon, was sitting on his red plastic chair on the verandah where he'd wave to passing cars that tooted hello.

The Fletchers' place was a version of a village store. There you could buy a flagon of milk or get a dozen eggs coated in dried chook poo and feathers. Frank kept a mental tally of how often people came for eggs and milk, who owed him money and who didn't wash the bottles clean. Frank was the only person other than Jen whom I saw each week.

'Oo go' some o' Mon-ay,' Frank said.

'I won't take any if you're short,' I said. 'I was going to make a frittata that uses eight eggs.'

He looked disapproving, probably at my extravagance; but then he could've just been disapproving of the food I cooked: 'that funny food' as he called the *osso buco* I once served when he came for dinner.

'Tha's awigh,' he said, 'plenny eggs. Ta' l'il brown ones on top shelf.' He gestured with his hand. 'When oo come ba' oo can do some'ing for me.'

I pushed through the screen door and headed down the passage to the egg fridge in the room with the four single beds and the bookshelf of recycled egg cartons.

Since Jack's death, our relationship with Frank had developed an almost symbiotic character. Jen looked after his fences and cattle; I read his mail, did his telephone banking and filled out forms and cheques.

After I'd set the eggs on the verandah balustrade, he handed me an envelope.

'From the council,' he said. 'What's i' say?'

It was a rates notice. I went into his bedroom to get the chequebook and, after I'd filled out the cheque, I handed it to Frank. There was an air of solemnity as he pressed down hard with the pen, carefully shaped the letters 'F. Fletcher' with a loop on the 'r' and then regarded his signature with pride before returning it to me.

How different we were: reading and writing were my lifeblood; to Frank they were mostly unnecessary mysteries. Lists and thoughts were only ever captured in his mind, and when he 'read' the *Rural Weekly* or the *Express Examiner* he looked only at the pictures and prices. And yet, when we asked Frank to get pollard and gumnuts from the rural supplier or a few groceries from the supermarket, he never forgot.

'Here's dog tucka,' Frank said, passing me an ice-cream container of kangaroo meat cooked up with pasta tubes. Same way, every Christmas he presented us with a fruitcake (a bit like those rock cakes he made for morning tea) iced white and each year with a new trim – pink one year, blue the next, then green.

Every couple of weeks we'd go over for 'tea'. Frank would direct me to get the cutlery and Jen to carve. 'Tea' was a plate crowded with wilted beans, dried-out roast potato and too many hunks of chicken drenched in salty gravy; for 'sweets' there was crumble or steamed pudding. Frank gave me a hard time if I didn't eat everything and I usually left with either a pain in the belly or a bad case of bloat. But we went back, again and again. To eat alone night after night spelled loneliness to me. Not that Frank ever said so.

One evening, after cattle work, after we'd had a beer, Frank beckoned me to follow him. I assumed I needed to do some telephone banking. In his narrow bedroom with its single bed and chest of drawers with the mottled mirror and boxes of blood-pressure pills, he handed me an envelope. He watched expectantly as I opened it. Inside was a wad of certificates from the recent Bonalbo agricultural show. I read out each one. First prize for fruitcake. Second prize for mustard pickles. Third prize for bottled apricots.

I looked up into his red face and proud broad smile and congratulated him. In months to come, a neighbour would pin those certificates to a corkboard and hang it on Frank's kitchen wall. In years to come, when the display faded and grew grubby with kitchen splatterings, Frank's pride held firm.

'How about entering in the Royal Easter Show,' I suggested. 'Jen and I could take you down there, to Sydney. It's fun and it's huge, way bigger than Bonalbo – there's wood-chopping, dogs, cattle and chickens. And they have district exhibitions where they make a big picture of something – like a cow – using all the produce grown in each area.'

Frank shook his head fiercely. He only wanted to enter the Bonalbo show, an hour away. He had no interest in the bigger world; he was satisfied with a world that extended no further than Casino. It struck me then how free and independent he was, how he didn't need to prove himself to anyone, how he was sure of who he was, what he did and where he fitted and belonged. He was content – even if he never used the word contentment, he embodied the state. Living as he did in the here and now of this place, he had all he wanted: his chickens and cows, beer and Bonalbo show, fruitcake and Fridays in town.

Over time, as the sheets of poetry stacked up and as Nessie became frailer, I contacted her son to discuss the book and told him how much it would cost to print. Could he and his sisters provide some photographs? And because I was no longer sure how Nessie's mind was working, I sent him the list of poems.

One morning he met me for morning tea at the Fletchers'. After we'd talked cattle and trees, after Frank had fed us rock cakes, he pulled out the envelope I'd sent. With his forefingers, he levered the top of the bundle back and forth and said, 'This poem here. It's not real happy. Do you think it should go in?'

Even before I looked, I knew which poem he was referring to:

*I know the time has come*
*To face the fact that I'm no help*
*To you or anyone.*

'It's your call,' I said. 'I put it in because I think it's a good poem, even if it's sad. Maybe I'm weird but I like books that show the real story, not just the jolly stuff.'

He nodded and looked down at the page. I wondered if he was torn between loyalty to his father and to his mother.

'You know better than me,' he said. 'I'll leave it up to you then.'

After Keith, the local steel fabricator and artist, had supplied a pencil portrait he'd once drawn of Nessie; after Jill, the secretary of the fire brigade, had desktopped the poems and photographs; after the books had been printed and stapled, we arranged a launch at the nursing home. Nessie was ninety-one.

In the lounge room of the nursing home, Nessie's friends from the Country Women's Association sat alongside the other residents and listened as I read out a couple of the poems. Nessie listened with her eyes closed.

Over tea and sponge cake with cream and jam, one of the ladies said, 'I liked the poems in the first book. That one about the rodeo.'

In that moment, I knew they'd never say they liked the poems that hinted at dissatisfaction or the challenges of relationships. They'd be considered too personal. Perhaps that was why Nessie needed my reassurance that they were worth sharing. She too may have considered these incidents and feelings too personal to air – she may only have been able to express these feelings in her writing, the truest of companions.

Should I have heeded her son's reservation given the book's likely audience? But then it struck me that the audience of country folk, with their reluctance to talk about feelings, might still appreciate reading these poems, might even get solace from them. Perhaps they were not so different from many urbanites who also didn't have the language to respond to others' shames and sorrows. Everywhere, different ways of being and communicating, and literature the gift that helps us understand the hidden and how much we all share.

I joined Jen who was chatting to the ladies from the Country Women's Association. She seemed to know some of them – and know how to talk to them. When they eyed me somewhat warily, my usual ease with strangers vanished: I just didn't know how to be myself with these women. Across the room sat Nessie, her legs cloaked in a crocheted rug. Had these friendships, I wondered, nourished her?

'Come, a photograph,' Nessie's son said, and I crouched beside Nessie. She was frail and a little confused, but with knobbled arthritic fingers she clutched her new book, *Dreams of a Dreamer*, and smiled for the camera.

A month later Nessie died. After the funeral I stood in front of the rosewood dresser Jen had inherited from her mother. On two of the shelves Jen had placed framed photographs, but the top shelf she'd reserved for my 'books', the law texts, the anthologies and journals containing my short stories, and the books I'd worked on as a free-lance interviewer or editor. I pulled out Nessie's first book, *Down*

*Through the Years*, and opened it to where she'd signed it, 'To my dear friend and helper, with love Nessie Bell.' Then I ran my fingers over her face on the cover of *Dreams of a Dreamer*, grateful that she'd seen it into being.

Nessie hadn't pinned her worth as a writer on a publisher's tick of approval. Once she'd had some reassurance – even mine – that the poems were worth reading, she'd seen no shame in self-publishing. It was a book, wasn't it, that others could read? A book of poems and illustrations she'd created and others might appreciate. Like Frank, Nessie had been proud of her creations, content with self-publishing her books. She didn't distinguish her book from those published by the big-city publishers. I'd been raised to spurn the parochial but was there perhaps some enormous benefit to living contentedly in a smaller world and finding satisfaction in one's work, whether it was validated or not?

As my eyes stuttered along the spines on the shelf, I wondered if I'd ever be able to operate Nessie's way. My work was only ever read if someone else published it. I didn't blog or post on Facebook or even have a website. Always, I looked for acceptance, socially and professionally, from the world 'out there'. I had to prove myself externally. But to whom and why did I really need to prove myself?

# 33.

# WISH YOU COULD BE WITH US

ON A BLAND MONDAY afternoon in 2012, just as I was about to head to the stables to feed the horses, the invitation to the wedding appeared in my inbox. Liora was getting married. Liora, matriarch of one of my 'happy families'. Liora, the only person from South Africa to visit the farm. She was seventy-six now, and recently she'd not been well. Now she was getting married to a man of eighty-one.

The invitation was from Liora's eldest daughter. The subject read, 'Wish you could be with us!'

I stared at the invitation – a simple font and layout, a request for no gifts, a morning ceremony in Cape Town followed by brunch. In three weeks' time.

An album of images of the family flooded through me and behind it was the soundtrack: 'wish you could be with us'.

The Freeds. Funny and fabulous. Seven of them – parents, three daughters and two sons – around the dark wooden table with the pewter plates. And always room for me, whether it was along the kitchen bench where we scattered matzah crumbs or shmushed ice cream with chocolate sauce, whether it was sleeping top-to-toe in the girls' bedroom with Lego-like bunk beds or squeezing into a train carriage to holiday with Liora's mother.

Friday nights, we girls would stand beside Liora who'd raise a single eyebrow if we were distracted and giggly. She'd wave her hands over the white candles and then, covering our eyes, we'd recite the blessing. Then one of the sons would sing the Kiddush and we'd sip sweet wine from the silver goblet and tear off a little of the challah that was passed around. As we hugged and kissed each other, we'd say, 'Good Shabbas, have a good week.'

Then we'd beg Rupert to tell the clock story and he, with bushy eyebrows and a crimson cravat, would glance up at the gilt grandfather clock behind Liora. He'd lean back in his carver chair and, with dramatic timing, tell about stumbling on the clock in a Belgian farmhouse when he was escorting one of his psychiatric patients home, and then how he brought the clock back to South Africa by duping customs officials and wearing the pendulum on his person. Each time, that story or its telling made our ribs ache with laughter.

I loved those Shabbat dinners – as a teenager I even tried to institute them in my mother's house. But they didn't work, couldn't, I suppose. Our blended family lacked the warmth and well wishes for each other, the accommodating unity.

The Freeds had always been my balm. They'd offered a refuge after my father left: from the loneliness that came with my older sister's sealed door, from my mother's grief and the revolving door of her dates before she remarried. They were there too later, when vitriolic voices spiked the Sunday lunches of our family.

Ah, the Freeds, my happy family. The family I'd always wanted to be a part of. But that was twenty-four years ago when I still lived in South Africa. Before I knew how life's anchors could be ripped out, how the stitching of family could unravel.

Now Rupert was dead, Dov lived in Israel, Mia in New Zealand, Joseph still in Johannesburg and Liora, Fenella and Ziva lived in Cape Town. I'd spent time with them all since my migration, individually or in small groups. But it was thirty years since I was with the Freeds all together. Thirty years since I was a part of the 'us'.

'Wish you could be with us!' I quickened inside. They wanted me there, like old times. Oh, and how I wanted to see Liora marry – a wedding, not a funeral. I looked up flights from Brisbane to Cape Town. I checked my calendar and balance on the credit card.

When I'd told a friend about Liora's impending marriage, she'd asked, 'Is she family?'

I'd said, 'Not strictly, but she's been like a mother to me.'

My friend understood; there was a woman in her life she called 'aunty' even though they weren't related. The same way Aboriginal friends talk of *tiddas* which means sisters; or how *ohana* is the Hawaiian word for family, whether it's blood or not.

Of course I'd go and celebrate Liora's marriage.


Marilynne Robinson's book *Home* was my companion on the flight back to South Africa. It too has a homecoming story but, in contrast to my excitement, Glory's return to care for her ailing father is reluctant. On the flight, I came across a passage about the emotional hazards of inhabiting the past as if it were the present. I read and reread that passage. And then I differentiated my experience from Glory's: I was going back just for a holiday to see the people with whom I felt most securely part of an 'us'. At 48A Fourth Avenue – the house I still labelled my dad's, the house where my stepmother, Genee, lived – I stepped through the giant-sized wooden door and set my foot on the stairway. I was back, somewhere I'd always belong.

Much of the house was unchanged: I slept in the bedroom I'd stayed in as a seven-year-old, dined at the same round glass table and set my cup beside the heavy glass ashtray my dad had used for his ubiquitous Havana cigar. There were some physical changes. The curtains in the room where I slept were patterned with fleur-de-lys rather than orange, red and white stripes. The wardrobe where I'd stretched up to borrow my dad's red cardigan had been knocked through to create a dressing room, and the storeroom that once held my childhood black box of 'things' for weekend visits was gone, as were the infantry of domestic workers. Genee now shared the house with Dieter, a man she'd married ten years after my father died.

It was lovely to again be in the house and to be with Genee, to talk of my dad as we sat in a garden where mop-head topiary nodded amid the purples of lavender, agapanthus and sage. I felt welcomed and loved. And yet, I found myself unsettled: the house seemed both full of the past and eerily empty of it.

Over the days I found myself quizzically examining the Louis XVI chairs, the urns and busts of Marie Antoinette and Kuan Yin. This wealth and luxury seemed now so unfamiliar. In response to my questions, Genee, who ran a décor business, told me about the various ornaments – the shells and family crests and double-ended scent bottles. I felt like I was in a museum, she the tour guide.

Sleepless from jetlag, a peculiar sadness stung me. The warm glow of belonging was dwarfed by loss more intense than I'd experienced on other trips back. The house now seemed to be my father's tomb. It made his absence palpable and reminded me of how long it had been since I'd known the safe comfort of family.

As the days wore on, I wondered if, like Glory, I too found it painful to have memory 'overrun its bounds'. Those wingback leather chairs, everything that had stayed the same, had sustained an illusion that what I'd loved in the past still existed. It didn't. Even if Genee would always welcome me, 48A was no longer my sanctuary, and I perhaps was a different person too.

The next day I drove towards my second sanctuary, the home of Daniel's family – my other 'happy family', where Jen and I had stayed years before. Confidently I set off, following the map in my head towards the house just a street away from where we used to catch the school bus. Instead I found myself at a dead end. My first sight of the house was also disorientating: instead of the tennis court where once we'd battled out tie breaks as Borg and Navratilova there was now another house. And then I softened with relief: there was the same high paling fence, the same white-walls and gateposts, the curved driveway and liquidambar trees, Evie in the kitchen. It was all still there.

Olivia, the family matriarch, was in the bathroom snipping stems and filling glass bowls with roses from the garden. 'Come, Hayls,' she said, and I followed her up the spiral staircase into the study where I sank again into the feathery couch, into the comfort of continuity. Apart from new upholstery and crowded bookshelves, little had changed. Neither had the ease with which we spoke. Here I was welcomed and loved, unashamed of my adult or child self. The safety and stability from the past existed in the present. But as in my dad's house, a shadow hovered.

Since my last visit, the father of the family, and a father figure to me, had died. And when Olivia had shown me photographs of the four boys – who now lived in America, London, Paris and Cape Town – there'd been no mistaking how time and distance had stretched thin my once-close connections. My attachment to these childhood houses, I realised, had passed its use-by date. Glory was right: the past was best kept 'in its place'.


On the morning of the wedding, Cape Town was foggy and drizzly. I was up early to prepare to meet the fabulous, funny and now famous Freeds.

And there I was, the girl who'd just shelved her novel and still hadn't published a collection of stories. Would they think me pathetic and a failure? Or would they just love me for who I am and for all the years we'd been so close, the kind of unconditional acceptance one trusts when one is certain of belonging? Walking the mental trapeze to keep my inadequacies in check, I put my faith in this amazing celebration. I lined my eyes with the kohl I rarely used, blow-dried my shoulder-length hair so that it curled rather than frizzed, painted my lips a deep red and, draped in a blood-red wrap, wound the black sash around my waist.

The marquee glowed with chat and buzz, but outside the air was fresh, the mountain doused in cloud, sunlight straining, cool and still and quiet. My mother was there too, her heels sinking into the wet lawn, her eyes moist with the delight of witnessing her dear friend's happiness – they'd been close since university days. And then I saw my first Freed: Dov. In a loose cotton shirt and fisherman's pants, he pounded a drum between his knees. Dov, who in his teens had worn a beard and braided cords and turned religious so that he ate only on paper plates in his mother's home and then, with his equally young wife, made *aliyah* to Israel.

My next sighting was the other son: Joseph of the body-building muscles and booming voice. He grabbed me in a hug and said, 'It's soooo good you're here.'

And then a golf-buggy chariot arrived, out of it climbed the three Freed princesses – glamorous and giggly – and then Liora, their beautiful queen mother, in her antique white suit with a floral fascinator pinned to her blond ringlets. She looked paler and frailer than I remembered. To cheers and applause, she skipped down the aisle towards a stooped man smiling in wonder.

After the ceremony I exchanged hugs and kisses and 'isn't it wonderful's. First with Ziva – once a Marilyn Monroe fan, now she was stark and dramatic with black hair, black tulle skirt and Yves Saint Laurent belt. Then Fenella, with her coppery hair soft down her back in a long dress that stroked her every curve. Mia wore a sleeveless dress revealing an upper arm tattooed with a spatula and coathanger. When I heard my mother ask about their significance, she laughed and said, 'Precisely because of that question. There is no answer.'

Over the kosher banquet of smoked salmon and scrambled eggs, Fenella said, 'I can't believe you're here. I never thought you'd be able to come. I sent the invitation almost as a courtesy.'

'One word from your gorgeous self,' I said playfully, 'and at a moment's notice I drop everything to fly across the world.'

The Freeds were all busy; there was little time for us to chat. But I didn't mind. They'd said they were happy I was there, and what bliss it was to feel the connectedness of being part of my happy family's celebration. It was a joy that swept its warmth from my feet up through my spine to my tight shoulders. I belonged.

'I'm in Cape Town for a week,' I said to the five siblings. 'It'd be lovely to catch up.'

They said, 'Yes absolutely,' and we exchanged numbers.

As I drove the winding back roads to Hout Bay past Cape Dutch gabled mansions and tin-shanty settlements, I told myself it was worth coming back for this celebration. But as the next day wore on, disappointment began to itch. I chastised myself for my hopes. They want to spend time with their mother. They're busy with jobs and families. They don't get to see each other often. They have a new stepfamily. There are too many people already. There's no longer room for you.

As things go in the Sea Point ghetto where I was staying in a cousin's flat, I ran into Mia on the promenade.

'Thanks for reading my book and for your comments,' she said. 'I was thinking we should find a time to meet.'

I suggested a time.

'I can't,' she said. 'I'm busy with the family.'

There it was. In one sentence, the reality check of my misguided fantasy. I was not part of this family, not anymore. I was not part of any family.

I texted the others. 'I have no time this week but I'll call for a chat,' said Fenella. 'Come for half an hour on Wednesday,' said Dov. 'Maybe we can catch up in Johannesburg,' said Joseph.


Leaning over the railing of the Sea Point pavilion, I hugged my arms across my body. My limbs ached and my throat was sandpapery. But

Mia had agreed to squeeze in a walk with me and soon she'd be here. As I turned from the railing, Mia and Ziva were striding towards me – long-limbed and slender in black leggings and runners, talking and laughing. Fabulous, funny, famous – and fit too.

Greetings were friendly and warm. This was good. It was as it used to be. I suggested coffee instead of a walk but apparently the pavilion's coffee was 'terrible'. So we walked, their one stride to my two. They glided; I waddled with seesaw shoulders and swaying hips. My bird's-eye view cast us first as swans and an ugly duckling, then as springbucks and a warthog, or perhaps whippets and a pug.

'Talk about bad coffee,' Mia said. And then she told how recently in New Zealand she was served sweetened coffee. When she complained, the waitress explained that they put hot chocolate in before the coffee. 'So,' Mia said, 'I said to her, "Are you stoned?" And then this girl burst into tears.'

'But who puts hot chocolate in coffee?' Ziva asked.

I nodded in agreement, but all I could think of was the woman who burst into tears. An extreme reaction perhaps, but I felt a flush of identification.

'Someone said to me that South Africans are sharp,' Mia said. 'Maybe we are.'

I said nothing. I'd certainly heard similar comments during my years in Australia. Now my first thought was to separate myself from other South Africans – even from Mia and Ziva whom I'd once seen as my 'we'. 'Sharp' now seemed connected to a kind of confidence and success from which I felt excluded. For a moment I even wondered if I'd changed, humbled by the elemental farm life. But then I had to admit that was semantics as on occasion I was definitely confrontational and defensive and impatient. And then it struck me: Mia had sounded unashamed when she'd described the incident, she hadn't shrivelled. In contrast, I was desperate for approval, desperate to separate and distinguish myself from any stereotype I regarded as negative. Any imperfection represented a roadblock to belonging.

As I skipped to keep up, I thought how this visit, at the point when I'd lived half my life in Australia, had a ghostly feel, an unfamiliarity. I'd assumed it was the passage of time, but as I listened to Mia and Ziva I wondered if perhaps I now belonged nowhere: never completely of the 'we' of Australia nor the 'we' of South Africa, nor even that of South Africans living in Australia. I, who'd so desperately needed and wanted to be included in the 'we' of Australians, to find my place in a non-Jewish rural Australian community and in a lesbian and gay subculture, had practised a kind of self-hatred that had turned South Africans into a 'they'. I'd judged and distanced myself from Mia's 'we' – a 'we' to which I would, if only by birthright, always belong. The eternal exile.

They asked me about my writing, and I told them about the rare highs of competition wins and publications, and the lows of packing away my novel after two years. I told them creative writing seemed to be my Goliath but was all I wanted to do.

Then I listened with a fan's fascination to stories of their next books' publication dates, the legal ramifications, the pending film deal with a famous director, the reviews, the other novels written. Success makes for more engaging conversation than struggle.

They told irreverent, funny stories. They laughed and said, 'Life is so cruel.' I listened and laughed with them, as I'd always done. But now, all these years later, I had nothing to add. This was their conversation.

After the hour they'd allotted from their busy lives, I returned to my borrowed flat with the shiny surfaces and manuals for machines we'd never run on our solar-power system. I listened to footsteps in the passage, to keys in locks, to doors shutting, to the pipes and groans of others' lives. This was how it had always been – I was inconsequential to the Freeds. When I was young, my mother had deposited me there and I was a guest of the whole family or played with Mia; later I'd hotfooted it the six blocks to the Freed sanctuary when the heat in my mother's house hit dangerous temperatures. But of course, when I left, the Freeds' lives continued undisturbed. No wonder the connection carried more significance for me than them.

I watched the darkening horizon beyond the high-rise beachfront buildings and told myself I should be happy. They'd made time for me; it was warm and friendly. But the sticky feeling persisted. The skeletal facts of my life were all they cared to hear. The adult me was not of interest to them – no longer a person 'like us', no longer part of this warm Jewish family. I wondered then if I'd have become a different person had I not emigrated at all or at least not alone, ahead of my mother. Perhaps I'd have been less sensitive and self-doubting, perhaps sharper and more sophisticated. Perhaps more interesting to the fabulous Freeds.

Out loud I said, 'Who cares?' At home in Australia I had friends who were kind and smart and funny and honest. They were my family. 'Put the past in its place.'

But it didn't work: the loss of inclusion in the 'us' of the Freed family made me weep. And as I wept for the Freeds, I wept for the shipwreck of my own messy blended family. Estrangement from the living, it seems, can eat at one more than loss of the dead; it can come to feel like banishment.

As I cooked myself eggs and spinach in the silent flat, I knew that just a few blocks away, the Freeds were having dinner together.

I knew too these good and kind people would never intentionally hurt me. They were simply a family and I the outsider who inhabited the limbo of 'old family friends': neither family nor real friends. It struck me then that it was the same with my other 'happy family' – there too, even if I'd stayed for a month each year, I'd been no more than a guest, and now I was no more than a long-ago connection.

When the red beacon of a boat glided across the water, I reminded myself, 'You have cousins and an aunt; you even have a mother who says she loves you.'

So why had I cemented the two happy families and their homes as my mental refuge, telling myself that with them I belonged? Was it due to a hopeful childish imagination? Or was this a mirage created by the terrifying loneliness of a young migrant, estranged from and silenced by her own family's unresolved conflicts, living in an environment where she'd come to expect people to be critical of white South Africans? Perhaps, in an attempt to construct an identity, I'd needed to be proud of something in my past.

Outside the ocean was coal-black and silvery. Untouchable and distant. Whatever the source of my deluded mythology, it was as if now, finally, my private fairytale had come undone.

On my last day in Cape Town, a cloudy tablecloth-over-Table Mountain kind of day, I visited Liora for morning tea in her new husband's beachfront apartment. In the passage was a collage of family photos. It was strange to see my childhood friends' partners and children, people I barely knew.

And then my role as voyeur was confirmed when I recognised the old photos, some of which I'd taken, of Rupert and Liora, their faces turned to each other, of the Freeds arm in arm in front of the grandfather clock.

Sitting and chatting with Liora, I was aware that on this trip the only real connection I'd had with any of the Freeds was with her. Suddenly I was assaulted by new questions: was that childhood inclusion solely because of my mother and Liora's friendship? Was Liora's interest and contact with me because she wanted to broker a peace between my mother and me?

As I left, Liora handed me a bookmark with a pressed bougainvillea flower and the words 'Liora and Michael'.

'Dov made these for the family,' she said. 'You have one, darling, you're family.'

In that instant, I understood my delusion. Happy families can be kind and generous to outsiders. They can even mean every word they say. Fences that are intact stretch to accommodate because they are sure and certain, but nonetheless they exist.

As I waited in the lobby for the security guard to buzz me out, through the glass doors I saw that the clouds had cleared. Into that crisp bright day I stepped, free at last of my fiction. Of course my two happy families' long-ago inclusion of me was loving and sincere, of course I'd celebrate their successes, mourn their sorrows and thrill when we exchanged emails. Always I'd be grateful for the good times and the vision they'd given me of a happy family. But it was I who'd held alive that connection too long and transformed it into something that spelled belonging. Their lives had moved on, as had mine. Finally, twenty-four years after migrating from South Africa, midway through my life, for once and for all, I let go of my attachment to those families and sanctuaries. What, I wondered, would fill the corner of my consciousness I'd signposted 'safety' and 'belonging'?

# VITAL AND BUBBLY

I'D CERTAINLY MOVED ON in countless personal ways, I thought, as I sat beside an elderly widower at my aunt Sheila's Shabbat dinner table in Johannesburg. The room was suffused with chicken soup warmth and the man and I chatted amicably. He told me he'd risen early to polish his beloved wife's silver.

As we all leaned in to scoop chicken soup, Aunty Sheila announced I'd made the *kneidlach* under instruction. My cousin Merle was amused. 'Are you going to make them for Jen on the farm, Hayls?' she asked.

'You have to get *schmaltz*,' my aunt said, her gold bracelets shaking as she spoke. 'They're just not the same if you use margarine.' She turned to her friend. 'Can you believe, where she lives there's no supermarket that sells *schmaltz*.'

The man raised an eyebrow and I explained that the supermarket where we shopped was over an hour away in Casino and definitely didn't stock *schmaltz*. As far as I knew, there weren't any Jews who lived in Casino or anywhere near the farm.

The widower was intrigued. He wanted to know more about my life.

I gave him the basic outline and told him the only Jewish tradition I maintained was lighting the memorial Yahrzeit candle for my dad. 'And now we light them for Jen's parents and Jack too, although my memory of the Kaddish has got a bit shaky,' I laughed.

My cousins listened. They knew that a parallel Jewish family life existed in Sydney, one that I'd been refused – and refused – a part of.

Auntie Sheila interjected, 'She can't just go out for coffee or to meet a friend. It's like when we lived in Wolwefontein when the children were little, but at least I had Maurice and the children and Marsha and Norman and their children next door.'

'And you've been there for how long?' the man asked.

'Seven years full-time,' I said. 'But with Jen for fourteen years.'

At the end of the evening, the widower took my hand and, sandwiching it between his large, soft-skinned palms, said, 'I can't imagine how someone as vital and bubbly as you spends so little time with people.'

My aunt stood with folded arms, nodding. The widower had articulated what she, my mother and all my beloved cousins thought, but now rarely expressed.

I told him it had surprised me too to discover how much I now enjoyed living on the farm, how I'd learned the pleasure of solitude. 'Sometimes I feel a bit bleak and cut off from the world, but then I also love living with Jen in our lovely little house and I'm lucky – I have the luxury of space and time to write. If I lived in a city I'd have to get a regular job. Swings and merry-go-rounds.'

In the early hours of the morning as I lay awake, the stranger's words swirled around my brain. What did he know, anyway? I asked myself. I'd drifted a million miles from the expectations of who I'd be when I grew up. This world of middle-class urban Jewish family was at once reassuringly familiar and strange. It might still haunt me but it was completely separate from my world – apart from my mother and Liora, only two cousins had even visited the farm.

And yet, the stranger had touched a truth: as much as I wanted the safety and independence of an inner sanctity, when I was with people who shared my passions I came alive, buoyant and engaged.

I was no monk wanting to leave behind worldly concerns for a mountain-top monastery to practise meditation. The rare weekend when friends visited, the few writers' residencies I'd attended and trips to town to meet my writing group or see friends didn't satisfy my need for human contact.

As light poked through the curtains, I admitted to myself that what really worried me about the stranger's words was the way he'd described me as 'vital and bubbly'. I no longer saw myself that way. I'd begun to feel socially awkward and anxious in groups. Perhaps the more time one spends alone, the more difficult it becomes to connect with others in groups, the more weight every encounter carries.

A few days later, after driving back from Brisbane airport, Jen and I called in at Frank's to collect the dogs. They ran rings around us, Lucy hugging my leg with both paws.

'How've you been?' I asked Frank.

'Good,' and then he told us it was hall night and we should have the steak.

'Amazing,' I said to Jen as we drove out his gate. 'Not the slightest acknowledgment that I've been out of the country for nearly three weeks. His world's so bloody small.'

Later, at the hall, I greeted Frank, who was cleaning the barbeque, and the blokes at the picnic table, and went in to buy drinks and order steak and salad.

'Did you have a good trip?' Rang asked from behind the bar.

I answered yes and told him about the wedding.

'Got any sheilas to introduce me to?'

'No, sorry,' I said, and laughed, baffled again how this kind of question and familiarity was as close as I now seemed to come to that mythical home of 'family'.

As I clustered close to the wood stove with three other women, I looked around the hall. 'God,' I said, 'we're almost the only women here.'

'Quiet night,' one of them said.

I laughed. 'You wouldn't know from looking at the parking lot. One person per ute.'

As we drove home, Jen and I did a mental up and down the streets tally: sixty-five permanent residents who came to community events – sixteen single men, a quarter of the households. When relationships had ended, the women and children left. The bright woman who'd sometimes been our dinner guest was gone, so had the 'princess', and there'd been one or two burly men who'd sat on our front verandah and talked about the grief of their wives leaving them – subsequently they'd avoided us, as if the spoken was shameful.

I lay in bed that night listening to a rustle in the orange jessamine outside the bedroom window. Was that stranger at my aunt's Shabbat table right? Had I, so beleaguered by shame and fear, sentenced myself to a strange exile away from people who shared my passions – from people like me? Was this rural area my 'proper' abode, the habitat that nurtured me?

# 35.

# RETIRED

'IN A COUPLE OF YEARS I'll be able to get my seniors card,' Jen said one night as we stood in a queue for movie tickets in town.

I blanched. I understood the need for her, a woman who'd worked her body hard for decades, to slow down. But I was only forty-seven. In the past we'd often laughed about the eleven-year age difference, how I'd been in primary school when she started teaching, still at school when she moved to the farm.

As the theatre lights faded to darkness, I wondered if perhaps, as we grew older, the age difference would become more marked, our differences more difficult to reconcile. As a retiree, she'd want to holiday whereas I wouldn't be ready to stop working: I had to keep writing if I was ever going to 'make it'.

A week later, as Jen helped herself to chicken and leek pie, she said, 'Why shouldn't I retire? You've been retired since you stopped working for the foundation.'

I held the serving spoon midair. 'Privileged' and 'self-indulgent' flashed in neon. My talons came out, my temperature rose. 'Then what's the writing?' I asked. 'The hours at my desk?'

She shrugged. 'A hobby.'

I stared at the peeling paint of the dinner table. I was swamped again by an all-too-familiar sense of how I'd failed to live up to the success narratives of my background and the Australian writing community.

'Your carpentry is a hobby,' I said. 'Not my writing. I can't believe you'd put them in the same category.'

'That's what I mean about a hobby,' Jen said. 'It's something you enjoy doing. You don't earn an income from it.'

I wanted to storm out of the house and down the road. But it was a dark night and there was nowhere to go.

'Obviously the small amounts I've been paid for stories or essays don't count.'

'They're hardly an income you could live on.'

My dinner remained untouched. 'What about writers who have to teach or do other jobs because book sales pay so little? Is writing just a hobby for them too?'

'Okay, okay,' she said. 'So, what should I call your writing?'

'My work. My purpose. I don't know – it's something bigger, the writing and thinking and reading. It's my anchor. My home. Vocation sounds up itself but it could be that. It's definitely not a hobby.' I turned my fork over and over. 'Jesus, Jen. A hobby passes the time. It's the pottery or scrapbooking someone does after a full and rich life. A mildly pleasant activity that gives personal satisfaction and pleasure. How can you put my writing in that category when it's what I keep at, hour after hour, year after year? It's what permeates everything: what gives meaning to my life, how I make meaning. Even my mood depends on it.'

'That's for sure,' she said.

'Okay, point taken. You go on about my incredible discipline, but I do it because I love it and I need it. I'm happy when I'm writing and reading. Admittedly, I want recognition, but it's more than that.' My eyes floated off through the glass doors to the dark night outside. 'I need to make sense of living for myself and maybe if I make sense of stuff it'll resonate for someone else in the same way books have helped me live, shown me how others experience the world – that we all feel, that our actions make sense to us.' I looked back at her. 'You know that's why I quit law, in the hope that I could write something that might do what law-reform papers hadn't – reach people's minds and hearts, help people understand others, maybe contribute to some positive change.'

As the words came out of my mouth, I felt my guts drop with the familiar challenge: was this personal writing mere self-indulgence? It was a question that burbled inside me every morning as I sat down at my desk. A question that unstitched the safety of the one place I probably felt most at home: work.

'So would you call my writing a hobby if I'd self-published a novel or a collection of stories or essays? Is a book the only thing that marks one a writer?'

Jen sighed. 'Okay, okay.'

I took a mouthful of dinner and chewed.

'Maybe,' I said, 'any occupation that's so solitary, that doesn't have contact with the bigger world – that isn't affirmed or recognised – is seen as a hobby.'

'Farming's solitary too.'

'To a point. You're still involved with animals, with neighbours about fences and roads and leases, with the stock carrier and agent and people at the produce stores. And then there are the sales. Think of standing there last week as the bids went up and up – that's when your work's visible and recognised.'

She smiled. The last line of calves had been in excellent condition and had brought such a good price it was even reported in the local paper.

'So, are you going to tell me now that my purpose is farming?'

I thought for a minute, searching for what in her life paralleled my writing. 'It's this place. Tywyah,' I said. 'It's what makes your life okay. Maybe why you do what you do. Like the dogs – for them it's mustering; they leap up as soon as you start the truck or pick up the reins. Even Lucy, too old and deaf to work, doesn't just swim in the dam, she brings me sticks.'

'Farming's just what I do,' Jen said. 'You're overthinking things. Farming's how I make some money. I grow food.'

The shame monster reared up again: I had no right to these feelings because I'd been able to support myself without a monotonous job. I sighed. 'I know I'm lucky money isn't my preoccupation or measure, and I'm grateful to you and this place for making life affordable. But that doesn't mean I don't need and want something that keeps me connected and contributing to the world. Maybe that's what the writing is for me.'

I couldn't seem to make myself clear – perhaps I wasn't clear. I chewed a forkful of pie.

'So, what is your purpose then?'

Jen shrugged. 'I don't think about it. I just do something outside each day, a little bit at a time. The sun comes up; the sun goes down.' She looked long and hard at me. 'I guess my purpose would just be to be happy in each day,' she said, sighing. 'I've got no great ambition, or plan or dream. We're all just grains of sand, Hayley. In years to come everything I've built here will be erased, forgotten. What does anything we do matter?'

'Oh, that's so goddamn Buddhist or existentialist or virtuous or something,' I said as I served myself more pie, remembering how, when I went on a Buddhist reading binge and to a few meditation retreats, Jen had simply said, 'I have my own way of meditating: it used to be milking in the morning, now it's when I'm out in the paddock sitting with the cattle.' Even if she didn't study the great thinkers and experts, she seemed to embody ways of living that continued to elude me.

'I guess I'm just way less evolved than you, Jen. There's more I want to do – aspire to, learn. I don't want to "settle" for a virtuous ordinary life.' I gathered the dishes in a pile and said, 'If I can't make some contribution beyond myself with the writing, I might as well be dead.'

Jen laughed. 'You might think you can be the boulder on the beach but eventually even that boulder will get worn away.'

I covered my ears. 'Now I really just want to slit my wrists.'

# 36

# CREATIVE SOLITUDE

A FEW MONTHS LATER, on a grey morning in 2013, a very deaf Lucy a few steps ahead of me, I walked across the paddock to Terry's house – or the 'convention centre', as Jen and I affectionately referred to it. It loomed above our front paddock, longer and wider than a tennis court. Under my arm I clutched a sheath of papers, an essay on which some of these chapters are based.

Like Nessie, like wilderness woman Ana Maria Spagna and Henry David Thoreau, I'd started to write about the material world around me. When I'd enrolled in a master's degree in creative writing the year before, I'd been introduced to the essay form. Deadlines for the degree gave me structure, and even though most of my contact was electronic, it connected me to the 'bigger' world out there.

The French word *essai*, I'd discovered from Michel de Montaigne, meant 'to try', and in my essays I tried to make sense of life on the farm. The essaying became a written internal dialogue, a space to question and understand the world and myself. It was a blend of the creative and the critical. I was compelled – possessed. Now more than ever I felt at home in my work, but this time, unlike in previous careers, I was completely and authentically myself. No fictions or facades, no silences.

Now too I no longer felt confined by the farm: everything in the bush was material for inquiry. As each essay led me somewhere surprising, my world seemed to expand. I was on an edge, discovering how and why, attention yielding amazement. I didn't much like digging out the compost from the long-drop toilet hole but I liked that we were taking care of our own shit. I despised the murderous ticks of a north coast summer, but they led me to consider parasitism. Experiences I'd struggled with resurfaced, now ready to be re-examined – if not to be published.

'Live to work' or 'work to live': the conundrum of contemporary life, and my personal struggle since I'd quit legal academia. Yet now my living was my writing, and my writing was my living. They were indistinguishable, equal.

In the evenings from my study on the verandah, I'd see the truck's lights and think I should stop and go inside and cook dinner. Soon, I'd bargain with myself, at the end of this paragraph. I'd hear Jen come in to get the dog food from the fridge and then go out to feed the three dogs. And then, what seemed like moments later, freshly showered, she'd stand at my door rattling the chip packet, saying, 'Chippies, chippies.' We'd laugh and I'd save the document and shut down the computer.

That morning, as I walked over to Terry's, I wondered if I was on my way to the gallows of neighbourly friendship: perhaps Terry would feel betrayed simply because I'd written about him and Shell. Although I barely saw him these days, our conversations had been more self-revelatory than any of my other local interactions. I wondered if it was only permissible to breach privacy if the other consented to be written about from the start. But prior consent would've been impossible. Although I'd chatted about the parallels between our creative processes over Christmas drinks, back then I'd not considered writing about this process. At that stage I wrote only fiction. Somewhere I'd read that having a writer in the family is like having a murderer in the family – perhaps the same applied to a small community? I might feel like an outsider now but if I wrote about the locals, would it lead to my being truly cast out?

Terry and I sat in camping chairs, drinking milky instant coffee and looking at the king's view. The house had verandahs wide enough to live on, a roof, walls, some doors, solar power and hot water, a toilet and a kitchen with benches of Sydney blue gum. But Terry didn't have the money for bathroom tiles or a shower recess and he was still sleeping in the caravan because the bats had moved into his future bedroom.

He told me he'd been applying for work in the mines where some of his mates were making big money working three weeks on, one week off. He needed cash to finish the house.

After I read Terry the essay, there was silence. I looked up at him. He was wet-eyed. 'You okay?' I asked.

He nodded and thanked me. He said he felt understood. Then he corrected me about the timing and how many tonnes of cement went into the house.

As he looked down into his cup, he told me his doctor said he needed to spend less time alone. 'It's hard going,' he said, 'day in, day out, on my own all the time, keeping myself going.'

'I know exactly how you feel,' I said. 'And I've got Jen around. I only seem to be happy out here when I'm having a good time with my work.' I looked around at the house. 'Why haven't you quit this, Terry?' I asked.

'How can I?' he said. 'I've sunk so much money and time into it. Lost Shell after twenty-two years. If I'd have known...' His voice trailed off. 'I'd never have started. I was building it for her, to hear her say, "Wow, he built this for me. He's gone through hell to make this for me." That's what I wanted all along.'

I followed his eyes as he looked around at the verandah posts, the bubble wrap over the window gaps, the sleepers. How tragic that the creation of a home had divided their relationship.

I remembered Shell's concerns about life in the bush and wondered whether either of them had really known the realities of rural life when they'd first bought the block and dreamed of their bush home. Was Terry really building the house for Shell or had he simply wanted her approval for the grand design that had got under his skin? Could work ever be enough on its own, without approval from others?

And what then was my motivation for writing? Had I been writing for my ego, or intellectual entertainment? For the canon of world literature? For myself or to prove myself to my mother and my estranged family, to people from my past, to my friends or different communities or to the big world out there?

I was slipping into that maze of 'why do I write' when Terry stood up.

'No,' he said. 'I've got no choice. I can't quit. Not now. If I do, I'll feel like a failure and look like a failure to my family and all those other people who've judged me. And what would I have? Who knows what I'd get for the place.' He paused. 'No, I wouldn't be able to live with myself.'

I felt deeply sad for the way things had turned out for Terry and for Shell, for the crippling emotional and financial costs they'd both sustained.

'I guess you can't shove your grand design away in a box in the shed like I did mine,' I said, 'and move on to the next thing.'

'Not likely,' Terry said with a slight grin. 'This place would weigh about 250 tonnes, the concrete's at least 150 tonnes.'

It was the first time I hadn't envied the tangible satisfaction of manual work. Sitting there with Terry, it struck me how fortunate I'd been. Each time I'd left a job I'd wound up embarking on something challenging and interesting, and possibly of use to others. Leaving something, I'd discovered, can be strategic – a positive rather than a negative. Again I reassured myself – as if I no longer itched with the shame of failure – that quitting the novel had been right. I was happier for it.

Perhaps one day Terry would complete his 'something different' kind of house: a house you can't buy, a house to outlive generations, a house to withstand storms, cyclones, summer heat and bushfires. For generations to come, the Parthenon would stand on its hilltop, a citadel of tenacity. Perhaps Terry would even feel it had all been worth it. But could a place, I wondered, ever really be a happy home if there was no one to share it with?

# PART FIVE:
# SAFETY

*home: in games, the place in which one is free from attack*
**– Shorter Oxford English Dictionary**

# 37.

# COMMUNITY

AN ADVERTISEMENT in the classifieds section of *The Land* news-paper announced that Macquarie Energy had applied for a petro-leum exploration licence, or PEL, to mine for unconventional or coal seam gas over an area of 1275 square kilometres, which includ-ed our local area. The map showed two adjoining rectangular boxes superimposed on the veins of rivers and roads. The squiggly line at the bottom of the skinny rectangle on the PEL's map was our road. Halfway along was the farm.

Malcolm, the contact person listed in the advertisement, assured me coal seam gas mining could coexist with agriculture. He'd only ever heard of two landholders refusing access, and one of them had changed his mind. He rattled off a list of draft guidelines and codes of practice that protect farmers and the environment.

'Nothing to worry about,' he said. 'They won't drill within two hundred metres of a residence.'

I looked down past the post-and-rail fence of our front yard to the paddock of blady grass and spotty gums where Topdeck grazed. As if on cue, a wallaby sat up on her hind legs, ears twitching.

'Two hundred metres from where I'm standing, Malcolm, is just past the vegetable garden. Would you want a drill rig just outside your front gate?'

Malcolm didn't answer my question. He suggested I call back if I had further questions.

The advertisement said we had twenty-eight days to lodge written responses to the application with the New South Wales department of trade and investment. I knew little about gas mining, other than what I'd learned from US filmmaker Josh Fox's documentary *Gasland*. Along with cattle drench, we'd brought home a copy of the film from the rural supplier. We'd watched images of industrialised farmlands, sick children, toxic spills and contaminated water that billowed into flame when ignited. We'd sighed about corporate greed and environmental degradation and unsafe mining practices in America. But that was there, not here in Australia.

I had looked no further. Despite seven years of living on a farm with a standalone solar system and rainwater and being aware and concerned about the environment, I didn't answer to the name tag 'greenie'. My version of environmental activism was signing online petitions or donating monthly to Greenpeace and World Wildlife Fund. Even if I cared about the logging of old-growth forests, I didn't have the slightest interest in chaining myself to bulldozers to protest. Human rights violations like violence against women and children and refugees, racism, sexism, homophobia, any form of unjust discrimination – those were the issues that made me burn.

But suddenly, with the news of the exploration licence, I had to know if they really could mine the farm. Surely we had a right to participate in any decision that might affect the land where we lived? Surely home is somewhere safe, somewhere one has some control?

As I read through the *Petroleum (Onshore) Act*, I discovered we couldn't stop the government from granting an exploration licence because we don't own the minerals underground, but we could refuse access to our land. If we refused access, the company could force us to arbitration. If the arbitration failed, we'd have to appeal to the Land and Environment Court. There were no precedents. This type of mining had only recently begun in New South Wales.

Two days later, Jen and I drove the forty minutes to a neighbouring village for a public meeting. In the community hall, with its mudbricks and stained-glass windows, wartime honour rolls banged up against pictures of evaporation ponds and the post-mining wastelands of Pennsylvania and Queensland. Trestle tables were swamped with scones and photocopied reports from the National Toxics Network. The dreadlocked drummer sat labelling little brown dropper bottles with the word 'Focus'. A woman in polyester trousers who told me she was a self-funded retiree strung up sheets of paper that listed the chemicals used in coal seam gas mining and their known health effects. A man with a porkpie hat and a white fuzzy beard sold yellow triangles with 'Lock the Gate to Coal Seam Gas Mining' in bold black letters.

In the crowded hall, I recognised those farmers whose paddocks of canola and corn I often passed to get to our place, the guys I'd met out fighting fires, Keith, the local steel fabricator turned sculptor, and our neighbours. This was a gathering of the wider community, well beyond our little community at the end of the road. When I bent to pick up my dropped pen, I saw thongs and blackened toenails, muddy workboots, sensible shoes, sandals, and a single pair of high-heeled boots – ah, the cattle farmer who'd once been the three-day-a-week mail contractor.

On a small television with poor sound we watched segments from current affairs programs about coal seam gas mining and saw images of the gas fields of Queensland. A man in shorts and sandals introduced himself as Ian, a carpenter from an area two hours away. He told us Arrow Energy was going to drill a well next door to his property. I felt a little ashamed of my ignorance. Clearly, coal seam gas mining was very much here in Australia, even in the Northern Rivers area. In fact, the industry was growing so fast, government regulation, it seemed, was struggling to keep up.

Ian told us we could take action to stop this: write submissions opposing the application and lock our gates to the unconventional gas mining companies so they couldn't come onto our land. If we put up 'No Trespasser' signs on all access gates and the 'Lock the Gate' yellow triangles, they couldn't legally come onto our properties. Onto the screen flashed a quote attributed to Margaret Mead: 'Never underestimate the power of a small group of concerned citizens.'

Concerned voices pinged around the hall. An elderly woman said she was worried about what it would do to the native animals. A farmer in an akubra yelled out, 'They won't care about that – all they'll care about is that this isn't prime agricultural land.'

Someone else was concerned about the narrow potholed roads and the single-lane bridge. 'We don't have the infrastructure for their trucks and pipes. And what about the tree plantations and the state forest?'

The captain of the fire brigade added, 'What about that flaring they do with the gas, and all that methane? We don't want another bushfire.'

Everyone nodded, everyone applauded.

As I listened to the community's outrage and concern, I thought about that statute and administrative structure, the conversations I'd had with Malcolm from the mining company and the bureaucrat from the department. The whole system seemed to be geared to granting mining companies licences to explore and produce gas. I wondered whether we'd be able to stop them, whether people power really could overcome governments and multinationals. The mounting rage was inspiring but no one seemed to be mentioning the system that governed these licences.

After years of being so inwardly focused, I was out of practice at speaking in public. My heart pounded even at the thought of standing up. But surely to challenge a system, we needed to understand how it worked? I raised my hand. 'I've been reading the department's website,' I said. 'Can I just check: if we lock the gate, can they still force us to arbitration?'

'Yes,' Ian said. 'But we have no examples of that in New South

Wales yet. We have to start by showing that we don't want them here. Write submissions and letters and say you don't want it.'

I wondered if this would be enough. In administrative law classes, I'd taught students how government decisions could be challenged on different legal grounds. A decision-maker's failure to consider public submissions could be challenged as a failure to take into account relevant considerations. But how did this work in practice? If government decision-makers didn't listen to the community's voice, would there be sufficient funds and energy to take the matters to court? And then, if it could be proved that the government had erred in making their decision, would this make any difference to whether the mining went ahead?

We had to try anyway, I supposed. Our sparsely populated community leapt into action. We formed a group and called ourselves the Mid-Clarence Group Against Gas – MCGAG. Now, with a common care rather than only geography, I felt something akin to what I understood as friendship with the locals and people from across the river.

In those early days after we'd heard about the application over the area, our phone ran hot. Emails with scientific reports flooded my inbox. None of the science made any sense until Geoff, a neighbour I barely knew because he didn't come to hall nights, explained that the shaded blobs on the geological map were the coal seams, the layer that the mining company would drill into in order to release the gas. In some areas, where there weren't coal seams or the coal seams were deep and impermeable, they'd need to fracture the rock to release the gas. Fracking involved pumping a mix of water, sand and a cocktail of chemicals down the well. The geology of our area suggested the companies would probably want to mine here. Together with Geoff, for weeks I toiled over a submission.

Bev, the local mosaic artist, rang to say she was organising an information night at another local hall in three days' time. 'I feel like Erin Brockovich,' she said. 'We can fight this. Would you speak about how the process works like you did the other night? And maybe give people some ideas about how to write a submission?'

I felt unnerved, hesitant to take the role of 'knowledgeable expert', particularly about something to do with the environment. There was always too much I didn't know or understand, too much information, too many competing views from informed people.

'I don't know much about it,' I said.

'You know more about law than anyone out here,' Jen said. 'And even if you're out of date, you know how to deal with the system.'

Despite the short notice, the hall was crowded with fuzzy white beards, thongs and blackened toenails, dreadlocks, farmers in checked shirts and women in floral frocks.

Geoff pointed to some areas on a geological map. 'The problem,' he said, 'is if the companies drill into the sandstone layers and then frack the sandstone to liberate the gas, that would lead to the contamination of the Clarence River, and if you live over the coal measures – around Bonalbo and Mallanganee – then the creeks would be in danger of contamination too.'

There was a hum of conversation, concerned looks. 'Not the mighty Clarence,' a bearded man with long grey hair said, 'the biggest river in New South Wales. They can't let that be contaminated.' There was a smattering of applause.

Someone called out, 'What about the eastern freshwater cod? The Clarence is its only known habitat.'

Then it was my turn. Suddenly I was explaining legal and administrative processes to the farmer from whom we bought corn to make lick blocks, the operator of a kayak business, the postmaster, the couple who ran the food co-op and the owners of the petrol station. I was back in the public world. My eyes, my pores, all of me came alive with the giddy joy of sharing what I knew, seeing people nod with understanding, wake up and register the need for community action.

When I fielded comments, Steve, the 'weatherman' on local radio, disputed the research on fracking.

'I'm no expert on this, Steve,' I said. 'We're all just trying to get a handle on it. Anyone else want to answer?'

Later, someone up the back called out, 'We should get a referendum on the issue'; someone else suggested a class action.

An elderly woman with long hair and liver spots said, 'You've got to bombard the media.'

'How about we focus on step one,' I said. 'The closing date for submissions about this PEL is in a few days' time.'

Afterwards people whom I'd never had much to do with lined up to talk to me – a mother from the school, one of the farmers Jen described as 'squattocracy', and two Aboriginal women who told me one of their kids watched a DVD about the issue and said it was 'scary'. The sense of community, of unity, was magnificent.

As we drove home through the mists, avoiding a calf sleeping on the roadside, a barn owl crossed our path. The joy of solidarity. Even if I was a little anxious about the limits of my knowledge, I felt elated – and I had skills to offer, skills that could protect people's homes. Writing creatively in my study on the farm certainly didn't give me this feeling. Again, the question pinched: what was the value of scholarship and literature? Should I go back to law and do something tangibly useful rather than pursue this much more difficult and solitary creative path?

# 38.

# CONTROL

AFTER PORING OVER REPORTS and news articles, I finally sent off the twenty-six-page submission to the state government opposing the granting of an exploration licence. I'd loved doing community work that used my skills. I'd loved loading placards reading 'Our Land, Our Water' and 'Mid-Clarence Group Against Gas' into the car, driving the hour and a half with Jen to attend marches in Lismore, to rally outside our state member's office in Grafton or join the Lock the Gate dragon-boat team. Each time I marched with Jen and our neighbours and looked around at our little group within the broader crowd, I'd flush with the recognition of belonging. We shared an affinity, belonged to a tribe. The connection was more than geographical accident. And yet, in all truth, the environment was not my burning passion. I was impatient to get back to my real work and fascination: writing stories about people and relationships, not trees and water and air and wildlife.

It was different for Jen. For Casino's beef week parade, a group was getting together a Lock the Gate float to raise awareness of the threat of gas mining. Jen fashioned a gate from bamboo and we joined the float. When interviewed by a journalist as to why she was marching, Jen said, 'I want to stand up and be counted as a farmer who doesn't want to see our rural farmlands industrialised by coal seam gas.'

As I listened to Jen's mounting fury, I realised that her motivation and rage about this issue was grounded in her daily reality and a sense of being what she'd often described as 'a caretaker of the land'. Place was core to her. How different it was for me: I might have lived on the farm for seven years and worked with Jen in the yards but no way would I have commented as a 'farmer'. After all these years I still wondered if it was fraudulent to call myself a local.

From a woman named Michelle who'd once been a stock inspector I heard about the 'resource reality tour', a kind of environmental freedom ride to raise awareness about mining in Queensland and to offer support to the locals enduring it.

'Bus trips and cruises aren't my thing, Jen,' I said. 'Not yet, anyway.'

'We won't know what it's like unless we see for ourselves.' she said. 'How can you not care?'

'Of course I care,' I said. 'What were those weeks I spent on that submission? I just also care about other things – like refugees – and I'm not exactly flying off to WA or Melbourne to visit detention centres.'

She gave me one of those 'I don't understand you' looks and headed outside to saddle her horse.

She never even got the chance to say she was going without me. I realised she was right. I should eyeball this industry that might come to our backyard. What's more, I do love an adventure and Michelle, that sassy woman in a cowboy hat, would probably tell a good story.

So, a couple of months later at half past six on a cold Saturday morning, we squeezed into the remaining seats of a twelve-person bus. Annette, the organiser, told me, 'It makes it much more real when those who are living with it show and tell people.'

I sat beside a fit, grey-haired British expat. As she poured herself a cup of milky coffee from a thermos, she explained she'd come on the trip because 'this is an issue you can do something about. It's not like wars.' Behind me, a woman with a lilting Irish accent said, 'I thought gas was clean until I looked into it because they're going to frack our little county back home.' In front of me was Anne; proudly seventy-four and a National Party voter, she wore stylish leather boots and regularly touched up her lipstick. 'CSG has changed my life,' she said. 'Now I go to demonstrations and talk to reporters – and did you hear we're doing *CSG: The Musical*?' Mohammad, a tall and lean young man, was a PhD student from Norway researching community participation in decision-making. He wasn't an activist and considered them anti-development and against progress. Squeezed into the very back corner was a woman with a long plait and deep black eyes who offered around almonds and goji berries. She didn't know much about CSG but she needed to get out and meet people. I wondered for a moment if this anti-gas movement would be good for me too – a way to have more social contact, an opportunity to be part of a broader community, to experience solidarity. Belonging.

Two men, ten women, mainly over forty, most of whom seemed to know a lot about coal seam gas mining. I fished out a pencil and notepad.

I listened as people talked about the millions of gallons of water pumped at high pressure into the rock to release the gas. How gas and fracking fluids creep up through cracks after the fracking. How it produces huge quantities of wastewater containing salt, which they don't know how to dispose of. How the process sucks dry the water-table and saps aquifers and rivers. How poisonous chemicals used in drilling can migrate to the bores of groundwater users. How no one knows what the long-term impacts of drilling will be on groundwater and farmland. How volatile organic compounds released during drilling contaminate the air. How there are risks associated with the flaring of wells.

Everyone seemed so informed and articulate. I scribbled down what they said, my mind dog paddling around facts I'd heard before but still struggled to retain.

Before long, my attention strayed from the cavalry of comments to the paddocks of broccoli with rich dark green leaves, millet and peas, and fluorescent green winter oats. In the distance, horses grazed and a red tractor ploughed a paddock of dark soil. The cattle looked fat and happy. This was such good, fertile country compared to our rocky little block. I wondered what it would be like to live among this rural community. Michelle pointed out the old Federation barn where she got married, the little town where her brother was posted for his first teaching job. I craned my neck to catch her landmarks and imagined her in wedding whites.

And then, on the outskirts of a small town, I saw the first sign of the unconventional gas mining industry: a billboard featuring a smiling man in a hard hat and the caption 'Careers are built here'. When we passed sheds the size of airport hangars and Olympian car parks jammed with white utes, Michelle said, 'Training school for drill pigs.' I wondered what the 'drill pigs' called themselves.

Our white bus was following a line of white cars, white SUVs, white utilities and large trucks carrying pipes – all mining vehicles. Now the roadside paddocks alternated: plastic-wrapped bales and irrigators, then piles of black coal, then paddocks of bobbly white cotton, then a gas-fired power station with towering funnels and drills and pipes and wheels and valves. And what was the next field of steel with pipes and machinery painted in the primary colours of playground equipment? A compressor station to liquefy and compress the gas.

The bus was quiet except for a rattle.


At an old timber country hall, the handshakes were firm all around. Joe had the logo of his cattle brand tucked into the brim of his akubra, and around his neck he pulled out a medal on a red ribbon to show us the inscription: Cranky Old Bastard.

'One of the ladies decided to give me a medal,' he said. 'And one for me mate. He got Whingeing Old Bastard.'

In the kitchen, a tall, graceful woman in an apron embroidered with the hall's logo, lifted the teapot in its padded tea-cosy and poured me a cup of strong black tea. I asked if she had gas wells on her property.

'No, but we've got the coalmine next door,' she said, and then told me her husband can't sleep because of the noise. They go to bed and moments later he throws back the covers, gets up and paces up and down beside the windows, raging against the mine. All night they hear the groaning and shunting and cranking of the motors and trucks and dozers. It's not just the coalmine either. Her husband's been battling a gas company for compensation after a salt spill on a neighbouring property contaminated the soil and creek water.

She told me her husband was a good man, a good husband and father; he'd never been cranky like this. But since the mine and the salt spill, he was always fighting – with the mining companies, and with some of the neighbours who 'sold out' to them.

'We've worked hard to get our cattle stud going,' she said. 'Not that I'm complaining. It's been a good life here. It's a good community.' Her smoky blue eyes filled with tears. 'But I don't know now, since the hall committee accepted money from the mining company.'

She paused. I wondered if it was her husband who'd been awarded the Whingeing Old Bastard medal.

'One night he brought us down for the annual dance,' she said. 'The girls were all dressed up; they looked so pretty. But he just sat out there in the ute with his mate, drinking beers.' Tears trickled down her cheeks. 'He wouldn't come in. Wouldn't talk to anyone.'

We stood together with our backs to the room. I was surprised by this matter-of-fact countrywoman's tears. She dabbed at her cheeks with the corner of the apron.

'Probably seems like nothing,' she said, and forced a laugh. 'But he's powerless against all the companies, we all are. I don't blame him. The noise, the salt spill, always on the phone to the companies, all these papers to read, letters to write. It's a full-time job on top of the farming.' She looked out the window at the men, some clustered around the barbeque, others near their utes. 'This mining,' she said, 'it's bad for the family, and for the community. It divides us.'

I couldn't shake off the image of that salt-of-the-earth woman's tearful blue eyes. As we drove along back roads seeing how native bush was being destroyed to make way for the pipelines – one for each gas company – her story clung to me. As it did when we met a wiry, tanned farmer dressed in faded blue jeans and scuffed workboots, her hands shoved deep into the pockets of her red fleecy vest. She swung her leg over her quad bike, her kelpie leapt up onto the tray behind her, and we followed her to what used to be her all-weather access road.

She stared at a mucky watercourse with blue metal dust and gravel dumped over the wettest area, and in a low voice said, 'I used to get nice clean water coming, now it's filthy. They change the way the water goes. The environmental assessment, that's written by them for them. Nowhere do they mention livestock or people.'

This farmer had done it tough but persisted through drought and flood and interest-rate hikes. Now it seemed the gas company's pipeline across her property might send her under. It had taken ten months to build and was still not finished. During that time, wild dogs began to use the cleared pathway as their highway – 127 sheep had been killed. When she mustered, the sheep slipped under the pipeline, but she couldn't, she had to go around, and by then she'd lost the mob.

She nodded as Joe, with the Cranky Old Bastard medallion, said, 'They tell us gas is compatible with farming but it's as compatible as a high-class restaurant in the same room as a dog-grooming business.'

As we drove away, no one spoke. I wondered at the system's stubborn refusal to see what gas mining was doing to the environment, and if this woman would wind up losing everything to legal bills and bank foreclosure. I knew all too well how for the farmer 'home' is both a place to live and a livelihood – perhaps even a self: farmer and farm are a single bundle. Driving into the area of Tara, we saw the creep of steel, swarms of mining vehicles, drill pad after drill pad, compression stations and production plants. The gas fields.

On a property with a yellow 'Lock the Gate' triangle on the gate, I met a woman in her late thirties with freckles and red hair, six months pregnant with her sixth child. She had burns on her hands from doing the family washing in the twin-tub machine. It wasn't only the water that was affected, it was the air quality too. 'Whenever they're working,' she said, 'the kids get burning and irritated eyes.' When they drilled the first well, her ten-year-old son started getting headaches and nosebleeds, then asthma. She told me that one day a week she worked at the Vinnies opportunity shop in town. 'Every second person I talk to knows someone who's sick. There are twenty-six families who are experiencing health impacts. There's a little girl, ten years old, vomiting and having nosebleeds. One kid's had seizures of unknown cause and rashes. For many people, it's because their bore water is contaminated.'

'Is the whole town against it?' I asked.

She shook her head. 'Some people still think the gas wells are good for the economy. Even with some of their neighbours having to move 'cos they can't afford the rents anymore. And half the shops have closed down in town because the DIDOs – the drive-in, drive-out mine workers – don't shop locally, except maybe at the pub.' She sighed. 'After I wrote to the local paper, the teacher at my kids' school went on in class about "the feral blockie who wrote to the media". That's what she called me – "the feral blockie" – and then she went on at the kids about how the mining is good for our community.'

'So how do your kids go with it all?'

'I complained about the teacher but eventually I had to move the kids to another school. It's further and more expensive, but at least they're happy.' She paused. 'It's a bit tricky for the kids. My boy, the one who's working at the supermarket, he tells me, "Don't talk about us in interviews, don't say our names." And if the girls get on Facebook when we're doing a blockade, the town kids will say "feral blockies", and if it happens to rain they'll write "hope youse all catch cold and drop dead". The kids just want to leave here.'

Jen and I barely spoke on the drive home from Queensland. The weight of what we'd heard and seen hung over us – divisive, apocalyptic, catastrophic for land and water, and for communities. This was happening seven hours from where we lived – and it was coming to an area near us. I'd thought it unlikely any mining company would choose to squiggle its way down the narrow winding cutting and along our rough country roads, but after driving the back roads of Queensland, clearly the mining companies would go almost anywhere.

I visualised Tywyah's future: there'd be a labyrinth of pistons and pipes and pumps rooted to a cement slab. The slab would be surrounded by denuded dirt, fenced in with crosshatched wire. We'd hear humming and droning, monotone moaning. A chemical smell would replace the manure-eucalypt scent that fizzes in the summer heat. The cattle and horses, kangaroos and pretty-face wallabies, magpies, kookaburras and parrots would all disappear. We'd have no leafy greens in the vegetable garden; we'd no longer be able to drink the creek water or inhale clean air. Divisions would flare up in the local community when some might get jobs on the mines and others would oppose it. We'd wind up with nosebleeds and persistent headaches – and take it out on each other. And all of this would've been imposed on us by multinationals who had no connection to the land or the community.

In Queensland I'd seen small towns with boarded-up family businesses, Lions Club and volunteer fire brigade signs swinging off their hinges, rents too high for local families, schools with noticeboards thanking mining company sponsors, and pubs selling expensive beer to DIDOs while slot-machines pinged and clattered. Is this what would happen to our area?

I kept thinking about those three brave and embattled women. They weren't complainers; they were brave, tough countrywomen fighting to protect their families, communities and homes. I thought about the words embroidered in white cotton on miners' high-visibility vests: 'See something, say something, do something'. Should we buy that mother an automatic washing machine? Encourage others to go see what was happening? Find pro bono lawyers? But donating money had never felt like an adequate response to injustice. So I sat down and wrote about those three Queensland women. This had ceased to be some intangible environmental issue I couldn't get my head around. Now, as I wrote about these women as wives and mothers and income-earners, I began to see it as a human rights issue. It was about people's right to a clean environment – about a right to exercise control over one's home, the place where surely one should be safe.

# 39.

# PROTECT

ONE QUIET WEEKDAY AFTERNOON some months later the phone rang. It was Annie, the inspiring woman who'd encouraged us to survey our community and get all our roads 'locked' against gas mining. 'Can you girls be at Pollocks Road by six tomorrow morning?' she asked. 'And bring a shovel. There's a direct action against Metgasco.'

Metgasco was the company mining for gas in the area. They were digging an evaporation pond at Pollocks Road.

'I'm definitely going,' Jen said as she charged over to the shed to find some shovels. Over the months she'd become increasingly possessed by anti-gas fervour, learning about the processes and following the growing movement on Facebook. I too was interested in going to the protest, just as I went along to marches and rallies outside our MP's office, but I didn't want a charge for malicious damage, particularly in an area an hour's drive from home.

The following morning I peeled my fingers from the frosty front gate and we drove towards town, headlights lighting kangaroos in the fog. An hour later, as the sun poked up above the red horizon, we turned off the main road onto an inconspicuous country lane, Pollocks Road. An excavator sat silently beside a large hole that was to be used for water produced by drilling. The crowd – mostly grey-haired – carried 'Water Not Gas' and 'No CSG' placards. A group of women who called themselves the Knitting Nannas sat on campstools knitting yellow triangles from canary-yellow wool.

I carried a shovel, still gold from when we'd painted it the previous year for a Wild West fire brigade fundraiser. I wasn't sure I wanted to put dirt into the excavated hole. I ardently believed in the right to protest, and since I'd lived in Australia I'd been to countless rallies and marches, but I'd never tangled with the Australian police. My experience stemmed from South Africa during apartheid: police and soldiers with their quirt and sjambok whips, guns and tear-gas canisters, and alsatian dogs, teeth bared, straining on leads.

'What if the police turn up, Boudicca?' I asked. Boudicca was a woman I'd consulted when I was working on our submission. She understood the science of gas mining, the aims and processes of the Lock the Gate movement, and seemed a sensible and measured person.

She explained that if we stepped inside the fence surrounding the hole we could get charged with trespass or malicious damage. We could get a fine of five hundred dollars but there was always the chance of a section 10, which meant no conviction was recorded even if found guilty.

'There are no leaders in this movement,' Ian said, who we'd met at the first community meeting. 'You make your own decisions.'

A woman from Queensland said, 'With the Kerry blockade we found we had to use our resources strategically.'

'This is not a blockade,' Ian said. 'It's a non-violent direct action. We don't have the resources for a blockade right now. I'm a carpenter, I need to get to work.'

'So is it strategic to get charged for this?' I asked. I understood that given the government was doing nothing to stop the mining company, direct action was all that was left, but would this action achieve anything? Who would represent people in court? Who would meet the fines? The ramifications rolled out ahead of me before anyone even went inside the enclosure. Political action, out-of-date knowledge of legal process and a vivid imagination make uneasy bedfellows.

The conversation went back and forth within the group. There were no leaders – and no consensus.

'I just want to do what I want to do,' a woman said and stepped through the gate.

Others followed. Some wore jeans and gumboots and wielded shovels fluidly; a woman in a dress and leggings dangled her shovel like a handbag; another stood atop a mound of dirt, ball of yellow wool and knitting needles in one hand, shovel in the other. Some of us – including Jen who was filming on her iPad – stayed outside. Cameras clicked, a newspaper journalist took notes. Of course there was no way the hole would get filled in by those few shovelfuls, but the action might lead to some publicity, perhaps send a message to parliamentarians and the public that the community opposed mining in this area.

I watched and jotted down thoughts on an old envelope, wondering about my choice not to enter the fenced off area and shovel dirt. As students at university in Cape Town during the state of emergency, we'd broken the law when we'd protested and when we'd worked in townships. I'd been frightened but I'd done it anyway because I had to: the injustices burned so deep I knew I couldn't live with myself if I did nothing. So did my choice to stay outside the hole now reflect my lack of commitment to this campaign? Would I have gone in if this was closer to the farm, or was my connection to country and environmental causes just not as deep as it was for those who were willing to risk arrest? But then I couldn't be sure I'd have chained myself to that excavator if this were a protest about issues I cared even more deeply and passionately about, like violence against women and kids, or asylum seekers being held in detention centres. Perhaps I just didn't have the fearless and selfless personality for frontline action.

'How was that?' I asked a woman as she walked out after digging a few shovelfuls into the vast hole.

'Great,' she said. 'At last it felt like we were doing something.'

We drove home past the Wilkinsons' place and past the sign declaring 'This is a Gas Field Free Road'. We'd erected it one grey day, twenty of us gathering for a photo shoot to represent the ninety-seven per cent of our neighbourhood who'd voted to keep our area free of gas fields.

I'd not met Ross Wilkinson before that day. He was a fourth-generation farmer, a cousin to Nessie the poet and the son of Isabel, who'd written the history of the area including a book called *Forgotten Country*.

'That's my life: the land and the river,' Ross had told me in his slow, wry manner for the press release I was writing. 'We went through twelve years when it never rained and we had to irrigate. Without good water you've got nothing. You can't grow anything, you can't live. You'd have to walk off your place.'

When Ross, his son and toddler grandson had stood in front of the sign for a photograph, Ross's comment – 'We don't own the land, we only look after it for the next generation' – became palpably real. I pictured Ross's grandson grown up, wearing a flannelette shirt, akubra and workboots. This was a deep attachment and a generational commitment to land – to country. A true belonging.

Towards the end of that year, Jen had begun doing regular daytrips to Glenugie, two hours' drive from the farm, to a blockade outside one of Metgasco's drill sites.

'But what do you do down there?' I asked after her first trip.

'Just be there,' she said, 'that's what a blockade is. You're there to show opposition whenever Metgasco tries to get into the drill site.

You don't have to get arrested if you don't want to. We're just there protesting, not doing anything illegal.'

'But what do you *do* all day if Metgasco doesn't turn up?'

'Hang out. Talk to people, maybe paint a banner, do some kitchen duty. You'd like it, there are lots of people to chat to.'

I wasn't so sure. Non-violent direct action seemed the only avenue left to stop the mining, but I didn't want to just 'hang out' at the blockade; I wanted to – had to – keep writing; I had deadlines for my master's. Yet each time Jen drove off to the blockade, a 'you should be going' voice screamed at me – after all, I didn't have a boss who'd dock my pay. What did my writing and degree matter in the face of this?

One December day Jen came back hot with stories. A truck with a huge generator for the drill site had attempted to get through the blockade.

'There were only three local officers,' she said. 'No way in a pink fit could they control the crowd. And then when they came up to the gate everyone sang Christmas carols.' She produced an A5 booklet – the *Gasfield Free Hymn Book* – and there on page one I found 'Jingle bells, methane smells/ salt won't fade away/ so much better is to use/ solar, wind and waves'.

'See,' she said, 'you'd have loved it.'

'Did Metgasco get in?'

'No. They just kept going past us. They must've decided to go back to Lismore.' Jen was pumped, victorious. 'Would've cost them heaps. It'll show them – and the public – that people here don't want the mining. Metgasco's got no social licence. They'll have to break the blockade to get into the site.'

I was sceptical: was it enough to just delay Metgasco and cost them money?

After I'd met my deadlines, I went down to Glenugie to see for myself. It was a beautiful area adjoining the Yuraygir National Park; a half hour's drive to the east were the blue seas of Minnie Water; half an hour west was the regional town of Grafton. We stayed a few days, sleeping in the swag on the back of the truck. During the days we hung out around the area outside the gate to the drill site, beside the farmers' loading ramp. A tepee had been erected and fences and gates were draped with the Aboriginal and Eureka Stockade flags, yellow 'Lock the Gate' triangles and signs that read 'Water More Precious than Gas'.

One evening a man produced a metal sleeve. The 'dragon', as it was called, was a lock-on that could be cemented into the ground. This was Frontline Activism 101. I shoved my arm inside and felt a bar at the bottom.

'You wear a chain around your wrist and lock that to the bar,' he explained, 'and then you can't unlock yourself.' He said it was much more effective than a bicycle lock.

'Effective how?' I asked.

'Because it takes the police hours to get the person unlocked. Usually they have to get the search-and-rescue team. They have to dig out the cement, use grinders for the metal, and not injure the bunny. It can take hours, even days.'

'Bunny', it seemed, was the word for those who strategically put themselves in 'arrestable situations'. An odd word to describe people who seemed so fearless.

'Weren't you scared?' I asked Stella, a middle-aged woman who lived just down the road. A few weeks earlier she'd locked-on to the back of a truck carrying fencing materials. I pictured her neck attached to the underside of the truck in front of the back wheels of a B-double truck.

She nodded. 'Yes, but I knew the truck wouldn't go anywhere.' She laughed. 'And I could hear someone up the road shouting, "Lie down like Gandhi, lie down like Gandhi." To be honest, all I was thinking was: I hope this doesn't take too long. Dad's at home on his own and he's not well.'

I admired her bravery and respected her willingness to get arrested – and I doubted I was bunny material.

Phil, a local man with a big warm smile and laugh and a few missing teeth, told me he was furious mad; ready to 'go' Metgasco as soon as they came. 'How can they do this to this country? Look at it,' he said, his eyes softening as he gazed around at the banksias and eucalypts.

'I don't know that violence is gonna get rid of them,' I said. 'More likely you'll wind up in jail and then what help will you be here? I'd just hate to see you get in a blue with a copper, Phil.'

He smiled at me and laughed. 'Dunno if I'll be able to control myself. They can't do this to us. It's our home.'

If the Queensland women had shown me how 'control' was part of having a home, Glenugie was showing me home was something one protected.

'See,' Jen said, as we drove away a few days later. 'You enjoyed yourself, didn't you? All those people to talk to.'

'Absolutely, and I still don't want to spend days there. I have to keep working.'

'I feel bad leaving,' Jen said. 'I wish Christmas wasn't happening.'

It was the third Christmas since Jen's mum had died. 'What? You'd spend Christmas down there?'

'Some of those people need a break. They've been there for weeks.'

'But what about Pen and Jill?' They were our good friends in Lismore; more like family. Six years earlier Pen had been given nine months to live following a cancer diagnosis. Every Christmas was possibly her last.

Jen shrugged. 'I guess Metgasco won't come over Christmas.'

Just before we left for Lismore, Jen checked Facebook for updates. She checked on Christmas Eve, first thing on Christmas morning, midmorning while Jill was helping Pen get up, before we sat down to lunch, after lunch, during the afternoon. 'Look how they're celebrating Christmas down there,' she said, showing us Facebook posts of a tree decorated with tinsel and 'Our Land, Our Water' signs.

'They're not going to come till the new year,' I said, irritated by

Facebook's intrusion.

'I've got to keep up with what's happening. It's any day now,' Jen said. 'Everyone's on high alert.'

By the fourth of January 2013, Jen was heading back to Glenugie. I went too, partly because to stay alone on the farm during the holiday season felt grim, partly because I was giving myself a 'holiday' from writing and even if I wasn't quite as passionate as Jen, even if I wasn't volunteering to be a bunny, I believed in the need and right to protest against unconventional gas mining. I had to participate. Jen parked the truck on the narrow country roadside and rigged up a tarp for privacy and to cover our 'kitchen'. I unrolled the swag in the back and found a torch I could use as a reading light.

The days were hot and sticky; the nights noisy with cicadas and mosquitoes, voices and music and cars driving on the road right beside our heads.

Camped on the back of trucks, in tents or under tarps were people I now recognised from public meetings and rallies. Seventy-five-year-old Anne, whom I'd met on the trip to Queensland, said it was her first time in a tent. I met countless new people too – accountants and artists, farmers and free spirits, people who were new to the area, or third generation. I loved hearing people's stories but when I began to feel lectured about the horrific state of the world, or when the 'gas bagging' began – as conversations about gas had come to be known – my interest dwindled.

One hot afternoon, I perched on a wooden fence beside a yellow 'Lock the Gate' sign. Five hundred metres up the quiet country road was the blockade. Across the road a herd of Santa Gertrudis cows flicked their tails at the buffalo fly. Willie wagtails swooped and dived. I heard the hum of an approaching car and a crackle from my walkie-talkie. I was on lookout: if I saw anything or anyone suspicious, I was to call it in on channel 27.

I sat there, a breeze filtering my hair and my hat, writing in my journal. I doubted blockading was for me. Again last night I'd had no sleep, but physical challenges weren't the foundation of my doubt. Unlike Jen and the other blockaders, I didn't follow what was happening on Facebook and didn't read anti-gas material voraciously. I was deeply concerned about the potential impact of gas mining and climate change and I wanted to *do* something, but I didn't burn with Jen's evangelical fervour and concentrated focus.

During the days Jen was busy: hammering signs, building structures, giving information to newcomers – being useful. She was blooming in this new environment, all her skills invaluable. I did the odd shift as lookout or washed dishes in the communal kitchen but mostly I was unsure what to do – what I *could* do. And wasn't work what was required in order to belong in any community? I'd been making notes in the hope I'd write something about the blockade but I didn't yet know what angle I'd take. Often I found myself wandering around, playing with the kids and chatting to people who were painting signs or setting up camp, to a man who was whittling a great big planet out of a huge block of wood, and to the people building structures from rope and bamboo. Jay, a tree lopper by trade, scaled the trees and rigged flags and banners high across the road. Ray, a pixie man who scurried around barefoot, was making an elaborate structure out of bamboo and rope and attaching it to the trees opposite the gate. The precision and professionalism reminded me of military operations; the ingenuity and creativity were the signs of the artist.

'It's good there are some people here who've done this before,' I said to Ray.

He'd been part of the North East Forest Alliance and protested against the logging of the area's old-growth forests.

I asked my favourite question: 'Don't you get scared?'

Ray laughed. 'Nah, I've built the structure so I know it's safe. Cops aren't going to want to hurt me – and if they do, they'll have to answer for it.'

I cringed inside, ashamed of my resistance. I was fearful of police and selfishly reluctant to wind up with fines or criminal convictions that might someday mean I couldn't take a legal job or travel overseas. Was there a place for me in this movement?

In the evenings everyone gathered in a circle outside the gate. Word was the drill rig would turn up on Monday; someone had seen a busload of riot police in nearby Grafton. A tremor of expectation rippled through the meeting.

By Sunday night the crowd had swelled. A red alert that the rig was expected had gone out to everyone who'd ever signed a petition. There were more familiar faces, including my old workmate from the university, Aiden. After years working for the North East Forest Alliance against logging in the area, he'd gone on to specialise and publish a book about activism and the law. 'Good to see you here,' he said.

Ian, whom I'd first met at the that initial community meeting, spotted me. 'Will you be a legal observer when the cops turn up?'

'I'm not a lawyer, Ian,' I said. 'And anything I remember is out of date.'

'You don't have to be a lawyer. All you have to do is record what you see – keep an eye on what's going on, particularly for the bunnies.'

As I took the little plastic badge, although flattered to be asked and pleased to have a job, I felt a flicker of concern: did I want a public role? A responsibility? Were my commitment and skills commensurate with a responsible role?

But how could I not? Here was something I could *do*.


Well before dawn, we heard the clang of the saucepan bell. The police had been spotted leaving Grafton. We gathered around the gate, some three hundred of us, bleary-eyed and pumped with conviction: we were peacefully stating our objection to what Metgasco was doing. People power could win. The mining company couldn't silence us. I was swept up in the fever of the moment. Jay and Ray climbed up their trees, Neil went up the tripod and Bart, who'd been wearing a white cotton glove and a padlock round his wrist for days, locked-on to a dragon in front of the gate. I hadn't even known a dragon had been cemented into the ground there.

I tugged the sleeve of the man whom I'd heard play flute and said, 'Can you help me keep tune please? This waiting's hell.' I launched into 'We Shall Overcome' and when a few people joined, I opened up the *Gasfield Free Hymn Book* and suggested 'Kookaburra sits in the old gum tree/ Sees them drill for CSG/ Laugh, kookaburra/ Laugh, kookaburra/ Fools these men must be'. Others joined us and soon our hearts and voices soared in the early morning quiet.

When the large bus arrived and officers dressed in flak jackets pressed down on us, we pushed in closer to each other and our voices rose louder. Tension now clung to the air. For some, the moment was the pinnacle, the end all the weeks had been working towards; for others, a first-timer's terror. I looked around at the pressing crowd, at faces tightly screwed up: what would the riot police do? Standing just metres away from the gate, my eyes flicked from lock-on to lock-on. What should I keep a record of, I wondered. Who would ever use this information? Can one ever really know where to focus or what's relevant in the midst of a dangerous or heightened experience? On my notepad I wrote:

*7.25 Standing between Bart and tripod. Officers dismantled stuff in front of the gate. Threw mattress and pillow over the fence into pad area. Now Bart is lying on rocky dirt. Take Bart's water away, leaving some just out of his reach.*

'Move back, move back!' officers in riot gear yelled. 'Come on, come on.'

I felt the crush of people. I anchored my feet, trying to keep my place so I could check on Bart. With his arm in a dragon cemented deep in the ground, he was so vulnerable, so exposed.

'I'm a legal observer,' I said to the officer, pointing to my badge. 'May I please stay here with Bart?'

'Everyone's to move out of the area. Back you go, come on, back you go,' he said, marshalling me with his hands.

I wanted to check Bart was okay and I didn't want to get arrested, but how far should I push it with this cop?

'Can you at least give Bart his water, please,' I asked the officer who towered over me. 'It's warming up. He's got a right to have a drink of water.'

'Move back, come on,' the officer said, as he planted himself in front of me.

Beside me was a woman dressed as an angel, an expression of sadness embroidered on her white cloth-covered face. Behind me I heard singing. I joined in for a verse but stopped when, over at the tripod, an officer began to dismantle the artwork. I could just see Neil who was up the tripod. Then the police unlocked the padlock that bound surfie boy to the arm of the tripod. This sweet man who'd told me it was his first blockade and he couldn't get any of his mates interested was marched away by the cops.

A truck with a cherry picker drove up beside the tripod. Officers wearing harnesses were raised to the tripod's platform. An officer gripped Neil's arm; he tried to swivel away out of reach. I held my breath.

'Back you go,' the officer in front of us yelled again. 'Come on. Back.' There was jostling and shuffling, the press of other protectors being forced back by the line of officers. Someone cried out. I lost my view of Bart. Lost my place. Found myself further back. And then there was Jen who'd been filming with her iPad.

'Did you hear?' she said. 'They've arrested Ian for tossing Benny a bottle of water. Now we've got no police liaison.'

The police liaison, we'd been told at the meeting the night before, was our way of communicating with the cops. What would happen to us now? My heart pounded, adrenaline rushed. Suddenly everything seemed risky and consequential. Standing on my toes, I looked across and there was Benny, dressed in his full black suit and gas mask with a 'Fossil Fool No More CSG' sign, tall with dignity, as he was escorted down off his platform by three police officers.

People were milling around; some had sat down in the road. A Knitting Nanna told me they'd arrested five people already. I heard a woman shout, 'Let go of me. Leave me alone!' Heard someone crying. Then another voice, a man, 'I'm not resisting. You don't have to do this to me.' Another voice, 'Don't hurt him, he's just a boy.' I couldn't see past the crowd to the source of those voices. Then an officer ran past with bundles of cable ties. Were they going to use those as handcuffs? What should I do? Where should I go? Where was Jen? Was she okay?

Then I heard a voice beside me. 'They say they're going to use section 186 of LEPRA to close the road for a "temporary purpose". We don't know if they can. Aiden's got the computer at the info tent. Will you take a look?'

I dodged others, past Alan and Deb, arm in arm, sitting on the road. What were the cops planning? Would a road closure mean we'd lost our right to protest? Would the cops arrest everyone? What then would the crowd do? Where was Phil?

At the info tent, Aiden was busy tweeting. It was years since I'd been on AustLII, the database with legislation and case law. LEPRA, I discovered, was short for the *Law Enforcement (Powers and Responsibilities) Act*. I'd never seen or even heard of this statute. I keyed in section 186 and began to read, flicking back to the definition section. In the distance I saw an officer twist a man's arm behind his back. Eighteen arrests, someone said. I looked back at the computer: did they have the legal power to close the road? What about our right to protest peacefully? The air filled with more crying, more entreaties. I didn't know the law; I was so out of practice. How could I make sense of this statute, here, now? I looked up to see officers marshalling the crowd down the road. There was the woman with the walking frame.

There was the young woman who'd camped near us. As her gorgeous dark-haired baby wriggled and wailed, she pleaded with an officer.

'The road's closed,' an officer said, standing in front of our computer table. 'Come on, move on with the others, down the road.'

Where was Jen? Had she been arrested? Our truck was parked in the opposite direction, north of the info tent.

I slipped out the back of the tent and ducked through a barbed-wire fence into the bush. Crouched over commando-style, I scurried through the bush, skirting the road until I caught sight of our camp. And there, miraculously, was Jen, lying completely still and silent on the bed, wondering where I was.

That's when I saw Ray was still high up in the tree. Those of us who'd managed to get back to our camps gathered at the police barricade. We waved at Ray and he waved back and smiled.

I was hot and sweaty; it had been a long and emotional day. Even the cops looked tired.

'Would you like some water?' Jen said to an officer. He refused.

I bit my lip as I stared up at Ray. Even if he was a monkey-climber, how was he going to get down safely? Out of the corner of my eye I noticed the woman who was his ex-partner and mother to their thirteen-year-old twins. She was watching too.

Then it came from the north, a slow and steady towering convoy of B-double trucks with diggers and excavators and other unrecognisable machinery. Rolling in, rolling over that hopeful opposition. People took up the 'Our Land, Our Water' chant. I stood silently. This was just all wrong. Inside me, lodged between my spine and sternum, was a hollow empty wasteland. Standing on that quiet country roadside, as each truck rolled past, I cried. For the defeat, for the people for whom this was home, for all who'd come to help protect it – and for the fact that the police had supported a mining company against a group of citizens who were peacefully protesting.

I crossed the road and was staring through the chain wire fence at the trucks driving into the drill-pad area when I heard shouting from behind me. Crossing back over the road, I saw Jen filming, and then I saw a grey-haired woman I'd later come to know as Maggie. She was on the ground, an officer holding her in a headlock, his arm pushed against her throat, her arm pinned to her back. She was begging him to stop hurting her and saying, 'He can't hear, he can't hear.' Beside her an elderly white-haired man, skinny legs poking out from his shorts, stood pale and trembling. Mick, I would come to learn, was a retired university professor. He was eighty-one and very hard of hearing.

People were calling out 'Let her go'; some were filming. Minutes later, when a couple of other officers appeared, Maggie was released. She gave her name to the officer, and I wrote down his name.

In the hot sun, Maggie and Mick clung to each other, trembling and crying. Maggie had a red mark around her neck. Someone produced rescue remedy, someone massaged her shoulders, someone made cups of tea.

A rhubarb of outrage tripped around the crowd: He can't do that. Abuse. Unreasonable violence. We're non-violent. We weren't doing anything wrong. We have a right to protect our land. We have a right to protest peacefully. How dare they.

Statements, that's what would be needed later, before people who'd been eyewitnesses forgot the details of what they saw. Away from the others, I transcribed a few people's stories.

When I again looked up there was no sign of Ray up the tree. Please, I prayed, please let him have got away.

A short time later, Jen heard a red-faced officer bragging to another. 'You wouldn't believe that little fella. Should've seen him run. If he hadn't had harness gear on I'd never have caught him.'

After the trucks and the police rolled away, an empty silence swamped us. Others who'd been marched down the road returned to their vehicles. They'd been standing in the blistering sun at the bottom of the road, no water, no food.

At sunset, after we'd all packed up, on public land down the road in among the gums, we sat in a circle, tired, shocked and sad. Some had bleeding wounds from where they'd been forced to the tarmac by the cops, some had grazes and cuts or pulled muscles. It was a day that would later be referred to as 'Bloody Monday'.

'What do we do now?' people asked. 'They can't do that.'

Absolutely not, I thought. I burned with rage and fervour: this was Australia, where we had a right to protest – and where, if I remembered the law correctly, the ombudsman oversaw police practices. 'We can complain to the ombudsman,' I said.

'Are you a lawyer?' someone asked.

'No,' I said. 'I taught law at the uni years ago, but I'm not a lawyer so you have to talk to one first. But as far as I remember, anyone can lodge a complaint.'

The next morning, as I filed into the back of the Grafton courthouse for the bail hearings, I was filled with the warmth of belonging. Our motley crew was a team, a community supporting those who'd refused bail and stayed in the lock-up. How heroic they appeared sitting in the little wooden dock, in their shorts and 'Gas Field Free' T-shirts, listening to the magistrate. Bail, I knew, was the straightforward part. What would the consequences be for these protectors? Who, I wondered, from the small pool of local solicitors, would be able to represent them for these criminal charges? They wouldn't get legal aid, the legal centre wouldn't have the resources to represent them, and wasn't the underfunded Environmental Defenders Office running a case against Metgasco in the Land and Environment Court? For a moment I wished I still worked in law.

Back on the farm I typed up my legal observer notes, forwarded the information on the ombudsman's process to others and discussed what had happened with my legal friends. I offered to write fact sheets or run training for the Community Legal Centre but discovered the Environmental Defenders Office was already doing that. I was relieved: I didn't have to get my head around all this. I could pop my extant legal self back in its dusty box.

At a small country hall in Doubtful Creek for a training session, I learned about the history of non-violent direct action, of Gandhi's work, of other communities where it had succeeded.

I nodded with purpose and pride. Non-violent protest was something I believed in passionately. Here was the possibility of using law for good means, here was the world where I'd once felt at home. I made notes about the right to lawful arrest and processing through the court system and what penalties might be applied to what offences under the *Crimes Act*. I found that the *Petroleum (Onshore) Act* had introduced a new offence of 'obstructing or hindering the holder of a petroleum title' with a penalty of $5500 but as yet it hadn't been used.

When the group split in two, Jen went along to the peacekeeper training, and although I'd been reluctant to even take the legal observer badge, now my long-ago faith in law's role in righting injustice led me to the police liaison training.

After the 'mock-ade' training, Aiden asked, 'Could you write the general complaint about Glenugie?'

I laughed, tickled to even be asked. 'I haven't done law for years.'

He sighed. 'Someone really needs to do it – my dean's breathing down my neck about how much time I'm spending on this.'

'Bugger,' I said. 'I thought I'd done my legal bit.'

Around me milled people I'd known from the Glenugie blockade and from that Pollocks Road shovel-dirt-into-hole day. If I didn't do this, would anyone else have time? If nothing was done then what happened that day would never be independently investigated; the New South Wales police wouldn't be pulled up for contravening fundamental human rights at a protest – and we'd be in even deeper trouble at the next blockade.

How could I say no? He and all the other legally trained people had 'real and important' jobs, whereas I only had my unpaid writing – and hadn't yet worked out how to write about the blockades.

I grimaced. 'I guess I can have a go, but you'll have to look at it.'

At my desk I logged into AustLII and pulled up the legislation. As the rusty cogs of my legal brain clanked and groaned, I wondered what the hell I was doing. My knowledge of law had only ever been academic. I'd never practised as a solicitor, and the only criminal law I'd researched since law school related to breaches of apprehended violence orders. Law was an old home I'd left behind, wasn't it? I'd moved on to creative writing, hadn't I?

Yet there was that image of Maggie in a headlock. That cocky young cop.

I might barely remember what I'd studied in first-year criminal law but I did remember the topic of my essay: 'Public Disorder and the Defence of Necessity'. Even if, as far as I remembered, that defence of necessity wasn't likely to succeed, Australian police had to respect the right to protest. These were people protecting their homes. I'd once been able to write and think legally. Surely, if I just used the legislation, others' statements and what I'd seen and heard at Glenugie, I could put together a complaint to the ombudsman? It was meant to be an accessible agency, wasn't it?

I worked long days outlining the causes for complaint using the administrative law grounds I'd once taught. The way the police had defeated the protest and rushed everyone down the road without regard to participants' personal safety. The excessive, unlawful and unreasonable force. I inserted quotes from the stories I'd heard from the bunnies: *The police took away my water and shelter. They used tools near me and didn't give me any personal safety protection. I got injured when they extracted me from the lock-on.*

There were quotes, too, from people who'd not put themselves in arrestable positions: *I was pulled from out of the line of protesters, pushed facedown on the road, my arms pulled behind my back, handcuffed and dragged away. I was dragged along the bitumen road. I was tackled, my head in a lock pushed to the ground and it bled. They used verbal intimidation even though I said I was moving. They told us it was an offence to film or take photographs. They were so rough it aggravated my frozen shoulder. I wound up with grazes and scratches. I said 'I'm not resisting' but still they pulled my arms behind my back and twisted my wrist.*

At the same time, in a fervour of righteous outrage, I sent a link for the ombudsman's web page to people who might also want to lodge individual complaints. I encouraged them to get legal advice.

Before I had a chance to finish the complaint, the red alert call came: the drill rig was moving from Glenugie to Doubtful Creek. Again we loaded the truck, dropped the dogs at Frank's and drove through the hinterland, along winding country roads with lush paddocks of fat and happy Herefords. This time we knew what to expect. We parked on a grassy patch just off the road and set up camp, calling hello to Boudicca who'd helped with the initial submission writing, surfie boy and the man we called 'Mr Incognito'. Then we heard someone was in a Mad Max–style armoured vehicle – later known as the Trau-matron – outside the gate to Glenugie. The drill rig wouldn't be able to get out to drive to Doubtful Creek.

This protest was on the rise of a road flanked by cleared paddocks dotted with pale grey Charbrays. The actual drill site was a way off the road, accessed through a state forest pine plantation. A tripod with an Aboriginal flag, the Eureka flag and the Australian flag stood in front of the plantation's gate, the barbed-wire fence draped with the usual 'Water is Life' and 'Can't Eat Gas, Can't Eat Coal' banners, and 'Lock the Gate' signs dangled from the nearby trees. Car wrecks littered the entrance: red, blue and metal grey, parked at different an-gles. Bunnies would lie in them with their arms in dragons cemented into the ground beneath the cars. A banner read 'Sovereignty: Our Culture, Our Lands, Our Time'.

There were dozens of familiar faces. In the grey evening light a tall articulate Githabul man cloaked in the Aboriginal flag welcomed us to country.

At night on the back of the truck, I lay awake listening to the occasional car and the crackle and pop of frogs down in the swamp, wondering if we were about to face the riot police again. Next morning, the fog still hanging in the valley, we heard the drill rig was still stuck at Glenugie. The Traumatron was proving difficult to move.

As the hot summer sun moved across the sky, I sat under a makeshift shelter talking to an older Aboriginal man. He sat in a camp chair with a cup holder in its armrest.

'We got to look after our land and our rivers, it's all part of us here. It's good we're all combining here as one people,' he said. 'It's the only way.'

Certainly, this movement seemed to have crossed so many boundaries and led to unlikely alliances including farmers and free spirits, National Party conservatives and Aboriginal people. The older Aboriginal man was right: working together for a common interest was the only way, not just to defeat a mining company against the gas invasion but also to connect with people from different backgrounds or cultures – it was a way that didn't feel artificial or smack of 'do-gooder', a way that was about protecting something universal: home.

I walked back up the road to the tarped truck. As I waited for the kettle to boil, I looked out at the road lined with cars and vans and tents and thought about the Aboriginal connection to land, and how different it was from the 'ownership' model of the coloniser. Then I remembered our neighbour, old Ross Wilkinson, and how he too, like Jen, talked of a responsibility to care for the land.

How different I was from them and from so many others at the blockades: they seemed so deeply connected to country in a way I, a Diasporic Jew, had no experience of. Perhaps my migrant self would never truly know such a deep and earthy connection.

With renewed rage after the horrors of the blockade, I returned to writing the group complaint. By late March, I'd sent the draft to other legally trained people. By late April, Maggie, the woman who'd been held in a headlock and dropped to the ground, who'd lodged a complaint with the ombudsman, had been charged with assaulting a police officer. I shrivelled with shame, convinced everyone in the movement blamed me because I'd encouraged complaints to the ombudsman. By late July, she'd been found guilty. Although I'd encouraged Maggie to get advice from a solicitor before lodging her personal complaint, and although on appeal she was finally found not guilty, still I blamed and shamed myself.

When a solicitor in town who'd not been anywhere near a blockade read the general complaint, she rang me and said, 'The statements need to be de-emoted.'

As I looked out my office window to the wayward bougainvillea over the vegie garden gate, I sighed and said, 'That's how it was. It was emotional.'

Once again I was flooded with fear and frustration with the law. A decade earlier the law hadn't listened to the women's stories of police failure to respond to breaches of domestic violence; this time it was activists' stories. The law robbed events of story, labelled people 'criminal' and 'guilty' and wiped away feeling and backstory.

How foolish I'd been to encourage people to make complaints about police behaviour and become invested in impossible outcomes. My desire to expose injustice and reform the system stuck to me like velcro, but I wasn't a real lawyer. It was all a dangerous mix: rage against bullying and injustice combined with those intoxicating words: 'Can you help?' Dangerous because it flared not only my ego but also my desire to belong. I'd written the combined complaint as an oral historian or artist, revealing experience by staying true to what people felt and said. How stupid. I should've written a story, not a police complaint. Art, not law or political manifesto, was where I wanted to be.

'Can I get the protectors to contact you directly?' I asked the lawyer.

Yes, at some point. There was no hurry. The general complaint was on hold until after the criminal proceedings had been finalised.

I bundled my legal notes into a blue folder and emailed the others an update. Job done, I thought. Brief and misguided foray back to law work over. Perhaps we only truly find our place when we let go of old identities and the recognition they once gave us. I could keep boomeranging back to that old image of self I had in my efforts to help others and gain approval, or I could take my place as a writer – even an obscure one. I cracked the spine on a new notebook and opened to a fresh, blank page.

# 40.

# 'WE'

A YEAR AFTER THE OTHER BLOCKADES, in March 2014, Jen and I pitched our tent in an empty paddock at Bentley near Lismore. Metgasco was soon to start drilling for gas on the neighbouring property. The blockade was taking shape: a farmer had lent this paddock to the anti-gas movement, and an information tent and a roster of workers had been set up. I too was more comfortable with the ins and outs of frontline activism – as long as I steered clear of law or leadership. A couple of months earlier, we'd wound up with penalty infringement notices after Santos's security guards had filmed us standing on a road at the Pilliga camp protesting against Santos's Narrabri gas-mining project. After requesting a review we'd got off. I'd begun to wonder if maybe the consequences of frontline activism – or of others' disapproval – weren't as dire as I'd feared. When we'd been asked to take a shift on the roster for the Bentley blockade camp, I'd been keen. Our first shift was the following night.

That night my stepmother, Genee, was shot dead in her bed in Johannesburg. Two days later I was on a plane to South Africa. Three days later I drove up the driveway of 48A and climbed the long staircase as I'd done as a six-year-old. Four days later I was staring at Genee's dead body. Six days later I told a crowd in the Johannesburg Country Club's rose garden – a place that had once had signage declaring 'No Jews No Blacks No Dogs' – that fairytales have it wrong: stepmothers aren't evil, they're kind and loving. After the service, again and again I heard 'this isn't usual for South Africa', 'it must've been an inside job' and 'make sure the police don't lose the docket'. Eight days later, at the request of Genee's children and nieces, I combed cupboards and bookshelves. I found photographs and books that had once belonged to my father and Lesley, the woman he'd left my mother for. Nine days later I was talking to police detectives and private investigators. Had Genee been murdered by someone she knew and trusted?

Over the phone, Jen told me that the Bentley blockade was expanding daily, that she'd done shifts on the gate, in the kitchen, at the information tent. I told her about meeting a private investigator at the Fire and Ice Hotel, and another at a highway service station. I was in a bad B-grade movie, but what else could I do to ensure Genee's murder was investigated?

I was in the departure area of Johannesburg airport much earlier than needed. I'd never wanted to leave my homeland – anywhere – so much. Sitting in the restaurant, I shuffled some of my father's books into my hand luggage, sent the last thankyou text message to my aunt and cousins, and gave away the SIM card. Out on the runway, swallows swooped and dived and I stared at the new South African flag painted on planes parked against a Johannesburg blue sky of puffy white clouds. I thought of the times I'd returned over the years, how there'd be an intake of breath as the plane's wheels hit the tarmac, marking that sense of returning to a homeland, my adult Australian self suddenly evaporating.

When I heard clapping, I turned to see a table of bald men staring up at the television screen: football. I drank the last of my beer and toasted my dad, Genee and 48A. Twenty-five years since migration, I had a surge of 'get me out of here – I never want to come back'. I doubted I'd return, not even to see my aunt and cousins.

Back in Australia, the queue for Australian passport holders was long. As I looked at the others in the queue, I wondered if my ties with South Africa were now truly severed and played my usual game of demographic definition. Who was a true-blue Australian, who was born elsewhere or had parents or grandparents from elsewhere? Who could claim to be 'made in Australia'? My perennial questions: how do you integrate your past with your present self? What is it to be you?

I stepped out into the bright Brisbane day, into Jen's faded cord-jacket hug, softening into the safety of her familiar smell and touch. 'Welcome home,' she said.

At the first glimpse of Wollumbin, the high cloud-catcher mountain of the north coast, I rolled down the window to breathe in the fresh air. What a long way this was from a murder in Johannesburg. I was back in the peaceful green and clean. Back home in Australia. Back home with Jen. Surely this was where I was safe? How I hoped I'd be able, at last, to shuffle those signposts that read 'safety' and 'belonging'.

'Let's drive to the farm via Bentley,' I said.

'You sure?' Jen asked.

'Yup, it'll be good to see it after all you've been telling me. Just quickly. I don't have much left in me.'

What had been an empty paddock dotted with a few tents when I'd left was now a village. A community.

At our tent, Jen said, 'See, your pillow's waiting for you.' Then she led me down roads with names like No Fracking Way lined with tents and caravans and vans, blue tarps and rainbow flags. There were toilets, a kids' tent, a meeting area, a fire pit and a kitchen that was even equipped with a steriliser. I greeted the people I knew and was introduced to some of Jen's new connections.

At the neighbouring property where the drill rig would enter, the area in front of the gate was crowded with tripods and tents, banners and flags, hearts and yellow triangles. Car wrecks and cement culverts with buried dragons blocked the gate itself. This was the Glenugie blockade magnified, organised, professionalised. And I wasn't a part of it.

'Can we get out of here now?' I asked.

Back on the farm, bewildered by the complicated nature of grief and the injustice that someone might get away with the murder of a kind, loving woman, I burrowed down, picking over photographs and memories of Genee, and of her and my father. As I mourned Genee, I realised I was mourning my last tenuous connection to my father and to South Africa. Along with it came a strange discovery. As I examined the photographs and books I'd lugged back from Johannesburg, I found myself charting timelines from my childhood and confronting the bewildering realisation that although my father had left our nuclear family when I was six, it seemed he might've been with Lesley from the time I was three or four. Betrayal and silence – persistent threads of many families' stories.

When I ventured out the farm gate to the supermarket in town, I inevitably ran into people from the gas field–free movement.

'I saw Jen out there last week. Were you there too?' a woman I knew from the Doubtful Creek protest asked.

'No,' I replied.

'You should've seen it. Did Jen tell you? There must've been two thousand people to greet the dawn. People are coming before they go to work. The cops better not try what they did at Glenugie or Doubtful. We'll get thousands more protectors 'cos people have woken up and this is close to Lismore.'

I nodded but the sense of urgency and significance of the blockade now seemed completely unfathomable. All I could think was: Genee's dead. Murdered. And by whom? Was it someone she knew?

Jen was absorbed in the excitement of the blockade. With all her practical skills and her steady, friendly diplomacy, she took on roles as a meet-and-greet person, as a traffic controller, as a builder, as an organiser, as a peacekeeper, and as the 'buddy' to the woman dressed as an angel who stood on a tripod with a platform metres above the gate to the drill site, where at dawn each morning hundreds of protectors converged. Someone had made Jen a badge that read 'Farmer Jen' and she wore one of the angel's white feathers tucked in the brim of her hat. She'd found her place in this community built on a cause that mattered profoundly to a diverse group, Aboriginal and non-Aboriginal, farmers and townsfolk. She camped at the blockade for three or four nights each week.

'You should've been there,' Jen said as we sat on the couch at home looking at her photos. 'It brought tears to my eyes. There must've been three thousand people, all standing united against gas mining, watching the sun rise and singing freedom songs, the angel up on her platform.'

Yes, I wished I'd been there for just that moment too. I wished I'd found a role for myself at blockades, one I felt comfortable with. I wished too I'd been able to be 'with' Jen – we'd made a solid team at the other blockades, a refuge people could turn to for a meal or a chat. We'd both loved being part of the community and what our partnership could create for ourselves and others.

And I wished Genee hadn't been murdered just weeks earlier.

'I just can't do it,' I said. 'If it was close enough to go in for a few hours and come home, maybe. But it's all too much. I feel so paper thin. I never sleep when we're at blockades and now I'm not even sleeping at home. I'd be no use.'

'You could still come,' she said. 'People come in all sorts of states.'

'Yes,' I said, 'and maybe that's not always wise.'


With Jen away, I wandered through the silent house, every window framing a landscape painting. Here is where we made love and where we argued. Here is where we laughed and wept with each other, and with friends. Here were the *wakis* I'd bought in Cape Town, the tables and bookshelves Jen had made for me, the paintings by friends, the red-tailed cockatoo feather from our Alice Springs trip. We'd lived together in this house for nine years. Everything here was made beautiful by its use and story; everything should've anchored and comforted me.

And yet now the world seemed upside down. Now it all seemed to magnify my loneliness and disconnection from my last tenuous link to South Africa, from my mother and the rest of the family, from my friends far away – and from Jen.

Into the loneliness and intensity of grief, my shames multiplied. 'Self-indulgent, spoilt, privileged, jealous, useless, failure. You live in a safe and beautiful place, have a loving partner and no money troubles and still you're not happy,' I harangued myself, borrowing negative stereotypes and creating my own.

Outside I heard cows and calves tap-dancing on the checkerboard of blue and white tiles that was the kitchen of Jen's first scantling and bush timber shack. I wandered over to the horse trailer that was a monument to the fire that had burned down her second home. Listlessly, I fossicked through the shards of tiles, the bits of aluminium, the horseshoes. Everywhere were spectres of Tywyah's past embedded in the present, a past that now I saw only as Jen's, not mine.

'It could be the farm,' my closest friend said over the phone from Sydney. 'It might be easier if you weren't spending so much time alone at a time like this, if you could just pop round to a friend for a cuppa.'

'I can't face going to town and staying at friends' houses. As kind as everyone is. Not now,' I said. 'I probably just need to get back to work. That'll sort me out.'

After a nod to my 'Virgin in a Strange Land', I sat down at my desk to write the story of Genee's murder. I put one word in front of another but they were just words, they shed no new light. Where solitude had often nourished my writing, now the terrifying loneliness seemed to undermine it. Where scratching around in the past had helped me settle some of the shattered glass, now it was neither refuge nor cure. I was not writing fiction where characters could wrest me away from reality – I was writing about a murder and this, the worst form of betrayal and silencing, brought other betrayals and silences hurtling towards me. Writing the real might help one clarify and understand – might free one – but it may also push one deeper into grief and depression, deeper into the mire of unresolved silences.

A note in the red mailbox invited us to the hall for morning tea.

'As if I've got time to spend my morning having cups of tea,' Jen said.

In the wake of Genee's murder I was working on an essay called 'My Father's Four Women', but thought perhaps it would do me good to get out more. Like stagnant water, I needed oxygenation. If I didn't want to drive hours for a chat with a friend, didn't want to spend days away from home, if I didn't want to join the packing of the beer fridge down at the hall, then this at least was a way I could just pop out for a few hours and see people.

The first woman to greet me when I walked into the hall's kitchen said, 'Oh, what a surprise to see you.'

Fair enough. Years earlier I'd begged off carpet bowls, and after a few sessions I'd not gone back to linedancing or to the art group. Always for the same reason: I was working.

I levered my legs under the wooden bench of the picnic table. Everyone seemed to have brought plants in damp newspaper, tinfoil or pots. There was advice: keep them contained or they'll take over, shade or sun, not too much water. There were stories: 'They used to say my mother grew the best ...', 'It was given to me by those people who used to live up on Bulldog'.

If only I'd read the notice properly. But even if I knew who'd given us the blood orange, lemon myrtle and magnolia, even if I weeded nutgrass and oxalis, I wouldn't have known how to take a cutting or what to bring along without asking Jen. I loved to anchor my hands in the dirt, to smell the roses, pull weeds and pick vegetables, but the actual growing was not my preserve or passion.

When Heidi offered a jar of pickled cucumbers and one of cauliflower, I realised I could've brought my chilli jam or bottled tomato sauce. It was just about bringing something to share and show. This was such a warm and welcoming community. It was forgiving too – absence was no obstacle to belonging, and anyone who'd once lived here, even decades earlier, was welcomed back.

Judy told a story about the plant she'd brought, and Ruth placed a cutting in the middle of the table and said she had more if anyone wanted one.

Sipping coffee and listening, I felt as though I was watching myself go through the motions of social interaction. Here so much of me felt hidden, so many of my interests seemed irrelevant or invisible. I peeked at my watch. Most of the crowd were retirees, well into their sixties or seventies. Sure, I sincerely liked and cared about everyone and it was good to see people other than Jen and Frank. Sure, I got a kick out of being part of the history of a place, knowing the people whose photos featured on the memorial wall and the stories behind the horseshoe nailed to a post. Sure, I needed conversation – but not just any conversation. I just wasn't that interested in talk of plants and produce, nor even of cattle and coal seam gas. To communicate is to be understood, surely, not just to talk and listen. To be with people is to recognise ourselves too.

A few weeks before at the Friday night bar and barbeque, I'd joined the smokers at the high table outside and someone had said, 'I'm not lazy, I just couldn't be bothered.'

'What's the difference between being lazy and couldn't be bothered?' I'd asked.

'That's a bit deep, Hayley,' someone countered, and the conversation had reverted to wisecracks that made fun of people or jokes about alcohol.

Now, my mind wandered into a what-if game where each person at the table morphed into a writer or poet I was reading. What an absurd fantasy. A conversation with a neighbour came to mind. When I'd talked about the writers' festival over at Byron Bay, she'd said, 'I love reading books but writers are crackers.'

'How's the strudel?' Heidi asked.

'Delicious,' I said. 'I've never made one – are they hard?'

She assured me it was simple. I said I'd have a go.

One night, as I pulled a head of garlic from the plait hanging off the pantry architrave, I looked over at Jen on the couch with her iPad. On the days she was home from the blockade, when she wasn't busy with cattle and farm jobs, she read and posted gas-related information and photographs on Facebook. Her iPad pinged with messages. Facebook had expanded her world; she preferred connecting online than by phone.

'Won't you come chat while I cook?' I asked.

'I've got to keep up with what's happening,' Jen said, barely looking up. 'The rig could come any day now. We have to be ready.'

We. I looked up from the bench at her head bowed over the iPad. Suddenly I realised that Jen's 'we' didn't include me: it was 'the movement'. She'd found another place to belong.

'I'm just saying I miss you,' I said tearfully.

'What do you want from me, Hayley?' Jen said. 'I'm home for half the week. I've been here to talk about Genee and the murder.'

'Physically, yes, you've been here – but you're still at Bentley. You're always on Facebook. I'm just asking you to be present when you're here, to connect with me, to talk about something other than CSG, and to stop bringing the bloody iPad to bed.'

'You read all the time. What's the difference between doing Facebook on the iPad and you reading a book?'

I struggled to articulate the difference. Lack of authenticity and genuine connection, creep factor, was it personal or public, real or fake. Every distinction I raised sounded puerile, snobbish, inflexible – demanding.

But mostly, I just couldn't bear to look at Facebook: it magnified my cavernous sense of outsiderness. It represented the fast-moving, colourful merry-go-round of life beyond the farm gate: 'the unlived life'.

'You're overthinking things again, Hayley,' Jen said.

'Well then, it's the glow from the screen. I have a hard enough time sleeping without you looking at the iPad in bed.'

Jen shook her head. 'This isn't about Facebook or Bentley. This is how it was when Mum was in the nursing home. As soon as my attention is on something else, you get jealous.'

'So again, this is about what's wrong with me,' I said, my tears shaken up with frustration.

'Come with me to Bentley,' Jen said one Saturday. 'I'm only going in for the day. Farmers are being encouraged to come. We'll just go for a few hours. I can show you what I've been doing.'

I trailed her around a campsite mucky with mud after rain, smiled and shook hands with people she introduced me to, photographed her curled up in the concrete culvert with lovely Louise from Chooks Against Gas. After the four years of caring for her mum and then her deep and persistent grief after her mum's death nearly four years ago, it was beautiful to see Jen so social and easy in herself, so liked and respected – so happy.

I greeted a few people I'd met at other blockades, but I had no filter and when asked how I was, I said too much about murder. My grief seemed to fall on disinterested ears as grief is wont to do. Everyone was consumed with what they saw as consequential. The blockade was not the place for me – or perhaps grief rarely has a place anywhere but in private.

Jen ducked away to shift some timber before someone tripped over it. The woman smiled gratefully. How, I again wondered, could I 'go with' Jen into this anti-gas world? How could I find my place? In the aftermath of Genee's death, my confidence and capacity to chat had vanished. With Jen busy, I needed the security of a job more than ever before. If not law then what?

Countless people seemed to be documenting the blockade experience and posting on social media or in local papers. So what original insight could I add to such an avalanche of comment? Before Genee's murder I'd written a few pieces for the local papers after we'd gone to the Pilliga forest to protest against Santos's mining project, but I was uncomfortable with writing such call-to-arms pieces. I was no journalist, confident of answers and facts; my writing was more reflective, more curious about complexity, more personal.

I looked around at the crowd: some were couples who were both actively involved, some were married or partnered but came alone to blockades, some were not in relationships or seemed to be in a revolving door of love affairs. The blockade had certainly been fertile ground for romance. How many of the people here had got involved in the movement partly because they were unhappy at home or needed something in their lives? What was the effect of an activist's consuming passion on their long-term relationship? Did those stay-at-home partners see themselves as helping a 'war effort' or like me were they ashamed they missed their partners who were so consumed by the movement? These were the questions that burned true for me: the private side of the public, the inner life that so often seems invisible and 'unimportant'. I wanted my writing to be a socially vital activity – an action in itself, not just a description of action. But how, I wondered, could I unhook myself from the urgency of it all to create something universal and timeless?

I thought about famous couples who might've faced these issues, and how political complexities had translated back into daily lives. About the Mandelas, how their relationship had endured the separation and abuses of the apartheid years but shattered after Mandela's release. I thought about Martha Gellhorn, the journalist, and how her husband Ernest Hemingway had cabled her in 1943, complaining, 'Are you a war correspondent or wife in my bed?' I didn't want to be a Winnie Mandela or an Ernest Hemingway. I didn't want to douse Jen's consuming passion or sabotage her connection to her new community. And I couldn't spend days and sleepless nights as a frontline blockader, particularly so soon after Genee's murder.

I set aside my notes for the essay. There was no place here for my kind of personal writing. This was not what the movement needed at this urgent point. At a moment of such intensity, who would care? What solace or guidance – what value – would such an essay provide? It might even be seen as sabotage: politics opposed to art. And was it fair to ask anyone else for their story when Jen and I were struggling to accommodate our differences?


Ten weeks after Genee's murder, the government suspended Metgasco's licence. Jen rang from the blockade with the news; in the background I heard the music and singing. 'It's amazing,' she said, tears and laughter spooling over the phone line. 'I wish you were here. We've won. For the first time.'

The police – having assessed the physical situation – were concerned about the possibility of human deaths should there be another encounter between police and protesters. The thousands of people who'd turned up most days to greet the dawn must've persuaded them. The Bentley blockade had proved the power of peaceful protest.

From a distance, I rejoiced. I listened to news broadcast after news broadcast. I read the articles online. I heard updates from Jen as she danced and partied with everyone at Bentley. I wished I'd been part of the blockade; I wished I'd known the community's triumph. I'd known only the losses. It was sealed: I was not part of this 'we'.

# PART SIX:
# THE HEART

*Home is where the heart is.*
**– Pliny the Elder (AD 23–79)**

# 41.

# WHERE AM I?

THE FOLLOWING JANUARY of 2015, on our seventeenth anniversary, wrapped in humidity and the soundtrack of cicadas, Jen and I sipped champagne on the front verandah. Lucy, now an old deaf dog, slapped down on the cool cement, and the horses milled around the front gate.

'Seventeen years, ten of them living here,' Jen said, disbelieving.

'Who'd have thought,' I said, laughing.

Seventeen years, I've now discovered, is also the length of time that the North American nymph cicada *Magicicada* lives underground before emerging for six weeks of sex and song that culminate in eggs and then death.

For the next four days the summer rains sheeted down, tumbling water down gullies, swelling the creek, ripping through flood fences, submerging the causeway and flooding us in. Then it was back to muggy heat and the screams of the cicadas, back to my work. I was sick of my self-reflective writing; I was sick of being inside myself. This, not the temporary isolation of a flood, was the cabin fever that undid me.

At my desk I fiddled with my pen. I fantasised about a movie or an art gallery, people watching or wandering through a bookshop or down a city laneway. I fantasised about seeing a friend in the flesh.

I stared at the blank page, and then at the collection of quotes written on scraps of paper and tacked to the wall. Again I read Mary Oliver's poem 'The Summer Day', in which she asks readers what they intend for their life. One life, one singular life: that's all I had. What the hell was I doing with it? I pushed my chair away from the desk – but to what?

Lugging the wheel of plain wire, I trudged through the long grass in Jen's wake. I stood in the creek wrestling logs caught in a tangle of leaves and cat's claw vine, branches and barbed wire. The barbs tore at my skin, the water weighted my feet, flies and mosquitoes buzzed around me. I was uncertain which bit of the wrecked flood fence to unhook, whether to cut the old wire and reuse it or introduce new wire.

'I just make it up as I go along,' Jen said.

I traced the wire to a log snagged under some rocks and tugged.

'Don't do it like that,' Jen said, 'you'll hurt yourself.'

'Let me just *do* something other than pass the bloody pliers.'

'You have to learn how to be a follower, Hayley,' Jen said, cutting the wire free of the snagged log. 'It took me years to learn how to do stuff like this.'

For the umpteenth time on the farm, I felt wrong, useless, bad.

And then it hit me with a blinding clarity: I was over farm work, I was over trying to adapt and prove myself, over battling my defiance and limitations. I didn't care if I never became adept at fencing or any of the other farm work that still eluded me. I didn't care if I couldn't measure up to Jen. I didn't care if I had no place, no home here. I didn't want to do this anymore. I didn't belong here.

'I'm just not cut out for this life,' I said to Jen as I snipped through the wire. 'I'm so worn down, it's like I don't even know what I *can* do anymore. Or even what I *want* to do. I'm not passionate about farming, I'm not willing to put everything aside to fight gas mining. All of that's you, not me.'

'I haven't asked you to be anything you're not,' Jen said.

The cicadas' chorus hit a crescendo. I had exiled myself from everything – including myself.

'I know that. I chose to come live here and go along with you, in all these things that I cared about or liked doing – a little. But now I just feel ... I barely know myself.'

My hair was greying, my skin wrinkling. Over the years I'd wanted to do and be so many things, repeatedly allowing pivotal experiences to trigger self-redefinition. I'd told myself that I had no need of my family's expectations and conventional structures. I'd insisted I didn't believe in the notion of 'people like us', and yet I'd ceaselessly worked up a sweat in my efforts to fit in – to belong.

'I'll be fifty in less than two years,' I said. 'Is this it? Is this it for my life?'

'Every paddock has its problems,' Jen said, yanking more wire free from snagged logs. 'There's nothing out there that's better than what you have here.'

Utopia: the word comes from the Greek for 'no place'. Of course, Jen was right. The years at Tywyah living the 'rural idyll' and being a member of a small community had shown me how easy it is to glamorise and oversimplify lives not our own.

'If you leave here you'll just have to deal with a job that stresses you out.'

Right again.

Jen stopped and turned. 'I'm not keeping you here, Hayley. You've lasted longer than any of the others.' She listed her previous partners, and then added, 'I've always said the gate's open.'

'Is that what you want?' I snapped. 'For me to go? To live separately?'

She stared at me, and then very softly said, 'I can't make you stay.'

'No, and you never have,' I said, gathering up the boltcutters and coil of wire. 'But if it weren't for you I wouldn't be here. I'd probably have moved back to the city years ago.'

Over dinner that night Jen said, 'It's not Tywyah. It's the monkey on your back you've got to deal with.'

'Here we go again: it's always about what's wrong with me.'

'Hayley,' Jen said, grabbing a box of matches, 'it's like these matches.' She took one out, burned it and jammed it between the table's palings. 'There's this perfectly good box of useable matches with one tiny little match that's burned but your brain lets the one match take over and forgets about all the unburned ones. Can't you just see how magnificent you are? How everyone sees you that way? You don't have to prove anything to anyone.'

Tears streamed down my cheeks as I shook my head. 'You'd be better off with someone simpler than me, someone who's more of a party girl and good at physical stuff, someone who doesn't get jealous, someone who's not tormented by a murder and a complicated family. There are heaps of girls who'd jump at the chance.'

'And I could say you'd be better off with someone more intellectual, who feeds that part of you.' She sighed. 'I don't think like that. I love you – all of you. This conversation's stupid. I'm going for a shower.'

She spent the next day out on the horse. In the late afternoon I watched her ride up the driveway. Sitting in the saddle, she looked smaller than usual, as though she'd wilted.

At the dinner table she said little other than, 'I'm allowed to have bad days too,' and in bed she curled away from me.

Two days later she said, 'Alright, if you find a job that can support the two of us away from here, I'll move with you. We'll find a way to mothball the farm. Reorganise the cattle – go into steers rather than breeders – so we just have to come home every month or six weeks.'

I choked on my sip of tea. Never before had this even been an option.

'That way you can open doors instead of wondering what's behind them.' Then she laughed. 'You should see your eyes; they're wild. You're like a young filly, all excited, the gates open, you've bolted off to see what's out there.'

As I skittered about online, I marvelled at how, after more than twenty years in country Australia, city life now seemed so exotic. Having been out of the conventional workforce for more than a decade, I didn't even know what sort of a job to aim for. But my imagination was irrepressible. I'd take my CV to a human resources agent. Surely someone would employ me. Surely I could again be a worthwhile, contributing member of society. Again catch trains and smile at strangers, debate ideas around the water cooler or advocate for clients.

The news that night was about the vigil for Reza Barati, the man who'd died while in detention on Manus Island. As I listened to the radio broadcast, I charred eggplant over the barbeque's flame. I pictured myself in the crowd, my voice and heart surging with the collective chant. When the arts show came on, I saw myself in the audience watching the play, seeing the paintings in the gallery, at the Wheeler Centre listening to writers. Melbourne was a poker machine of stimulation, sensory and cerebral. How would it feel to regularly spend time with people passionate about literature and scholarship and the process of writing?

The week before, at the Wednesday cattle sale, as we'd leaned over the rail and stared at our pen of black steers, our stock agent had joined us.

'I keep looking in the bookshop but your book's not there,' he'd said jovially.

'I'm afraid not,' I'd said. For a moment I imagined voicing the challenge of work that doesn't have immediate concrete results, a 'product' or 'property' to which a 'right' might attach. I'd draw the parallel with cattle farming or building a house, observing how most of the work is invisible to everyone else but still one works at it daily, gets knocked down and gets up again. Instead I said, 'Books take much longer to grow than calves.'

As we'd chewed roast beef and gravy sandwiches in the cafeteria, I thought how I'd been humbled by farm life. The tangible always seemed more pressing, more valuable than the intellectual lauded by my background. It was nature, food, water, shelter, life itself. It was the same at the blockades where I'd found myself questioning whether frontline activism was more important – more worthwhile even – than anything I might be able to do with words. Action, product, result. That's what seemed to matter. Not words, not thought, not inquiry.

Now as I imagined a life in a city like Melbourne I wondered if I might stop questioning the value of the work I found so compelling. How would it feel to be somewhere where there was room for more of me?

As I walked through the paddocks, I spied a family of kangaroos, ears flicking, each sitting up on hind legs with their arms hanging in an O, front paws clasped. 'Lucy, come here,' I called to my walking companion, but of course she was too old and deaf to hear, and when the roos saw her they took off. I watched them hurtle through the bush, dark tails and rear ends surging and sagging. Creatures at home in their habitat.

# 42.

# PARTNERSHIP

AT THE BIMONTHLY fire brigade meeting, someone proposed we send flowers to the captain's wife. The captain looked down at his hands as he rolled a cigarette and said, 'You don't have to. She's out of hospital.'

I leaned on the slab that served as our bench and said, 'So, everyone, will we organise flowers anyway?'

The vote was a yes.

'Don't send them home,' the captain said and rattled off an address in Casino.

While I ate my sausage and tomato sauce sandwich, I asked the captain when his wife was coming home.

He took a swig of his beer and, looking down at the cigarette between his fingers, he said, 'She's not. She wants to live in town. She's too isolated out here.'

Out of the corner of my eye, I noticed another member of the brigade listening to our conversation. 'Have you heard something similar?'

He nodded. His wife also wanted to move closer to her family now that all her friends had left the area. 'I don't want to go though,' he said.

For many, it seemed, a partner – a love – is not the salve to loneliness, not enough to make home. I looked across at another neighbour who'd admitted she'd leave if she could afford to – living away from town was certainly cheap. Perhaps many rural people craved more social connection and weren't satisfied simply by nature's quiet bounty. Perhaps it was not simply my personality failure.

'Will you move to town?' I asked the captain.

He looked forlorn. 'What am I going to do there? Here, I've got my golf, the bus run, the brigade, the property, the jam sessions at the hall.'

I nodded. 'Whew, that's tough – for both of you.'

The captain nodded and looked over at the table where some of the recently single men stood. 'Seen it out here heaps,' he said.


From my desk I watched Jen and the next generation of dogs, Tim and Bounce, come through the front gate. Jen dismounted and unsaddled Red, and then, head bowed, she led him slowly back to his stable. Unlike the men at the fire brigade, she'd said she'd come with me. But was it fair to uproot her from her life of thirty-four years and drag her to an unknown fate in a distant city?

While walking that morning, after a night of blustery wind, I'd come upon a bird's nest on the track, finely crafted from twigs and bark and grasses. They'd have to build yet another home, I mused, as I looked up into the branches of the spotty gum. Just as Jen had done three times on this farm using the sand and dirt and timber of the land. Repeatedly she'd invested in this place – rooted herself in it – whereas I, with my litany of changes, had never felt grounded in any place.

I thought of our holiday the previous year at a friend's house at the coast near my former Mullumbimby home. One morning as we'd walked along the beach Jen had said, 'I don't know what I'd do with myself if I lived here.'

'You'd garden, maybe help out at the community garden,' I'd said. 'You'd finally have the time to paint and draw. You'd find things to do.'

I'd smiled at a woman tossing a ball to her kelpie.

'This has made me think of Dad,' Jen had said. 'When the Galls sold the farm, Mum and Dad had to find somewhere to live. Dad must've been about sixty-three, a few years older than me. They found a place – a tiny house in exchange for Dad doing some maintenance. Mum was working at the pub so they were fine for money, but Dad got quieter. And later, when they moved to the Gold Coast, Mum was busy with friends and making clothes but Dad got even quieter.'

'You could become a Knitting Nanna Against Gas. That woman Judy told me the anti-gas movement gave her a sense of purpose after she retired.'

'Retirement has to be at the right time,' Jen had said. 'I'm fifty-nine. I'm not ready to stop farming and be completely financially dependent on you. When I'm older maybe, when I'm ready to retire, then I'd like to travel a bit.'

Timing: should it be mine or Jen's?

And if we did set up a home elsewhere, what would happen to the dogs, the horses and the cattle? What about Jen's community? What if I couldn't find a job and somewhere affordable and halfway decent for us to live? And what of our spark? Jen was both completely familiar yet also so very different from me. Did a tension between the known and the mysterious still fan our spark? Would our relationship even survive if I dragged her into what I thought was my world?

I looked up at the tiny black-and-white etching on my study wall. It featured distant, gloomy clouds and a wooden gate set in Hadrian's Wall in northern England. It was the title that had grabbed me: 'Who's to know if it's the right gate?'

I took the question to town to my friend Pen.

'I just can't keep living out there,' I said tearfully as I sat in my usual pink chair across from her. 'It's like I don't know who I am anymore. I'm living Jen's life.'

It didn't need verbalising: we both knew how ridiculous it was for me to cry to my terminally ill friend whose life extended no further than the lounge room.

'And now I've given Jen such a hard time she's agreed to move to the city if I find a job.'

'Oh, darling,' Pen said, laughing. 'I can't see that happening. You just carry on doing what you're doing. You love your writing and Jen loves having you there.'

'But I get so sick of myself, Pen. Out there it's just Jen and me. No real friends. And other than when I help with farm work or Frank or the fire brigade, all I do is write – about myself.'

'Everyone's like that, darling.' Her blue eyes sparkled. 'Except most people just think about what bills they need to pay and what they'll have left to spend on stuff and holidays.'

I stroked a clump of hair off the cat's back and watched it fall from my fingers. 'When I left law I hoped I'd stop being so identified with my work. But on the farm, apart from Jen, it's all I have. And I don't even know if it's worth carrying on with the writing. I mean, what good will any of it ever do anyone?' I caught Pen looking at me quizzically and laughed. 'God, Pen, sorry. I'm an idiot. How do you manage to be so bloody cheerful?'

'No point being any other way,' she said. 'And I've got no huge expectations of myself. I can just sit back and watch all of you who I love.'

As I drove the hour and a half back to the farm, I wound down the window and felt the wind against my cheeks. Was my thinking – the expectations, resistance, beliefs and patterns – my prison rather than my life itself? Had this always been my problem? Pen was the opposite: she'd found a way to let go of expectations and accept her fate and suffering.

Again, I heard Jen say: 'What if you hate the job? What if the next thing isn't what you'd hoped? Why do you have such high expectations of yourself and of life?'

Maybe a job in the city was a cop-out. To leave the farm would be to fail, to wimp out. Again. I had to get over myself: tame my appetites and be grateful for Tywyah's many privileges and for a fabulous woman who so patiently loved me, dark difficult bits and all. Perhaps partners – and places – who seem different from us are like havens. They give us something we lack, or think we lack, and compel us to see deeper into ourselves.

Late that afternoon, as we fed hay to the twenty-three weaners, I told Jen about Pen's pep talk.

'Phew,' she said with a glint in her eye. 'Does that mean we don't have to leave the farm and live in a noisy, smelly, ugly city?'

'Might have to take a raincheck,' I said as I walked over to open the iron gate where the Hereford cows stood, eyeing the fresh pick on the flat.


The first anniversary of Genee's murder came and went, and as 2015's summer heat ceded to the gentle pattern of autumn, the cicadas quietened. The cooler weather made it easier to work outside, and with my final deadline for the master's degree, I was again absorbed and grateful for the freedom and solitude of the farm.

One afternoon I got up from the desk. Jen had slashed the bottom paddock and my job was to bundle armfuls of the cut grass onto the truck, stomp it down, and then use it to mulch the garden.

'This life's just not for me,' I again said to Jen. 'Even if I'm not as useless as I think, there's not enough here that lights my fire. I love you and I love being with you but … I'm not living, not fully. The fire brigade and Frank's verandah and hall nights just aren't enough.'

This time I spoke in a tone of quiet acceptance. *Live each day as if it's your last* has a different tenor if it's theoretical. I wasn't on a palliative care bed like Pen, life didn't have to be a trial, and my continued efforts to recast myself as a practical countrywoman content with living away from 'the wider world' now seemed a form of starvation.

That night I looked up PhDs in creative writing and scholarships and flats to rent and did a rough budget for living in Melbourne.

'Melbourne?' Jen said. 'That's a full day's travel from here.'

'Lismore and Byron are too small,' I said. 'I need a city. I don't want to go to Sydney 'cos the family are there. Melbourne has art and culture and activism, and we know people there. Twenty, I counted.'

'I can't say you can't go,' Jen said. 'But what about us?'

'I guess I'll have to become a fly-in, fly-out worker. It'll be like our early years together – just a bit further apart and more seasonal. You can come down when things are quiet here and I'll come back for semester breaks or when you need me for cattle work. We could have the best of both worlds.'

As the days shortened and the winter cold crept in, Jen curled into the crook of my arm in front of the wood stove.

'I love having you here,' she said. 'It doesn't matter how much farm work you do or don't do or how well you do it. I don't know if I'll like living here without you.' She was quieter, softer, smaller.

'I'm sorry,' I said. 'I know this isn't what you want.'

She sighed. 'Maybe it'll be good for me. You've always challenged me to step outside my comfortable paddock.'

I pulled her closer.

A few weeks later, as I mixed pollard and gumnuts in Topdeck's feed bucket, a male wood duck hovered just outside the stable waiting for crumbs, a series of deep gouges across his chest. Further away, the female pecked at the ground. She stood on her right foot; her left leg dangled footless. As I stepped away from the stable, the female hopped over to join her partner.

Jen joined me and we stood together watching the wounded duck.

'I remember a poem we did at school about how swans mate for life,' I said. 'Do you reckon ducks do too?'

'Probably,' she said, 'it's easier that way.'

'Sounds like your attitude to human relationships.'

'That's right. You don't have to break in a new one.'

'God, you're romantic.' I laughed. 'You break in rather than tie the knot.'

She looked at me. 'I know young fillies, Hayley. They come back to their paddock for a feed. The flighty filly can have her gallop down the paddock to Melbourne and in a few years she'll be back when she's an old mare who only wants to do a jog.'

As I watched Jen saddle her horse, I marvelled at her forbearance and sensible stability: over the years she'd accommodated my volcanos and floods, now she was accommodating my whirlwind of uncertainty. What a precious love this was.

# 43

# MIRRORS AND MEASURES

WITH BOWED LEGS and wrinkled knees, Frank pushed the calves up the race towards the crush. Jen and I drenched, inoculated, castrated and tagged calf after calf. By midmorning Frank's face was placenta red. I asked if he needed a rest; he refused.

Job done, back at Frank's, I slumped in a padded dining chair and Frank shoved a bottle of beer at me. He'd kicked off his gumboots and now wore black slippers. His legs were skinny and spotty with patches without pigment and he lifted the leg of his shorts to show translucent white skin and a grape-purple bruise. When he said something I couldn't decipher, I assumed he was being crass and feigned incomprehension. But when he addressed me again, I sharpened my focus and realised he was blaming me – unfairly – because he'd been kicked in the yards.

When the clock chimed five he turned on the television. It was a quiz show for primary-school students. He swung his slippered feet back and forth against the bald carpet and called out the answers. Sometimes he shouted 'siwy bugga' at the contestants.

When I said it had been a long day, that I was tired, he called me 'city girl'.

In that tag I heard an echo of the line in Nessie's poem: 'It's no place for the weak'. I was about to leap to my own defence but I stopped myself. Frank was right, in a way.

'Will I ever be a country girl, Frankie?' I asked.

'May'e in a mon',' he said, 'when you come ba' from holidays.'

After a meeting at Melbourne University, I climbed the wide marble steps to the State Library's reading room. Settling into the hushed quiet, I smiled at the familiarity and comfort of a library with a collection too vast to be displayed.

I opened the yellowed pages of a book I'd been wanting to get hold of for some time, Susanna Moodie's *Roughing it in the Bush*. Published in 1852, part memoir, part novel, it was an account of her life as a Canadian settler during the 1830s. I jumped to the last chapter, 'Adieu':

> *… that was the last night I ever spent in the bush – in the dear forest house which I had loved in spite of all the hardships which we had endured since we pitched our tent in the blackwoods. … Nor did I leave it without many regretful tears, to mingle once more in a world to whose usages, during my long solitude, I had become almost a stranger, and to whose praise or blame I felt alike indifferent.*

Moodie's time in the bush spanned years, much like mine. It wasn't a brief respite from her usual home – it wasn't an 'experiment' like some of the other 're-wilding' books that contemporary readers seem to crave.

Perhaps Moodie and I were alike. Certainly, like her, at a distance from the farm, I too felt a deep affection and gratitude for the simplicity and space of that life, the green and quiet – and particularly for the freedom to walk and write at my own pace. And yet, unlike

Moodie, I'd not felt indifferent to the praise or blame of the outside world.

I looked at the people around me, reading, writing, texting, resting their heads on desks. Here, strangely, I felt accompanied, even if no words were exchanged. Common purpose, even if not communicated. I let the peace settle in my heart. Perhaps in the city, alongside other readers and writers, I would find my true home.

I looked up into the dome towards the natural light. But then how would it be to live insulated from the elemental and earthy life, away from the spotty gums and dogs and horses and cattle – and Jen. After decades in the country, might I find I didn't quite belong in the city either?

I flicked to the page in my notebook where, like a travel writer, I'd started making notes for my 'Love letter to Melbourne'. My eyes flew over my beloved's advantages: spontaneity and stimulation, opportunity and accessibility. A list borne of comparison between urban and farm life. How odd. I – along with Frank – described myself as a 'city girl' and yet my frame of reference – the structure that was now my baseline – was the farm. Perhaps the years at Tywyah hadn't only demystified life in the bush, they'd also seeped under my skin along with memories of blackened fingernails and bruises, scars and splinters. Wide skies and space, the gums, the roos and wallabies, the frosts and floods, summer heat and bushfires. This was what I knew now more than Shabbat dinners or city laneways. Places and their people have a way of shaping us too.

But did that mean I should stay on the farm?

'Susanna,' I asked, 'why did you leave?'

*To the poor, industrious working man it presents many advantages, to the poor gentleman, none!*

I smiled at the different meaning of 'poor' when used as an adjective to describe these two different nouns.

Susanna continued:

*The former works hard, puts up with a coarse, scanty fare,
and submits, with a good grace, to hardships that would kill a
domesticated animal at home. Thus he becomes independent, in
so much as the land that he has cleared finds him in the common
necessaries of life; but it seldom, if ever, in remote situations,
accomplishes more than this. The gentleman can neither work
so hard, live so coarsely, nor endure so many privations as his
poorer more fortunate neighbour.*

The economics of choice. Again, those 'necessaries of life'. Jen
was Susanna's industrious 'working man' – both before and after the
fire, she'd chosen farm life and identified as a 'self-made peasant'.
Self-contained and independent. In which case, urbanised I, with
the choices provided by my education and economic resources and a
body not built for farm work, was the 'poor gentleman'. I panicked.
I didn't want those descriptors: not 'poor' as an adjective, nor 'gentleman' as a noun.

A recent phone call with my mother came back to me.

'What two words would you use to describe yourself?' she'd asked.
The question had been posed at a dinner party.

'Oh god, that's a tough one, Ma.' I'd paused. Did I say woman,
feminist, lesbian? What about ex–South African, ex–legal researcher and educator, ex–city girl, Jewish? Terms of a past from which I
felt ambivalent and exiled, and yet defensive in the face of potential attack. It didn't feel true to say Australian, countrywoman, cattle
producer, landlady, writer. I refused to be defined in terms of Jen
as 'farmer's wife' or 'other half'. I knew I shouldn't use self-critical
terms: jealous, imposter, failure, childless, difficult, discontent, out-
cast. Each pigeonhole felt oppressive and not truly representative.

My mother had laughed. 'Yes, it would be for you. You are so
catholic, Hayley.'

'Mmm, the catholic Jew,' I laughed. 'What did you say, Ma?'

'Oh, elite South African.'

'You've got to be joking,' I'd said, shrivelling again at the thought that if she and I were truly as alike as people from our past used to say, I too could be tarred with that label and its associations of arrogance and superiority. So I repeated what I'd often said: 'We are just so different.'

'Oh, Hayley,' she'd said. 'I was being tongue-in-cheek.'

'Maybe,' I'd said, 'but you'd have no problem with someone describing you that way. You'd probably feel flattered.'

I sighed and set the book down. Mirrors and measures. How exhausting they were. By submitting with good grace to rural hardships the 'poorer more fortunate neighbour' becomes 'independent'. As Jen had done, as Frank had done. Moodie had touched my deepest nerve: a longing for inner wholeness and self-possession. For self-sufficiency. To me, the truest and only wealth.

Beside me a man with a cap and bomber jacket uncapped his flask. As I so often did, I wondered if he was Australian-born or if his family might've come from Lebanon or Israel or Palestine, and where they now lived. How did he walk through this world? Where was his 'home'? Where did he feel part of a 'we'?

It struck me then: the story I'd always told myself was that I didn't demonise 'the other'. I was curious and open, aware of the many hues and textures that make an individual, and how each fine thread affects the others to weave the whole. Yet when it came to myself I struggled to accept duality and the dignity in my difference, thinking always that I ought to prove myself a part of a group, or disprove the stereotypes attached to the labels of my identity. Unwittingly, as I'd separated myself from the cultures of my past, I'd also enacted a shaming which had made it harder to build my own solid raft. So afraid of loneliness and rootlessness, I wanted to belong everywhere, to be a someone everyone approved of. A ravenous hunger that had first taken root as a child. A ravenous hunger that had turned my many freedoms into a prison where I was the only guard.

I buried my head in my hands and listened to the turn of others' pages. I might think it was farm work I was sick of but, really, I was just sick of feeling embattled – of downplaying or neutralising or feeling ambivalent about parts of myself and my background. Sick of the unresolved hauntings and familial shames and silences. Sick of apologising for myself and the historical and collective forces that had shaped me. I was sick of shame and fear and their bedfellow: self-criticism.

Back on the farm, spring heralded the time to burn off paddocks that had been blanched by frost. In the late afternoon, Jen walked the track with the driptorch. I brought up the rear, driving the truck with the spray tank, waiting for enough of the bush to blacken before wetting the edge. How I wished I had to move to earn a living, in order to get medical help or to care for someone. Then the decision would've been clear rather than a tussle between independence and this beautiful partnership, between my intuition and the narratives and expectations that haunted me.

As I waited and watched, I thought about my vague Melbourne plan. The PhD application was due soon and still I wasn't clear about a topic, or even whether I should go. I thought too about my network of friends in Melbourne, how one had said, 'Just come, it'll work out,' and another had offered her front room and an introduction to a two-month house- and pet-sit. Stay or go, stay or go. Embedded in each action was a sense of loss, and exile.

I pulled the trigger on the hose and sprayed. A writing friend had recently led me to James Wood's essay 'Secular Homelessness' in which he coins the term 'homelooseness' to describe a state, with some component of loss, 'in which the ties that might bind one to Home have been loosened, perhaps happily, perhaps unhappily, perhaps permanently, perhaps only temporarily'.

Perhaps a nifty label like 'homelooseness' might provide the shelter of belonging I so craved. Perhaps it might reassure me that Jen and my love would survive even if we lived apart.

The night before Jen had said, 'Just make a decision, Hayley. Get your act together.'

White smoke enveloped me; it caught in my throat and stung my eyes. Like the future, I couldn't see the road up ahead – not for my independent self, not for our partnership. But I had to go. I would go. In the new year. In 2016. Like those summer cicadas, having lived hidden underground, engaged and absorbed and introspective, I had to surface: to move and sing, to flap my own unashamed human beat amid society.

I slowed the truck to a halt and sprayed a burning stump. Sometimes one risks losing a great love, sometimes one risks losing one's self.

# 44.

# HOMECOMING

AFTER A BALMY FEBRUARY day in 2017, I leaned on the stone bridge over the Yarra River watching rowers glide past. A saxophonist's 'Summertime' floated up from Southbank and up ahead Sandridge Bridge was a blue arc across the river. I wanted to freeze this moment. The next day I'd be leaving my beloved Melbourne.

Over the last year of 'homelooseness', I'd bounced between Jen and Tywyah, and Melbourne where I'd spent a total of seven magical months house- and pet-sitting. In Melbourne I'd had the stimulation of quality and quotidian time with old and new friends, conversations with strangers, writers' talks, films and plays, galleries and museums, marches and rallies. Amid diversity and choice, my litany of otherness and sense of 'missing out' had dissipated. I was a newcomer but not an outsider. There was no mould I needed to fit, no particular 'us' or 'we' to which I needed to belong. I was free to be my curious self, excited again to feel part of the diverse 'big world out there', and nourished rather than defeated by the solitary hours working at house-sit dining tables or libraries. It was as if I'd come out of exile, from wilderness to metropolis. My optimistic, vital and passionate self had been resurrected.

Along with an addressless life, this strength had allowed me to finally break my silence within the family. There'd been no resolution but my mother had finally stood up for me and spoken out too. And with that act, finally, she'd validated my truth. I no longer needed to carry all the responsibility. I felt solid in myself. Seen. Unashamed.

If my time in Melbourne had begun with a panel on 'Empathy in Australia' where I'd learned a new word from philosopher Roman Krznaric, 'outrospection', it was ending with a session that placed outrospection in context. I'd just left the air-conditioned quiet of an auditorium where writer Alberto Manguel had talked of his recent book *Curiosity* and how, on the path of self-discovery, 'books become compasses that embody the four cardinal points: mobility and stability, self-reflection and the gift of looking outward'.

I looked back at the Arts Centre lit blue, an Eiffel Tower in a city that was my Paris, London and New York all rolled into one. Now deep love and care were reeling me back to Jen.

A few days ago she'd rung, tearful. 'I'm so worried,' she said. 'I don't think she's going to be around much longer.' Jen's sister Kay had inoperable liver cancer. It was February now, three months since the November diagnosis.

In December I'd sat on the edge of Kay's bed. Until recently a strong and vital 67-year-old nursing sister, Kay's pallor had become yellow, and she was ten kilograms lighter and battling nausea.

After Jen's call, I cancelled the next three-month house-sit. So much for 'homelooseness' and utopian ideals about relationships. I had to be with Jen.

After a month beside Kay, Jen and I sat with her as she took her last breath. I held Jen tight.

'Thank you,' she said. 'My rock.'


Tim's howling and barking greeted us as we drove into Frank's yard after the funeral.

'He knows it's mummy and aunty,' Frank said as I unlatched the front gate.

'See,' he said as I hugged him. 'Told you you'd be back.'

Back at Tywyah, Tim, the only dog now, was watchful and whip-quick when either of us moved. The purple salvia over Lucy's grave was in full flower and the cardinal rose over Bounce's grave was bright red. From the kitchen wall, Jen took down an etching she'd once bought of a woman sweeping. Its title was 'Sweep more, think less'. In its place she hung a mirror that had been a fixture in her mother's and then Kay's home. The mirror was etched with a verse:

> 'Mid pleasures and palaces though we may roam,
> Be it ever so humble, there's no place like home

I shook my head in wonder. 'It's so simple for you, isn't it?'

'Yup,' she said straightening the mirror. 'But it's more of a home with you here.'

Over my 'homelooseness' year, I'd studiously avoided using 'home' to refer to Tywyah or to the house-sits. I'd been deliriously happy in my city life, convinced that like-minded friends and stimulation were key to my contentment, doubtful I'd ever return to live full-time at Tywyah. The hyper-mobile untethered lifestyle was probably unsustainable: it didn't meld well with paid or voluntary work, and adjusting to a new house and its resident animal was time-consuming and distracting from my writing, but I'd hoped I – we – could find a way. Now circumstances had brought me back. Was I being compelled to accept that despite my sense that I didn't want Jen to be the central pivot of my life, the unavoidable truth was that home was with her – where the heart is?

At the hall's Friday night bar and barbeque, some of the locals hugged Jen, some said 'Sorry for your loss', some couldn't find the language and just nodded. Everyone had known about Kay's illness.

'Are you over Melbourne yet?' they asked me.

'Not quite, I loved it down there,' I said. 'But I need to be with Jen for now.'

'You're lucky,' a local cattle farmer, said, 'you can fit in anywhere.'

I stared at her. Me? Fit in here? As I watched her walk away, dressed fashionably in high-heeled boots, I wondered if feeling like an outsider was something she, both cattle farmer and fashionista, also struggled with in this community. Perhaps countless people struggled with belonging.

'You'll have to come to yoga on Friday mornings,' Paul said as we stood ordering drinks at the bar.

'Yoga? Here? You've got to be joking.'

'Yes, yes,' Nadine said as she arrived, and threw her arms around me. Bringing her warmth and sense of fun, she'd moved to the area just before I'd left for Melbourne. 'I wanted to do more yoga so I enrolled in a teacher's training course and started running classes here and in the other halls in the district. There've been about eight people each week. And I found a "vino vinyasa" style that I'm thinking might be perfect for the area.'

I laughed with her. She'd found her way to fit right into the drinking culture.

As I waited at the kitchen counter to order steak and salad, I marvelled again at this forgiving community. Membership – the 'us' – really was based simply on the choice to live here. It was not defined by blood or marriage, similarity or shared interest, nor by work, appearance, achievements, culture, ethnicity or the company one keeps. Everyone was welcome at hall nights and people had the freedom to have a go. At one fundraiser I'd even earned fifty dollars for our fire brigade by singing karaoke – 'It's Raining Men' – something I'd never had the guts to do in my other worlds.

I felt a nudge and turned to see Kara, who'd gone off to Sydney for high school and then to university to study nursing. 'What are you doing here?' I asked.

'I could ask you the same thing. We heard you'd gone to

Melbourne.' Then gesturing to her boyfriend and sister, she said, 'We decided to come back to live with Mum. There's no community in western Sydney. Not like here.'

I laughed and said, 'Funny you should say that – in Melbourne I kept wondering if the people I knew had community or just groups of friends and colleagues. Some of my friends don't even know the names of the people in their street.'

At the scrape of metal against tiles I looked over to Jen, pulling up a chair for me at a trestle table. Conversation meandered from the fence that needed fixing over at Frank's front paddock to the fire brigade, to the new bridge across the Clarence River and the heritage value of the old single-span bridge.

These were good people, kind and helpful. People I respected and cared about, people I'd known for decades and would miss if I never saw them again. So why had I always felt so lonely here?

Was it that I, who'd known the intimacy and stimulation of truly great friendships, had expected too much from 'community'? Maybe the real challenge of living in the bush was not aloneness but how to be satisfied by connections with people whose passions and preoccupations and backgrounds differed from mine.

As Jen had said years earlier, 'They're your neighbours. You don't have to marry them.'


The next morning I set off to walk my old path down past the spot on the flat where the bombproof horse Boxer was buried, and past the gully where we'd saved a cow with calving paralysis. Just beyond the little gully where Lucy used to paddle, the white-winged choughs squawked and scrambled in the apple mahogany trees. In every direction were landmarks, each with a thought or a meaning, a feeling or a story. Each a symbol of the continuity and depth of my relationship with Jen and Tywyah.

At my special tree, a spotty gum that had bifurcated to form a bench, I sat picking at a slab of loose bark. My only certainty was Jen, our true and potent love. How it had weathered flood, fire and drought, how it had allowed us each to change, how it had grown wiser, how it had proved we were each autonomous yet supported by the other in deep and profound ways to become better versions of ourselves. Over the 'homelooseness' year we'd been finding our way with a new form of relationship, and yet in Melbourne when I'd slipped my spinning self between cold sheets and stretched my arm out across a bed so empty without Jen, I'd questioned my choice to cleave apart our daily lives. Often I'd wake and long for the sound of her steady breathing and warm body, often I longed to know her thoughts and wished she was beside me listening or seeing what the city offered.

But even if this love was as fundamental to my sense of self and safety as food and shelter, what about my individual heart? I didn't want to fall into the despair and alienation I'd known over the years here. If home for Jen for some unknown time frame was Tywyah, what then would become of my personal and singular life?

I peeled away the strip of loose bark. Could I find a way to carry that robust Melbourne self into this rural world? Could I find the mobility and outrospection, the stimulation and face-to-face companionship that had brought me back into myself in the city?

As I walked back to the house, I passed the three mounds of bark. They were shorthand for a monumental decision Jen had made: to have the place selectively logged. I remembered the day we'd spray-painted pink crosses on the habitat trees and how we'd listened to the urgent pulse and beep and thud of the harvester with its giant claws, questioning whether it was the right thing to have done. For months I'd avoided the killing field of fallen trunks and crowns. Now, six years later, the spindlier trees were filling out and growing taller, and those three mounds, once as high as funeral pyres, had composted down. Slow and gradual change: in physical landscapes, in small communities and in ourselves. Perhaps just as Jen had returned after the fire, now I too was being given a second chance – a chance to 'do over' life at Tywyah.

'Fifty-two cows and fifty-one calves,' I said, looking down at the clipboard. 'We better do up some new sheets for you to carry around. It's April and these were done last September.'

Jen slid shut the gate on the race. 'That wasn't so bad, was it?'

'Because that tetchy Brangus didn't put me up the rails,' I said. 'And you didn't yell at me.'

I carried the box of tags and the esky back to the truck and untied Tim. It was good to work physically again, to be in my body. Despite city walks and an hour here and there of 'No Lights No Lycra' dancing, I'd done more physical work in a couple of weeks on the farm than during the months in Melbourne.

I hopped in the truck and called out, 'See you at home for lunch.'

Jen raised a hand as she settled into the saddle, Tim falling in behind her.

I smiled to myself as I picked lettuce and parsley from the garden, and with my bare feet anchored to the teak boards I'd sanded all those years ago, I felt my belly settle and my tight shoulders drop as I mashed tuna with mayonnaise, parsley and shallots. I might've often felt dispensable and useless on the farm but in Melbourne I'd missed my kitchen and farm chores and routines. Familiarity. Simplicity. Ordinariness. Continuity. Stability. Responsibility. The hallmarks of home.

At the lunch table I said to Jen, 'You're right – that went well in the yards today.'

'Yeah, cattle behaved.' She winked.

'Maybe the time apart has been good for us. Freshened up how we behave towards each other.'

'Nah, you weren't trying so hard,' she said, turning up the volume on the radio in readiness for the cattle report.

I started to say 'I was doing what I've always done' but stopped myself. She was right. After being around writers and readers and philosophers, miraculously, I no longer cared if I wasn't any good at farming or building or gardening – they just weren't 'mine'. I didn't have to prove myself in Jen's farming world. Like writing, cattle farming's not a hobby. It's life and it's work, the relationship between the two is symbiotic, inseparable, personally significant in ways no one else fully understands. Perhaps just as Nadine was running her yoga classes, asking for help to chop wood or build fences – living her non-farming life in a rural area – I too could find a way to live my passions and interests in this district. My role on the farm was simply assistant or audience – label it 'farmer's wife', label it cheer squad. It was just one small part of who I was. No single tag accurately describes any of us.

At the end of that year at hall night I felt a tug on my arm. It was Mathilda whom I'd once helped learn the alphabet. Together with her siblings, she was back for Christmas to visit her father.

'How's school?' I asked.

'Good,' she said, before leaping onto my back and instructing me to go outside.

As I watched her sister Isa monkey-climb up the basketball hoop, I looked out to where the ironbark planted as a memorial to Jack was casting shadows on the lawn. Inside was the wall of photos, one of the ninety-year-old poet Nessie and her red-faced husband Lionel, one of Mathilda's grandmother Jeanie sitting on the front of the fire brigade truck. Above the bar was the bamboo gate with a 'Lock the Gate' sign from a gas field–free fundraiser, and an assortment of flowers cut out the year we'd had a Woodstock theme for the fire brigade fundraiser. All of these signified the privilege of staying in one place for a long time.

Inside the hall I walked over to the maps I'd pinned to the noticeboard along with a notice: 'Where do we all come from?' The map of the world was now dotted with eight coloured pins – South Africa, the United Kingdom, Austria, Hungary, the Netherlands, Germany and Perm in Russia. I was yet to meet the person who'd put a pin at Alaska. Alongside it the Australian map sported eighty pins, most clustered within five hours' drive. The population was tiny but here too everyone had come from somewhere, some just geographically or culturally further away than others. There really was no constant and amorphous 'them' for me to fit in with. Any 'us' was simply based on location, its seam plurality – each member of the community was an individual free to be whoever they were, in apparent acceptance of differences.

Since my return, I'd determined to feel less apologetic about my interests and background and resources. I'd taken to showing more of myself here, even wearing the fitted jeans and tops I usually only wore in town. The federal government's recent postal survey about same-sex marriage had certainly highlighted Jen and my difference from most of the community. Our lives – and political views – had seemed on public trial. Even though we'd long pushed aside self-consciousness and fear and taken to dancing together at the hall, even though many of our neighbours proudly told us they'd voted yes, I figured we'd always feel slightly 'outside' this largely heterosexual community. Or perhaps some outsiderness is inevitable and my expectations of community had been too high, my notion of 'belonging' utopian.

Paul joined me for a chat and pointed to his pin at Birmingham. We were the same age; he was a kind, respectful and friendly man, someone I'd liked as soon as he came to the area. Yet simply because he was a man and wasn't bookish, and our connection didn't have the kind of intimacy and intensity I'd known in friendships away from here, I'd never thought of him as my 'friend'. Perhaps I'd been wrong. Perhaps my expectations had again got in the way.

'Thanks for being so patient with me the other day on the fire line,' I said. 'I feel so bloody useless at all this physical stuff.'

'It's good you're coming out to fires now,' he said. 'We need you – and you're more experienced than most here.' He looked kindly at me. 'We can't all do the same things, Hayley. I can't write stories and books like you.'

I nodded. 'It is nice to feel more part of the brigade. You don't get that when you're doing admin.' I paused. 'You and Richard and Jen make it easier, and it helps having another inexperienced woman like Nadine. When we first started going out – after we did our basic training fourteen years ago – it was just the blokes who'd been doing it for years and Jen and me.'

'Oh, yes,' Paul said, stroking his goatee beard. 'I can't do anything either if I'm intimidated.' He paused. 'And what about Melbourne? Are you going back there?'

'Million-dollar question,' I said, looking at the map of the world. 'You just love it here, don't you, Paul?' This area was all he knew of Australia and he'd embraced it, becoming a friendly and helpful member of the community.

He nodded. 'Way more than Birmingham.'

'Lucky you to find a place that feels so right.'

'We see more of you than we ever used to,' he said. 'It's good.'

'Thanks, Paulie,' I said. He was right. My trips to town were rarer and briefer and we'd even borrowed a kayak and joined the river paddlers one day. 'I don't know,' I said, looking over to where some long-term locals were playing pool with a few newcomers. 'Things feel a bit different here now. Maybe it's me – or maybe the community's growing and changing too.'

He nodded. 'Not as caveman-like now.'


In the cool of an early morning as I squeezed through a barbed-wire cockies gate, my sleeve caught on a piece of tie-wire. How Tywy-ah slowed me up and tied me down! I paused to look east, at my favourite view of the caterpillar mountain, aware that I no longer felt trapped. I was surprisingly happy back in the quiet calm, walking through cattle and kangaroos and horses with Tim by my side, eating from a garden rather than restaurants, listening to the magpie carol from a branch near the outdoor dunny, watching wallabies graze near the house in the late afternoons and working on the farm with Jen or among my books in my little study on the verandah.

I thought again of an old friend's words on the eve of my migration from South Africa: 'You can be whoever you want to be.'

Over the years, when I became a lesbian, when I left the city, when I quit law, I'd repeatedly wondered if this was what he'd meant. Now I wondered if perhaps, like my childhood wooden babushka doll with all its embedded smaller selves, we are always still becoming. This rural life too was shaping me even if I hadn't become the Amazonian 'chop wood, carry water' type.

At my bifurcated tree I looked up at the two trunks. The spindlier one with its skinny boughs in multiple directions and cankers over old wounds had grown aslant, reaching for the light; the other trunk was too thick to hug, sure and tall and straight. It struck me then that these were my two selves, the younger and the older. The bridge between them was this life at Tywyah with Jen, a life that had taught me what no academic or literary education could. In a place that attracted people who lived by their own rules, where I'd had the luxury of deep thought and freedom from common pressures, I'd attended to my interior landscape. I was more solid and self-sufficient, more capable and less afraid of aloneness and attack. My observation skills were sharper, and I was humbler after living in a place where the glory of intellectual achievement mattered little if no water came out of your tap. My route to this sureness was of course different from Jen's because our primary languages were different: hers physical and accommodating, mine cerebral and questioning. I'd needed ordinary time with like-minded people in Melbourne to realise I didn't have to prove myself to anyone – or have their feedback – in order to feel 'valid'. I just had to have the strength to own my full self. Life, I now understood, was precisely where I was, not that merry-go-round 'out there', spinning brightly without me.

Back at the house, I eased the hayfork under a pile of horse manure. I stopped to change arms, to feel the sun on my skin, to listen to the wind form the bass to the magpie lark and noisy miners. I breathed in deep, my Barbie-pink gumboots anchored to the ground. The real secret of those gumboots – my ruby slippers – was that no yellow brick road can show us the way, no wizard can buttress us against the mystery of life. We can't shelter in a homeland or a new citizenship, in family or friends or communities, in religion or tradition, in ideologies or political movements, in work or even in texts. We can't take shelter under any label. We can't even shelter in a deep and true and generous love, although it might influence our choices. The richest and primary home, the only one that can keep us safe and offer us any certainty and continuity between past and present, is inside each of us. It's where the heart is.

As I hoisted manure into the wheelbarrow, I realised the real question was not 'Where and with whom do I belong?' but 'Am I truly here in this place, now?'

A willie wagtail landed on the barbed-wire fence. A Koori friend once told me, 'If you see a willie wagtail, listen,' so I stopped and watched it seesaw on its barbed tightrope. Seesaw, wobble, pivot. No burial can wipe out the past, no fence can contain all of who we are. Even if I belonged nowhere completely, I might find a measure of belonging everywhere, because chances were that like those Herefords down in the bottom paddock, at some point I'd unlatch Tywyah's chain – whether or not Jen wished to join me – and step through the gate into the unknown, to experience its divots and ditches, to shelter under its shade trees and sample the fresh pick of grass, bitter or sweet.

# ACKNOWLEDGEMENTS

THE STORY I'VE TOLD in this book reflects how I've experienced, remembered, understood and shaped events into a narrative using the techniques of fiction, personal essay and memoir writing. Memory is subjective and slippery and experiences, like ourselves, are complex. This memoir is my subjective and candid telling – it is not journalism or reportage, nor oral history. Others may recollect and perceive shared events differently. With that awareness, I've carried out my writerly responsibilities to the best of my ability: remained true to my recollections and the emotional truth of my story, and told only what the reader needs to know in order to understand why my search for 'home' has taken this course. It is in an attempt to deepen my, and hopefully our, conversation about the significance and meaning of home and belonging that I've shared my story. I've collapsed some time frames and omitted or changed some identifying details and names to protect privacy. Some people have chosen to have their names included. My thanks to you.

This memoir began in 2014 as a collection of essays, some of which had been published. My sincerest thanks to those who provide opportunities for short form writers – in my case: *Australian Book Review* and the Calibre Prize; *Griffith Review*; *Southerly*; *Going Down Swinging*; Queerstories podcast; Outstanding Short Story

Competition; the Nature Conservancy Nature Writing Prize; www. narratively; *Kenyon Review*; *Fourth Genre*; and anthologies *Split*; *Afterness*; and *Intimate Strangers: True Stories from Queer Asia*.

The essays were written while I was a student in the low residency MFA program at City University of Hong Kong, which sadly no longer exists. Thank you to Robin Hemley, Xu Xi, Ravi Shankar, Susanne Paolo, Madeleine Thien and Luis Francia for expanding my world, and to my lifeline writing group during that time: Jesse Blackadder, Sarah Armstrong, Amanda Webster and Emma Ashmere.

I am forever grateful to editor extraordinaire Nadine Davidoff who guided my reworking of these essays into memoir, first with the most incisive structural report in September 2016 and subsequently with editorial advice which blended her remarkable intelligence, kindness and professionalism. Thank you too to Jesse, Sarah and Virginia Peters for their wise and stabilising counsel during these last years.

I came to writing after law thanks to my acting teachers Linda Rutledge and Penelope Chater who encouraged me to draw on my inner self to embody characters and to attempt writing for the stage. Jesse Blackadder invited me to join her writing group in 2002 when I'd written nothing but law, and ever since she has lovingly encouraged, commiserated and cheered me on, always honest, always generous with her skills and experience. The ever-visionary Peter Bishop, then Varuna's founding Creative Director, and Amanda Webster encouraged me to turn to creative nonfiction and I met with them a number of times at Varuna, along with Leah Kaminsky, Catherine Therese, David Carlin, and Alice Nelson – thank you for 'homelooseness'. Emma Hardman, Jessie Cole, Lee Kofman and Mags Webster have been long-distance literary friends, and Charlotte Wood and her February 2019 Surge group accompanied me during a final restructure. My sincerest thanks to you all for feedback, inspiration and conversations about literature and the writing life.

During my years of writing fiction I was privileged to win a Varuna

Longlines Fellowship and two Northern Rivers Writers Centre Residential Mentorships where I benefited from mentor Marele Day's wisdom and encouragement.

Before she died in July 2018, my mother read and praised an even longer version of this manuscript – and insisted I didn't end a sentence with a preposition. I'm so very grateful to have inherited from her a love for literature and friendship. I so wish she'd lived to hold this book. My thanks too to my beloved Glazer cousins, my 'happy families', a generous and accommodating local community, new friends in the district, the Melbourne house-sits and pets, and my magnificent touchstone friends, far and wide. For the conversations and care that have helped me write and share this story, thank you especially to Sam, Lally, Louise, Harriet, Darby, Gina, Karen, Lib, Julia, Miche, Marianna, Jaye, Angelikie, Fiona, Andi, Jesse and Ruth. And Pen. And mostly, Madeline.

I was diagnosed with ovarian cancer in March 2019 and Ventura Press's Jane Curry sent me an enthusiastic 'yes please' in July 2019. Thank you so very much Jane, Zoe Hale, Sophie Hodge, Holly Jeffery and Simone Ford for 'getting' my book and nurturing it into being whilst I was undergoing treatment. Thank you Isobel, generous photographer friend, for capturing me when I still had my mane of hair. Thank you to Anna Lensky and the team from Pitch Projects for guiding me as this book became public. And a very special thank you to Dr Ellen Kennedy, Dr Marcelo Nascimento, Dr James Bull, the crew at the chemotherapy lounges, Angela Keating and Claudia Valenzuela who helped me be able to realise this dream.

And always, my deepest thanks and truest love to Jen for loving, challenging and encouraging me to be my full self.